JUSTIN RUTHVEN-TYERS

phoenix
from the ashes

THE BOAT THAT REBUILT OUR LIVES

ADLARD COLES NAUTICAL
LONDON

Illustrations by Justin Ruthven-Tyers. For more information
please visit justintyers.co.uk or contact justin@justintyers.plus.com

First published by Adlard Coles Nautical in 2012

ISBN 978-1-4081-5141-9
ePub: 978-1-4081-5924-8
ePDF: 978-1-4081-5588-2

A CIP catalogue record for this book is available from the British Library.

This book is produced using paper that is made from wood grown in
managed, sustainable forests. It is natural, renewable and recyclable.
The logging and manufacturing processes conform to the environmental
regulations of the country of origin.

Typeset in 10 pt Sabon by MPS Ltd
Printed in Great Britain by Clays Ltd, St Ives plc

Note: while all reasonable care has been taken in the publication of this
book, the publisher takes no responsibility for the use of the methods or
products described in the book.

I DEDICATE THIS BOOK
TO DAVID SPEARS WHO
SELFLESSLY INVESTED IN
ME YEARS AGO WITH NO
EXPECTATION OF A RETURN
ON HIS INVESTMENT... AND
WHO HASN'T BEEN
DISAPPOINTED

CONTENTS

1

A STRANGE MEETING

Now that I come to think about it, the old stone pier at Carsaig in Argyll, Scotland, was the perfect place for a strange meeting. It is a lonely spot on Scotland's fractured west coast – port of arrival for all Atlantic depressions – overlooking 4 miles of turbulent sea toward the remote Island of Jura.

The rude pier is a short strip of bumpy concrete splodged out from buckets onto a base of boulders, and is used by two fishermen whose boat leaves at five every winter's morning, and returns after dark laden with crimson langoustine – known locally as 'the prawan' – destined for markets in France and Spain.

We were just setting sail from there in our boat – which is also our home – when a good-looking, dark-haired man in his late thirties, immaculately dressed in a dark suit and trilby, strode down the pier toward us, his steel Blakey's clacking against the concrete. He looked as though he had come to meet a steamboat, but was 80 years too late. As we swung our bow out to sea the smiling stranger reached the end of the pier and called after us, 'I've heard the whole story!'

Were it not for the fact that we were the only other people around, we would have assumed that he was calling to some-one else. I liked him already but I was so busy wondering, 'Who on earth is this man... why is he dressed like that... and what the hell is he talking about?', that I only managed a feeble, 'How are you doing?'

He expanded a little: '...about the fire... and the boat-building, and everything... And I just wanted to say – if ever you write a book about it all, I want the first copy.'

This book is for him – whoever he was.

* * *

For seven years my wife, Linda, and I lived on board a 15-ton traditional wooden sailing boat, which we built ourselves as complete novices – starting with the trees. She's the prettiest boat you've ever seen.

Our voyages have taken us to Celtic lands – to Brittany, Ireland, Scotland, and to our usual over-wintering port in Cornwall, and between those few latitudes we found infinite variety of people and place, and every year we make fresh new travels in those old hunting grounds.

This was our second visit to Scotland in our boat – the first had been a summer cruise three years earlier. This was the real thing – we planned to find out the hard way if man could 'survive' a Scottish winter, living on a boat. Linda was born in Glasgow and knew better than I did that the days would be short, the nights long, the weather wet, and the temperatures often freezing; and that here on the west coast we would be hounded by storms – yet we were attracted by the idea of being cocooned on board our boat in a desolate place. We imagined evenings reading endless books by the cosy glow of our wood-burning stove in the soft yellow paraffin light; listening to gales singing through the rigging. And we imagined days walking the hills; foraging along the low-water shore for mussels and oysters; or searching in the woods for the dry firewood that would keep and cheer us.

We had sailed up from Cornwall on the south-west coast of England to arrive in the boisterous days of summer, when play-ful winds send white horses racing across the blue water and agi-tate the emerald pines and the knurled branches of ancient oak.

We had spent months studying the sea charts, pinpoint-ing likely 'hurricane holes' where we could anchor our vessel secure against the winter storms, and began immediately to search out these promising-looking spots. The west coast of Scotland is all rocks – a fact that prevents most yachtsmen from the 'softer south' from visiting it at all. 'Anyone who tells you he has never hit a rock is lying,' was our first local report of the kind of sailing we were in for. And we weren't long in finding out the dangers for ourselves.

Scudding down the coast off the small island of Kerrera one sunny afternoon, with a gale of wind behind us, and intending to turn sharp left around the heel of the island to enjoy the protected water in its lee, I made the decision to take a shortcut between it and an off-lying rock called Bach Island. There was plenty of room, probably several hundred yards, but I hadn't reckoned on the effect of the shallow water that formed a saddle between the two, or on the increased wind that would be funnelling through. The waves, which had been gently lift-ing and lowering us as they tumbled ahead, soon became short and steep – and took control of the boat. As the stern rose, the bow broached across toward the rocky shore, helped by the press of wind in the huge mainsail, which should have been more deeply reefed; and as the wave passed under us to lift the bow, *Caol Ila* spun her head the other way, threatening a gybe. The island shore was perilously close, the waves began to break with a roar, and sandy water crashed on deck. I forced the tiller – which bent with the strain – as far as it would go to one side, and a moment later just as far the other way, trying to maintain a straight course. A minute or so and we cleared the shallows, the waves lengthened, and we were through. It was the closest we had been to wrecking ourselves.

We were looking for places that were interesting, lonely, and beautiful, and would offer us protection from winter storms. Wind will come from all directions, and as it rises in strength, so is there increased danger. A sudden squall will sweep a boat clean off her anchor and onto rocks without warning. And having to move a vessel by night to avoid one danger – in the cold, the rain and the dark, where navigational aids are few – might lead to another. A good anchorage will offer protection from three of the four points of the compass; in a perfect anchorage, protection from the fourth point will only be a short journey away.

And we wanted comfort, too – living aboard doesn't inure you to incessant rolling, to always having to hold on when walking about, to wiping porridge off the walls... we wanted to be as still at night as a babe in its cot. In short, we were looking for places to anchor our vessel, here on the wild west coast of Scotland, that never get rougher than a farm pond.

Invariably, such places are difficult of access, being littered with hazards – submerged rocks, narrow channels and strong tides; seldom visited during a fine spell of summer weather, they were utterly deserted throughout the winter. Ashore, there may be no house for miles around, but exploring the area often revealed fascinating signs of a more historic habitation – a village abandoned in the Highland Clearances, of which only rectangular shapes of tumbled stone remained, with a sheep fank nearby; a graveyard accidentally discovered (hidden amid acres of dense fern, warm, musty, and head-high), with its tombstones carved in bas-relief depicting Celtic warriors dressed in mail, a claymore clasped to the chest and the flat of the blade pressed to the nose, or lichen-covered Celtic crosses unchanged since the days of early Christianity; a standing stone holding its solitary vigil millennia-long; and, on a raised beach where no wave has crashed for ten thousand years, the remains of a lump-rock wall half-concealing the entrance to a cave, a dwelling perhaps of one of the earliest inhabitants hereabouts. Inside the cave, digging at the floor would reveal darkened patches of ground where fires had burned, together with charred hazelnut, limpet shell and bone; and above, the damp rock roof would be discoloured pink-to-purple by heat.

The silence in these places was complete – on board the radio scanned, but found no station; the mobile phone received no signal. We stepped ashore, stopped, and wondered if our ears had dropped off. No cars; no tractor tilled a distant field; no planes; no industry; and no voices, because no one was there. No one to hear us – yet when we spoke, it was in a hushed whisper, not daring to trouble the silence. It was a world away from the world, and we had it to ourselves.

Having found places where we and our boat would be safe, we needed next to look for work and found, happily, that it had been looking for us.

'There's a bloke wants some work done on his fishing boat, and he's heard I'm good with wood... I'm going to see him tomorrow morning; d'you want to come along?'

Graham was a chainsaw sculptor – long-haired, short, wiry, and 52 – whose voice was never more than a croaky whisper. Owing, I suspect, to a mid-life crisis, he'd just bought himself an old wooden boat of 25 feet, his first, built in the 1930s for coastal day-sailing.

Craft of this era and quality of build send traditional boat-lovers dewy-eyed because there are so few of them left; but when I first met Graham, with his boat hauled ashore at a marina, he was busy chainsawing out the accommodation until nothing remained inside the shell but smoke and a liberal spattering of chain oil. Ignoring the vandalism to yet another piece of our maritime heritage, structurally speaking it was like taking the pit props out of a coal mine. But he sat serenely on deck in the autumn sunshine as smoke drifted out of the companionway hatch, nodding slowly to add conviction to what he told me: 'Next year, I'm going to sail her to Hawaii.'

'Why Hawaii?' I wondered.

'Why not?'

There are two types of sailor who ask *Why not?* The first are adventurers of unlimited resourcefulness, able to circumnavigate the globe on a piece of driftwood; the second don't know where Hawaii is.

It is a requirement on the CV of every blue-water cruiser that he is a dreamer, but he needs to be practical too, and the two don't often coincide. It was difficult to tell if Graham possessed both. From where we were standing, Hawaii was 7,000 miles away – by air. His boat was small, and though he wouldn't be the first to do it in a boat of that size, he would be one of very few.

It wouldn't be his first epic journey. He lived in a gypsy caravan that he had pulled, two or three years previously, the 600 miles from Kent on the south-east coast of England to Scotland, behind a draught horse, living off the land as he went, eating rabbits, pheasant, deer – or sifting through the bins.

Expanding on his life story, he told me without pride or regret that he had abused drugs for 30 years, but had stopped using hard drugs some years previously. Slow in thought and speech, the extremeness of his experiences had given him a strange kind of wisdom with one foot in reality and one in fantasy – sometimes absurd, sometimes charming.

I liked Graham, but I feared him too. People in the village that surrounded the marina preferred not to become involved with him, and I wondered if they knew something that I didn't. For all those reasons, I hesitated before taking up the offer of looking at the fishing boat.

At eight o'clock the following morning, as I climbed into the passenger seat of his ancient pick-up truck and settled myself down among the rubbish, he sat in silence, rolling a huge joint. 'Morning, Graham,' I said.

'Morning, Justin.' He continued rolling. I felt uncomfortable – I expected the drug squad to raid at any moment and arrest me for passive smoking. I shuffled lower into my seat and accidentally kicked a bulging carrier bag onto its side; as I straightened it up, I noticed that it was half-full of what I hoped was dried parsley.

'That'll keep you going,' I said.

'Not for long.'

At last, with a flicker of flame from his lighter, Graham disappeared into a cloud of blue smoke. After a while a hand emerged, turned the ignition key, paused there for ten long seconds, then turned the key to 'start'; the suspension bounced and the diesel engine clattered into life in the cold, misty air.

'I think we're going to be a bit late,' he said, cheerfully. 'I told John to expect us at half-past eight, but it'll prob'ly take us an hour to get there … unless I get my foot down.'

To drive in Scotland is to rediscover the joy of motoring. The roads are not busy – Linda and I once drove the 21 miles along Loch Awe, Scotland's longest inland loch, on an ordinary morning in April, and passed only one car. To delight the eye there is drama in both colour and contour around every bend of the single-carriageway roads. Around the worst bends there will be a bunch of flowers tied to a tree, which helps keep your mind focused on the road.

After heavy downpours – there's one an hour in Scotland – waterfalls seen in the distance as white lines threading sinuously down black mountainsides can be heard roaring from five miles away. When you drive over these cataracts, where they are forced sucking and gurgling through a conduit under the road, they fire out the other side like water canon, filling the air with noise, spray and rainbows in the newly emerged sunshine. I look forward to the ever-changing scenery of a car journey in Scotland, but I'm not a very good passenger.

Graham's pick-up truck had the unnerving habit of sliding at the rear when cornering sharply – so much so that it was easier to view the road ahead through a side window. Plunging downhill on the reverse camber of a wet road, this 'sliding' tendency worried oncoming traffic, too, judging by their faces. I began to wonder if I could get through the winter without work.

In one of those strange and unexplained ironies in life, Graham evidently imagined that I was sitting in the passenger seat wondering what the hold-up was: 'I always drive cautiously when I've got a passenger,' he croaked. We came over the brow of a hill and heard a clonk from all four wheels as their suspension springs straightened out, relieved of the weight of the vehicle now that we were airborne. We landed so hard, I almost expected to hear the sound of jet engines back-throttling, followed by the 'No Smoking' sign being extinguished.

'Well, that's very much appreciated,' I told him as I climbed back into my seat, 'because I'm a very nervous passenger.'

'You mustn't worry – I'm aware of everything around me… my concentration is right here,' he said, wafting the smoke in front of him. I almost wished that I hadn't complained because he was so taken aback that I should be afraid of his driving that he turned to face me – as far as his seat would allow – and leaned against his door while he described the scrupulous attention to detail he brought to it, with the result that any former objective to stay on the road was almost lost to this new purpose.

'It's not *your* driving,' I said, looking through the windscreen for him, 'as much as the driver in the oncoming vehicle – he may not be expecting to see you on his side of the road.' This note of humour drained from my face as I watched him straighten out another double chicane.

'Don't talk like that,' he warned, 'you'll attract it to you.'

That was enough for me. 'I cannot believe that someone in a car two miles away is being influenced by what I am saying to you right now.'

There was a screech of brakes that laid my left cheek and both palms flat against the windscreen as we skidded into a lay-by on the opposite side of the road, and stopped. Graham turned off the ignition.

'Why have we stopped?' I asked.

'I can't tell you this and drive at the same time,' he began. His tone was patient, but slightly hopeless, as though he were about to explain to a four-year-old what electricity was. 'You are in touch with every living thing around you,' he said with a majestic sweep of his hand, which reminded me of Yoda, '– the trees, the grass, and the leaves. Your spirit and their spirit are one. It doesn't matter whether they are right here, or on the other side of the world. You are in touch with everyone and everything – always.' He studied me to see if he was getting through, and then suddenly his wizened face lit up and he beamed at me: 'I don't know why I'm even explaining this to you – you know it! You know all this stuff!' he chuckled. The engine clattered back to life, and the adventure continued.

Graham

Arriving back at the loch, I saw the green hull of our boat *aol Ila* floating above her reflection; blue wood smoke curled zily up from the flue; a heron fishing from a rock at the water's lge let out a shriek when he saw me, and flapped clumsily way. The dinghy floated under the branch to which she was ed with a highwayman's hitch. This knot falls apart in your nd when you pull the bitter end – I only use it on still days calm anchorages, and it has become synonymous with time ent in paradise. I climbed into the dinghy, rippling the still-ss of the water, and rowed away. Back on board, the sight of nda's violin and books of music scattered about told me she d had a nice day too; she hunched her shoulders and flashed impish grin – then, with a self-deprecating reference to her olin practice, said, 'I've managed to clear the anchorage again!' From the oven came the smells of a home-smoked fish pie. ettled down by the wood-burning stove to enjoy simply ng here, and thought back to how it had all started.

Linda

Eventually we drove onto a pier in a well-protected harbour, and John – a giant of a man in his forties – stood smiling as he blocked the path of our vehicle, his thumbs hooked behind the shoulder straps of his regulation yellow PVC fishing dungarees.

'Aye, aye,' he said.

We climbed out of the car and stood chatting for a few minutes while our words drifted away as steam on the cold morning air. Over John's shoulder empty fishing crates, bearing the legend THIS CRATE HAS BEEN STOLEN FROM McCULLOCHS FISH WHOLESALERS LTD, were being loaded onto a fishing boat. I watched as they sailed through the air in a great arc, appearing from behind a building and disappearing over the side of the pier, thrown and caught by unseen hands.

We followed the heavy 'clump' of John's yellow wellies as he led the way along the pier to a motor launch and jumped on board. He laid a big hand on the starter-cord of the outboard engine and, with a mighty heave that left the boat rocking for about half a minute afterwards, stripped the line out to its fullest extent. It refused to start, despite reaching about 8,000 rpm. He gave the engine some good-natured rebuke under his breath while he checked that the fuel was on, the choke was out, and the throttle was open; and then, apparently concluding that he hadn't pulled the cord hard enough, got to his feet and took the starter-cord in both hands. Bringing his whole weight to bear on the problem, he stripped the cord again; nothing. He pulled again... and then again. The boat rocked so violently from side to side that I was beginning to feel seasick. But all of this was only a prelude to the frenzy of pulling that now ensued, and I could see that it was beginning to get personal – if he had just put the engine into gear as he pulled that cord, we would already be a mile out to sea. He brought his fist crashing down onto the outboard motor – the universal 'final warning'; pulled again, and it reluctantly spluttered into life with a tinny popping exaggerated by the glassy stillness of the morning.

We motored for 20 seconds to a fishing boat that lay quietly at its mooring; he killed the engine and climbed on board. I looked back at the distance we had covered; I could almost have leapt it. As John unlocked the wheel house, we idled around the decks of the fishing boat and poked investigatively at bits of machinery. It smelled damp, oily and fishy. Everything on board was heavily built, functional, and ugly, designed by hard-won experience and a shortage of cash. Down below, John showed us around the very basic accommodation by way of an example of what he wanted us to recreate on his 'other' boat. It wasn't going to be difficult. The bunks were bare plywood sheets screwed to a $4'' \times 2''$ framework. 'Well, this is it,' he said with pride. 'I'd have the accommodation just the same in the other boat if I could – but you'll see she's a slightly different shape up for'ard.' As we motored back to the pier I couldn't help wondering why John didn't buy himself a bucket of nails and a few bits of wood and do the job himself, instead of employing a couple of first-rate boatbuilders like me and Graham.

We stood in the forepeak of the 'other' boat like three men in a potting shed without windows, and because there were no windows we examined each other's footwear in order to avoid each other's gaze – John's yellow wellies; my leather boots of a style that I thought boatbuilders would wear; and Graham's hairy 'Yeti' boots. John described in his gentle Scots accent what it was he was 'after having': 'Two berths on that side, one on this with a settee berth below, a work surface athwart ships, galley, sink, and lockers wherever you can get them.' In the silence we tried unsuccessfully to imagine the finished cabin.

Graham threw back his head, shook free his long hair, and screwed up his eyes like a Native American summoning dead ancestors.

'What kind of a *feel* do you want it to have in here?' he enquired. John answered in that tone that lets the speaker know he has been heard, but imperfectly understood.

'Eh?'

'I imagine you work quite hard at your prawn-fishing?'

'Aye, we do.'

'And when you come in here you just want to relax and forget all about it... what do you want – some beanbags?'

John roared with laughter and winked at me edgement at what he supposed was Graham's wid humour.

Was it even remotely likely, I wondered, th would be the preferred seating arrangement of bl chuck 200 fish crates 50 feet in the air, and who here stinking of prawns to drink tea – so strong it it – from chipped enamel mugs? Surely they'd pro splintery wood with four-inch nails sticking out – up – to prevent their arses from slipping off as th gunwale to gunwale in a raging storm.

Graham blinked his way through the laugh work out what the joke was, but John choked saw that Graham was in earnest: 'Aye, I can see coming from... but really we just need it to be strong and easy to clean.'

'Like his other boat, Graham,' I hinted, be enquire about the drapery.

'I was just getting there,' said Graham, gett what's the budget for this?'

'I was hoping you'd be able to tell me.'

Graham thought for a long time, appearing price a series of possible interior designs. 'Well 'did you want to spend more or less than £5,0

'£5,000! Well, certainly no more!' John ga

Ignoring his amazement at the ruinous pri 'Ok then – but we won't be able to start for

In the 1980s I used to sell telecommunic for a PLC in London amid cut-throat compe never, never, heard a sale closed better.

Even though I put my chances of survi during the next three weeks at only 50/50, i found some work so that we could begin mer's sailing. On the drive home, I was l returning to our quiet anchorage and tellii day. I chuckled to myself when I thought yarn I would have for her, and it occurred would provide us with a good deal more

2 THE HOUSE FIRE

'This is Justin,' a friend said at a party as he introduced me
to an attractive, dark-haired woman in her forties, who had
every appearance of wishing she were somewhere else. 'He's
the one that had the fire recently.' Before I could say 'hello',
she flagged up her hand to stop me.

'Don't talk to me about fires!' she said theatrically. 'We
had a fire in our airing cupboard.' For the next 20 minutes she
described how a faulty switch had started a fire that scorched
her knickers, tea towels and pillowcases; how the house had
filled with smoke; how she managed to save the budgie; the
timely appearance of the Fire Brigade – what they did and said,
how she had made them tea, but couldn't offer them biscuits;
and how it had taken days to clear the smell from the house.
As I listened to her, I realised that sooner or later she would
ask me what happened with my fire. She did.

'Well... our house burned down.'

An involuntary hand climbed to her mouth.

'Oh my God!' she said. 'That sounds worse than mine.'

* * *

At three o'clock one morning I became aware that Linda had
whispered something to me and as the words seeped into my
drowsy mind, I awoke, frightened.

'What's that noise?' she'd asked. The noise was everywhere.
It sounded like the gnawing of a thousand rats. I jumped out

of bed. Upstairs our house had an open-plan sitting room – all the bedrooms were on the ground floor. It had been built 120 years earlier entirely from wood – timber frame with shiplap boarding on the outside; the floors and ceilings were planked; and all the rooms had panel walls... only the chimneys were of brick. I ran into the dining room, from where the noise was louder, and noticed that it seemed to be coming from the ceiling; so I jumped on a chair, and laid my hand against the boards – they were hot. I ran upstairs, expecting to be beaten back by flames when I opened the door to the sitting room, but was startled to find that all was quiet. I crossed to the fireplace to make sure that the fire was out, and found that the ashes were stone cold.

Relieved but confused, I turned to leave and cast my eye around the room one last time, and then noticed a wisp of smoke coiling into the air from one side of the hearth. I leapt over and tore the carpet away to reveal the floorboards, at which fingers of smoke slithered into the air from the gaps between the boards.

I phoned the emergency services and had just given them our address when the phone went dead; and then the electricity failed – but instead of plunging the house into darkness, strips of feeble orange light, which I hadn't noticed before, glowed from the gaps between each of the ceiling boards above my head, bathing every room thinly. The house was completely alight, but flames hadn't yet broken through into any room. We pulled on the odd clothes that came first to hand, and left the house – then I remembered the advice to close all internal doors in an attempt to contain a blaze, and rushed back inside. I hadn't been out of the house a minute, yet already things had changed. The house was hotter, airless, fumy, and for the first time felt threatening. I slammed just one door at the far end of the house, violently, by throwing my shoulder against it; and as it banged closed, a panel jumped off the wall behind me, sending a flame belching across the room. I gasped, and the fumes I breathed in locked my chest. I realised then that in a fire, it isn't the heat that kills. I staggered out of the house alternately choking and vomiting.

By the time we got down onto the road, the first fire engine screeched to a halt. I recognised the driver.

'Is it actually alight?' he demanded, throwing down the window of his cab. I felt a flash of guilt for disturbing him at this time in the morning – then, almost with relief, I remembered the flame.

'Yes.'

Doors burst open; boots rained down onto the road; locker lids were thrown open; hoses stripped from reels and the crew ran up the hill, dragging gear behind them.

The house was 70 feet above the road and from where we stood only a faint orange glow could be seen through the windows until, suddenly, we heard a crack and saw a roof tile shatter in the heat, allowing oxygen into the starved house. As we watched, the orange glow at the windows became yellow and, softly at first, we heard a low rush of air, which soon increased to a roar.

The fire crew were having trouble getting sufficient water pressure to fight the blaze. By inspiration, they dammed the mill leat that ran along the road with sandbags, and four men dragged the frame of a huge diesel-engined pump to the water's edge and threw it in. They fired it up – you could feel the growling of the engine through the road underfoot, and watch the level of the water in the leat falling as it drank. Just as the fire crew began to drench the house, its roof collapsed with a single catastrophic action. The deafening crash of tiles echoed across the night valley as the roof fell through the building, sending flames bursting out of windows whose frames rolled across the lawn in fiery cartwheels, chasing firemen into the darkness. The house was now a ball of fire too bright to look into, and flames rose into the night sky, setting light to the trees. The fire crew walked back down the hill – there was nothing they could do. I put my arms around Linda, who was sobbing uncontrollably, and said, 'Good will come of this.'

I don't know why I said that. All we owned now were the tatty clothes in which we stood, and an tatty car for which we no longer had a key. But as I stood there watching the house collapse in flame, all I could think was: 'Good will come of this.'

Later that morning, Linda went to the bank to see if she could get access to her account without documents. A few minutes later she emerged, in floods of tears again. She'd been explaining her circumstances to the cashier when a member of staff interrupted her – he worked on one of the front desks, selling insurance, and couldn't help overhearing the conversation. He shouted across in a supercilious voice, 'I hope you were fully insured?'

'No,' she said.

He crashed his hands down on his desk in exasperation and then, in a tone that implied she had exhausted the last of his patience, roared, 'Oh! I can't believe people like you...'

Over the months ahead a lot of people asked what had caused the fire, and it was a long time before we ourselves knew – but we discovered that some mortar had been missing from between the bricks in one of the chimneys.

We stayed with friends for a month, then began to rent a place in the town. The charred ruins of our house remained on the hill above, to tell the story.

I remember a few years earlier, while living in London, I had a burglary at my flat and set about repairing the front door myself. I bought a new lock and handles at a DIY centre, got them home, saw that I had bought left-handed handles for my right-handed door... but rather than change them, spent a day and a half rehanging the door to suit the new handles. It was only when I stepped back to admire my handiwork that I realised that there is no such thing as left-handed door handles: you've got both handles, you just install them to suit. I was a DIY botcher – so it came as a shock when one day someone suggested, 'Why don't you rebuild the house yourself?'

I didn't know whether to laugh out loud or pity them. It was about the most absurd suggestion I'd heard; yet, dangerously, it took root in my mind, and after that I kept asking myself, 'Why don't you rebuild the house yourself?... You can always hand the mess over to the professionals when it all goes wrong.' So I thought I'd give it a go.

In the paddock above the ruins of our house I began building a stable for Linda's horse, with the intention that we would live in it first. The day we moved in – with the simple furniture of a plank to sit on with plates on our laps, a camping stove for cooking one-pot meals, and a bed made from bales of straw – was one of the richest days of our lives. I was too excited to sleep much. Pasture smells breezed in off the field through the open half-door to mingle with the piny wood, and I lay listening to the sound of leaves rustling in the great oak tree that overhung the stable, until rays of golden sunlight striking the planked wall opposite told me it was dawn.

Using the foundations of the burned house, a team of bricklayers built up the block walls of the new house, and on top of those some carpenters erected the timbers for the roof. I laboured for them; watching and learning; and when they had finished I took over, beginning by felting and tiling the roof to create a dry space below.

I was nervous at first, and self-conscious, too – always stopping work when anyone visited, so that they wouldn't see how I fumbled; but as my confidence grew I began to enjoy the build. By coincidence, builders and tradesfolk would gather every morning and evening at the bottom of the hill – where a construction firm had its office – to sign in or out for the day. Standing in the road chatting to each other, they'd steal glances up the hill to see how I was getting on; from the fragments I overheard, it was going OK.

Linda worked for the National Health Service and was based at a hospital. Every morning she'd leave the stable early to go to the hospital for a bath, then begin her day's work. I bathed under a field tap – in the height of summer it was fun, but as autumn rolled in, quickly followed by a harsh winter, the cold water tumbled onto my head like bricks. One day I turned on the tap and found that the water had frozen – 'Thank God,' I muttered, and never used it again.

Fifteen months after we started, the house was finished; it looked great, and even featured in a magazine. We lived there in bliss for a few years, but our eyes had been opened to what we could achieve, our hearts became restless, and we yearned for some new adventure. We realised that we faced a choice – we could live in our pretty little house happily enough for the rest of our days, or we could sell up and take a chance on life.

Before meeting Linda, I had been on an ill-prepared and financially perilous year-long cruise in a yacht, and talk of it from time to time had sown a seed in her mind that she would like to try something similar... though perhaps with better organisation.

We began to visit boats for sale, but didn't like the light skittish feel of some, or the plastic-wood of others. Flush with the success of building the house, and easily prone to self-deceit, I began to wonder if we could build our own boat.

At first we considered building in steel, as a kind of insurance policy, whereby a steel boat would survive a collision if ever we hit rocks; but when we were invited to visit an amateur steel boatbuilder in mid-construction, and he showed us around his rusting hulk propped up in a field, and we saw the heat-distorted sheets of hull planking that made it look as though it had already fallen off a cliff, my heart sank. Although I felt we might be able to do better than that, I could see how hard it was to achieve a good result, particularly as I wasn't an accomplished welder... and anyway, what did *I* know about metal? We began to consider wood. It was hard at first to give up the feeling of security we thought would be ours from sailing in a steel hull; but we came to realise that we had no intention of becoming a casualty on the rocks, and that it was ridiculous to plan the boat-build around that eventuality.

Wood has gone out of fashion for boatbuilding because it's expensive and needs a lot of maintenance – but it remains the loveliest material to work with and, for appearance, nothing even comes close. We chose to build a wooden boat and to sheath the hull with fibreglass and epoxy resin – it would make the hull incredibly strong and the wooden planking would never feel a drop of water.

As for the design of the boat – it was suggested by the most enjoyable book I've ever read, *Sailing Alone Around the World* by Joshua Slocum. Actually, I've read it 20 times. In it Slocum describes his adventures as he became the first person to sail around the world single-handedly in his boat, the *Spray*. Setting sail in 1895, *Spray* was remarkable for being able to steer her own course without the need for a hand permanently on the helm – a fact that probably owed a lot to his deckmanship – but without which a voyage 'alone' was unthinkable. At one stage he sailed for 2,700 miles spending less than three hours at the helm. Three years later, having survived pirates, an ambush by natives, phenomenal waves, storms and uncharted reefs, he sailed home and tied his boat quietly to the same stump from which he'd left, to the astonishment of all who had resigned themselves to having seen him for the last time – bar one, who always said, 'The *Spray* will come back.'

We were romantically impelled to build a replica of his boat. We needed some building plans and found our man in John Hesp. Over dinner one evening, John explained he would do the drawing, but wished we would build a different sort of boat – one based on the Falmouth pilot cutter. Falmouth is situated in the south-west of England in the county of Cornwall, which overlooks the English Channel on the one hand and the Atlantic Ocean on the other; and was one of the ports from which, during the great age of sail, pilot cutters would head out over the horizon in all weathers looking for incoming ships and offer pilotage to their destination port. The rule was that the first boat to put a pilot on board an incoming vessel got the work; consequently the pilot cutters were sailed hard and fast as they raced to get their man on board. Over many generations the pilot cutter design was refined with this one object in mind – and they became, in their day, the fastest small craft afloat.

It was a romantic story and I found the designer persuasive, not least because he was prepared to risk losing our business in his attempts to get us to change our minds. I reasoned that he knew a lot about boat design, and I knew nothing – so perhaps I should listen to what he was saying, even though he wounded me when he told me he 'hated' the *Spray*.

My first impression of the boat he drew was that it was slightly quirky – a bit like a child's toy boat with its almost flush decks, and its long coachroof with portholes; but the lines were very pretty, and the gaff-rigged sail plan looked rakish. We soon warmed to the design and could imagine being proud to own a head-turning vessel like that – so we settled on building it.

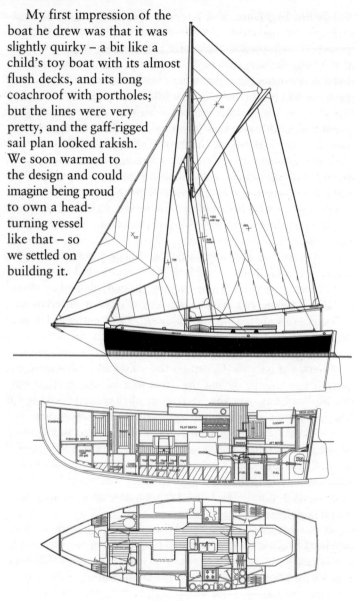

John Hesp's boat design

His brother, Dom, was building a virtually identical boat, and was six years into the project when we met him. We'd turned up wide-eyed to have a look around an actual example of the boat we were to build. Dom is a blacksmith, and by that I don't mean he makes horseshoes – he was a member of the team that built the £270,000 Winston Churchill Memorial Gates, with blazing bronze and wrought-iron spears, that guard Churchill's crypt in St Paul's Cathedral. He was building his boat with the same breath-taking perfection from, naturally enough, steel. I tripped around his boatshed – a dilapidated mill with a river running through it – and tried to make intelligent remarks. At the end of the tour Dom turned to face me, propped his hip against a vice embossed with the legend '3 Tons', and folded his arms revealing veins the size of garden hose running over the undulating hills of his musculature – the like of which I'd only previously seen on the back side of a racehorse.

'So you're going to build a boat?' he said.

'Yes…' I faltered. My courage was faint after all I'd seen.

He cocked his head to one side and fixed me with his eye. 'You must be f—ing mad.'

I struggled for an answer.

Dom went on, 'Tell you what – six years I've been at this – and it's not nearly finished yet… it's bloody nearly killed me, this has. If I'd known how long it would take, and how hard it was going to be – I'd never have let John to talk me into it.'

I nodded sympathetically. John lurked in the background impassively – this must be how they signed up all their clients.

'Tell you what – if you're thinking of building a boat, my advice to you is: don't-f—ing-do-it.'

I thanked him, and told him I'd consider what he'd said.

John estimated how much hardwood and how much softwood we would need, and sent through a cutting list so that we could begin to order the timber. Exmoor, where we lived, is a farming area and is quite well-wooded, so I began looking around for a sawmill. I hadn't visited one before and, when I found one, walking into the yard with all its machinery screaming as it cut through trunks of enormous trees, unmanned me;

but the sweet resinous smell of freshly cut boards was intoxicating, and I couldn't wait to get my hands on some.

It can't be every day that someone turns up at the Quantocks Sawmill – suppliers of fence posts and shed cladding to Somerset's sheep-farming community – and asks if they've got timber suitable for boatbuilding. I can see that now.

'What sort of wood 'as it got to be?' Mr Cowling, the yard owner, eyed me up and down doubtfully.

'Douglas fir – not too knotty.'

His gaze fell onto the 24-foot long boards that were stacked between us – and which I noticed were riddled with knots.

'Well, this is the Douglas we got – I shoont think twood be any good.'

I wasn't so easily discouraged – the way I saw it, if I was going to build a wooden boat, I'd need a *lot* of wood, and I'd just found some. I ordered 400 cubic feet ('4 undered coob,' he corrected me) of inch and a quarter boards.

Two weeks later I turned up to collect the timber and was shocked by the size of the stacks. I was planning to get them home in my beaten-up Land Rover, which had earned its spurs building the house.

'How you going to get 'em 'ome?'

'On my Land Rover.'

'On that?' he said, tossing his head in the direction of my pride and joy. 'What – a cuppla boards at a time?'

'No, I'll take… say, half of it – you'd be amazed what it's carried in the past.'

Ten minutes later, Mr Cowling's son gingerly lowered six tons of planked timber onto the roof of my Land Rover with his forklift truck, and crushed it, forcing the wheels up inside the bodywork. Then he lifted them off again. Point made.

I jumped into the cab, and was about to drive off to go and arrange some proper transport when I noticed that daylight was shining in around the floor – and that the cab was no longer attached to the chassis.

We also needed a lot of hardwood. Steve Groves had an old-fashioned sawmill close to where we lived, tucked away in such a private spot that I had no idea it was there. 'That's the intention,' he said.

Ostensibly Steve was selling timber, but unless you could explain what each piece was for, and satisfy him that you wouldn't waste it, he wouldn't let you have it.

He could supply us with all the hardwood we needed for the frames, deck, floor and accommodation of the boat. I can only imagine that he hadn't spoken to Mr Cowling, and therefore didn't know what he was letting himself in for, when he suggested that I come to the yard and help him saw the ash, oak, chestnut and maple that we needed. The huge circular saw blade of his mill, measuring 6 feet in diameter, was powered via a fabric belt, which whipped rhythmically up and down like a sheet in the wind as it streamed along at a terrifying rate. The belt was driven by a noisy tractor housed within the cutting shed; and when he released the clutch, the circular blade sang out with a windy, lethal note, above all of which you could not make yourself heard. As a result, Steve had developed a kind of mime language – working at his yard was like taking part in a Chinese opera. 'Yes' was a single nod; 'no' was indicated by shutting his eyes and shaking his head once. 'Don't do it that way' was meant when he frowned and drew in a long breath through pursed lips... whereas 'For Christ's sake, don't do it that way!' was indicated similarly, but with raised eyebrows.

At first I tripped around the yard in an amateurish way, Steve's skill and economy of movement making me more keenly aware of my own shortcomings. He moved tree trunks around first by tractor, fitted with a pair of forks, and then – once they were on the saw bed – by use of a crowbar, sharpened at both ends until they were brighter than a Japanese chisel, and with which he could line the trunks up for the blade with millimetre accuracy. He held out a crowbar and mimed a long nod – I came to collect it; he positioned me at the far end of the log by gesticulation and then, according to instruction, I flicked it in under the log as I had seen him do... but it didn't get under properly, so I gave it a manful thump with the flat of my hand, only to feel the keen edge of its other end sink to the bone. I looked at my blue puncture wound and knew it was going to hurt; then at Steve – but he had turned away, busying himself with something else, pretending not to notice.

Perhaps to put me at my ease, he told me the story of a 'know-all' that came to his yard once and wouldn't be told anything. Steve warned him not to leave the trapdoor to the sawdust pit – under the blade – open.

'I know, I know, I've worked in a sawmill loadsa times,' the know-all kept saying.

Suddenly, he fell through the trapdoor and into the pit, from where he would have a mole's eye view of the screaming blade and feel its gale of wind. It was a heart-stopping moment for both of them, but he bounced out and away – 'like a frightened rabbit,' Steve said – and then pretended nothing had happened.

'Course, I pretended not to notice, didn't I?' he said.

I couldn't help sympathising with the know-all and suggested to Steve that because he was so good at what he did he made us feel our inadequacies.

'Christ – it's me who's inadequate,' he said under his breath, walking away.

His knowledge of working with timber had been handed down through generations. He turned the process of planking a tree into a journey of discovery – he told me that he often found bullets embedded in a tree, explaining that saplings were used for target practice during the First and Second World Wars; and now that the trees were mature, 70 or 90 years later, bullets are found in the heartwood.

One day, sawing a huge trunk of ash, there was the usual 'Whump!' as the newly slabbed board fell flat on the table, exposing its grain to the air for the first time. It was a stunning example of the much-prized olive ash, where the dark brown heartwood is framed by the newer white growth. As I stood admiring it, and wondering where on the boat I could use it to show off the grain to full advantage, Steve had walked round from the business side of the sawmill; he passed in front of me and, laying two great hands on it, said: 'You in't gettin' that bit.'

He might have refused me his best bits of wood, but he gave freely of his knowledge – lifted me out of the junior class, and taught me to cut accurate joints. Within a few months our paddock was filled with stacks of drying planks, and I had a quantity of already-seasoned timber on which to start work.

To get the project off the ground, we had borrowed £10,000 from our good friend JFW, who had just sold his farm to go round the world on a motorbike. For the time being, Linda planned to continue working full-time; I would build the boat full-time.

I shut myself away in the workshop to make my mistakes in private. The workshop was actually the stable in which we had first lived; it had then been home to Linda's horse for a few years – but, sadly, he now trotted around a paddock in the sky. The stable wasn't big enough to assemble the whole boat, but it *was* big enough to get us started, to build all the component parts – the frames, deck beams, stem, furniture and fittings.

On that first day, leaning against the huge and pristine workshop table – which had neither a scratch nor spot of glue on it – I suddenly felt physically sick in my stomach; utterly daunted by the size of the project I'd taken on; I felt as though I'd been dropped in the deep water of mid-ocean and left to swim for the shore. Questions that I should have asked earlier crowded into my head now:

Where do you begin to build a boat?
How do you know whether the bits you build are good enough?
How long is it all going to take?

I looked out through the open door and into the sunshine which beckoned me away from all this; yet to either side I could see the thousands of pounds worth of stacked wood, which had turned the paddock into a timber yard. What on earth was I going to do with it all?

In front of me lay John Hesp's hundred pages of detailed drawings which used words I couldn't understand to describe parts of the boat I didn't know existed. As I looked up in despair I happened to catch a glimpse of my reflection in a dusty window and was shocked by what I saw – I scarcely recognised myself... it was me, and yet it wasn't me; I seemed so small, powerless and defeated. Self pity welled up in my breast. And I was shocked, too, when I heard a voice – my voice – hurl abuse at the image: 'Look at you – you idiot... what made you think you could build a boat – you're nothing but a pathetic daydreamer. You PRAT!

I turned away, feeling ridiculous, and began to wonder how I would explain to Linda that I couldn't do it, and rehearsed the excuses I could make to hide the fact that it was my incompetence that prevented me. I thought of all the money we'd wasted – all the time, and all the dreams we had for the future aboard our boat. I knew she'd be disappointed because she had *trusted* me.

In the silence I came to realise that I would do anything rather than lose that trust, tarnish the image of the hero she erroneously saw in me; and anything rather than spoil our dream.

I picked up one of the drawings, tried to imagine it in three dimensions, tried to work out how you would go about making such a component part; and slowly some answers came. I began with the frames.

At 12 ft by 12 ft (3.6 m × 3.6 m), the workshop table was big enough to draw the wishbone shapes of each frame or 'rib' of the boat, full size – though we didn't need to actually 'draw' the frame, merely to plot the position of 40 or so points along the frame's curve. These plots had to be millimetre-accurate, and to achieve that we drew a grid of vertical and horizontal lines, top, bottom and both sides of the table, with accurate measurements marked off along them. A straight edge (and it had to be straight) could then be laid across the table for marking off. The designer supplied us with the position of each of the 40 plots – which differed for each of the 19 frames – as a table of offsets. At each plot we marked an 'x' onto the table and screwed a short length of angle iron up to it. The idea was that we would create a formwork on the table from the carefully placed angle irons, to which we could bend and clamp our timber to form the sweeping curve of the frame.

We prepared our timber – ash, because it bends well – into long, thin strips, called laminars. The length of the laminar varied according to the size of the frame. The width of each one was around 2 inches, and the thickness of the laminar varied between a quarter-inch and three-eighths thick, depending on the severity of the curve it had to be pulled into – only thin laminars will bend into tight curves. Taking eight or so of these laminars, we wet-glued each one and stacked them into a slippery pile, building up the required thickness of the frame – then, turning the stack onto its side, we pulled them into the curve of the angle irons and clamped them into position for two days, until we were sure the glue had set. We used resorcinol formaldehyde for the glue – it is the purple/black glue you see in plywood.

We laminated the port and the starboard side of the wishbone frames at the same time and glued them together at the bottom, adding further support where the frames begin to separate with a structural member known as a 'floor'. The top 'open' ends of the wishbones were filled by deck beams, which were also laminated curves. The designer's instruction was that we should include in each frame the supporting timber for any accommodation that occurred at that part of the vessel – it might be a settee, or the support for the navigation table, for example. The idea was that when all 19 frames had been set up and the hull planked, it would be a simple matter to lay floors (cabin sole), attach walls (bulkheads), and build furniture if all the supports were already in place – and so it proved to be. Two days after gluing, we took the clamps off, cleaned the frame up, stored it away, and got on with the next, until all 19 had been completed.

Linda would help me in the evenings for an hour or two when she came home from work with jobs that I couldn't do single-handedly. We worked during the weekends, too, making great progress, but never seeing family or friends. We'd heard that 95 per cent of the people who start building a boat don't finish it – and we were frightened of being numbered among them. After a year either I alone, or both of us together, had worked on the boat on every single day, often until 10 at night, and we were beginning to irritate our friends – so we took Sundays off to socialise, and resumed visits to family events.

Because the stable was too small to accommodate a 37-foot boat, we had a lot of humorous jibes about the boat being too big to come out, but of course we were only building *component parts* of the boat, and I had measured everything – so it was embarrassing to discover that the biggest frames wouldn't go through the door. In answer to it, I bought a pair of the largest hinges I have ever seen, reinforced the corner of the building, and then hinged the entire wall.

After 18 months of building, we had made all the components for our boat that could possibly be made without joining anything together, including frames, stem, hatches, cockpit, tiller, bowsprit, furniture, doors and a hundred smaller items, and it was time to move everything to a huge barn we had rented 12 miles away so that we could put it all together. Linda gave her notice at work, and joined me with boatbuilding full-time.

Then something happened that I hadn't been expecting – I'd been working so hard on the boat that I hadn't even thought about it. In order to pay for the boatbuild, it was part of the plan to sell our house. Having built the house ourselves – together with its history of being built on the ashes of the one we had lost in the fire – it held a more important place in my life than even I had realised. On the day we were to move out, with all our possessions packed up and loaded onto a lorry, I walked around the empty rooms for the last time – touched the doors, the timber posts, and the stone fireplace, and climbed the stairs, running my fingers along the handrail with the intimate knowledge of one who has built them; and everything I touched brought back memories of the challenges and hurdles that had been overcome. Arriving upstairs, I looked out from my favourite window, out to the hill at the back of the house, and up the track leading to the paddock overarched with its canopy of trees creating a dark, secret place. At the side of the track there still remained a stack of 50 or so roof tiles, surplus to the roof build, and covered now by the leaves of eight autumns. I realised suddenly that the house was really a child of mine, and that this was our last day together; these were our last moments. A voice inside my head asked, 'My God – what have you done?' I wept. I thought of stopping the new owners at the threshold and telling them that I had made a mistake, that I was sorry but they couldn't have my house... but I knew it was too late for that. Linda came up the stairs and, using my pet name, laid a hand on my shoulder to turn me as she said cheerfully, 'Come on then, Alfie – we're all packed!' As she pulled me around, she noticed my face – there were no words – and she left me in private. For an hour more I stood there, asking: 'My God, what have I done?' Even today I still dream we've got our old house back; then I wake and remember.

At first we rattled around in our new boatbuilding barn, which was 90 feet long (27 m) and 40 feet (12 m) wide; but within a week or two we began to appreciate the extra room, particularly when we came to put the stem and keel together. The stem of a boat is the piece of wood that forms the 'cutwater' at the front, the bit you see coming menacingly toward you when the vessel is under sail – it plunges down through the water and bends round to become the keel. It is a huge structure, made, in our case, from 18 layers of wood 10 ft (3 m) long and 6 in (150 mm) wide, all bent through 90°, and it connects to the keel with a 'scarf' joint (a scarf is the diagonal joint that looks like the end of a chisel); then the joint was glued with epoxy resin and drawn together by bolts. The keel and stem together formed a single swept piece of timber 45 ft (13.5 m) long.

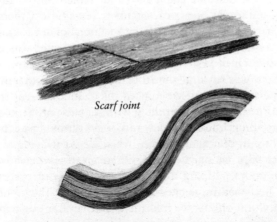

Scarf joint

Laminated curve

All 19 frames – which were biggest toward the middle of the boat, and took three men to carry – were then 'set up' like the skeleton of an upside-down dinosaur. We set them upside down, so that we could attach the keel easily. To set the frames up, we built a 'strongback' on the floor – a kind of wooden railway track. The strongback allowed us to stretch out a wire so that we had a dead-straight line for reference, and also to establish an absolutely level plane on the floor. With the strongback, we could set each frame the correct distance apart – dead centre and at right angles to the line; the correct height off the floor; and absolutely vertical to the level plane. It sounds complicated, but wasn't.

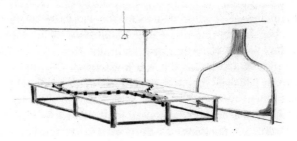

Laminated wishbone frames

For the first time, we could get an impression of the size of the vessel, and see the poetry of her curves. It was also a 'moment of truth', as we could sight along the keel notches in each frame to see if they aligned. The greatest error we found was one-sixteenth of an inch (3 mm) – with which we were thrilled.

The barn was open at the front, and its three other walls were only half-height, so we noticed the change in weather as autumn turned to winter, bringing with it gales that shook the asbestos roofing panels and blew tornadoes of sawdust around the building. In the evenings, too, when we went home to the holiday-let barn we had rented until Easter, the wind howled under the doors, keeping the curtains in a state of perpetual agitation and making it hard to heat even with the plentiful supply of wood offcuts we had for the stove. But our temporary accommodation was pretty, it had exposed timbers to the roof, and a gallery at one end on which was the bed, so we took it in turns to lie in bed watching the other prepare breakfast below – it was quirky and we loved living there.

We lifted the huge laminated keel and stem and dropped it into place. Once that was glued into position it secured the bottom ends of the frames once-for-all-time. We began planking near the ground (i.e. in the deck area of our upside-down frames), and when the first plank was fastened on either side we had locked the position of the frames, top and bottom, for ever.

I mentioned earlier that the Douglas fir boards we bought from Mr Cowling were 'riddled with knots'. We didn't intend to build with planks that were faulty, of course, and developed our own 'grading' technique. The boards we bought were up to 20 inches (500 mm) wide, and these we sawed down to 2½ inches (60 mm) wide for our planking so that, being narrow, they would plank around the hull with a sweeter curve – in the tightest curves, at the turn of the bilge, we used planks that were 1 inch (25 mm) square. Where a knot threatened to compromise the strength of these narrow planks we sawed it out and scarfed the plank back together. At first I wondered how strong the scarf-jointed planks were, so I supported the two ends of a scarfed plank on trestles and jumped onto the middle. When eventually I managed to break it, and several others I experimented on, they never broke on the scarf – the scarfed area was always the strongest part, so I stopped worrying about that. If we couldn't decide whether a particular knot was acceptable, the little test we developed was that Linda took one end of the plank and I the other, and we swung it sharply up and down until it was flexing like a bridge in an earthquake; as the plank flexed, a weak knot would give a little 'click', which you could both hear and feel. If the plank made no sound we accepted it; if it 'clicked' we scarfed. We carried on sawing, checking and scarfing until we had 140 planks, 40 ft (12 m) long and 2½ inches (60 mm) wide. Over the next couple of months we planked the hull amid the delirious excitement of watching our boat take shape – they were screwed and glued both to the frames and sideways to each other. The finished upside-down hull was an impressive size, towering above all our visitors and stretching far back into the darkness of the barn.

We were building our boat amid the Devonshire rolling hills and patchwork fields of farming country, which boasts the highest sheep population per hectare anywhere in Europe. Over the road from us was a sheep transport depot and consequently a lot of our visitors discovered us by chance as they nosed around the nearby barns, waiting their turn to unload. Great was their astonishment, once they had satiated their appetite for derelict balers, wrappers and muck spreaders, to come around the corner and discover a ship-in-build. They soon became regulars, coming in to chew the cud and check on our progress. In fact, it was mutually beneficial – we hadn't appreciated what a fund of knowledge existed among sheep farmers concerning boatbuilding; nor did they make us beg for their advice – they *insisted* we had it, and didn't stop until we had *all* of it.

Having built the boat upside down, we had to turn it the right way up to fit tanks, engine and furniture. At this stage it was 37 ft (11.3 m) long and weighed several tons – that's a couple of tractors – so we called on our farmer friends to help. Word went round and 20 people arrived on the day we had appointed as 'boat-turning' day. One of those who came was an old neighbour of ours from Dulverton. He'd never seen our boat, working offshore as he did, but he'd promised us about a year earlier that he would give us a hand turning the boat when the day came, and he was well qualified to do so – he was one of the 'sky monkeys' who had helped set up the pre-construction of the Millennium Dome in London, and worked as a rigger on oil rigs. Walking into the barn to see the boat for the first time, he was caught off guard and staggered backwards at the size of it – he'd misunderstood and thought we were building something about the size of a rowing boat. Then a stranger walked in – wiry and in his thirties, he had the lively step of a practical man; he clapped his hands, once, rubbed them together, and announced: 'I hear there's a boat being turned here today... I've done a couple of these before, I'll give you a hand.' The two of them took charge – and a great job they made of it, sticking with us for the two days it took to gently heave her over.

For the spars – the mast, the boom and the bowsprit – I was guided by advice of John Leather in his lovely book *The Gaff Rig Handbook*. He seemed to recommend Sitka spruce, plenty of which grew in a small forest owned by an estate just along the road from our house, so I went to visit the owner who himself was nearly as tall as a tree, and was fascinated to hear what we were up to, as we walked through his forest – he taking a long easy stride with his hands clasped behind his back – we marked three trees for felling. They grew straight and reached right into the canopy where I could see their needles gently dance. On the way back to the estate house, I raised the subject of money: 'What price did you have in mind for the trees?'

'I was just thinking about that,' he said. There was a long silence as we walked, and only when we got near the house did he straighten up and say, 'Would £30 be all right?'

A few days later I was there, alone, with my chainsaw. I kissed the tree, promised it adventures new, and then, following the advice in my Husqvarna chainsaw users' guide, cut the bird-mouth scarf one-third of the way through the trunk, completed the back cut, and watched the tree fall in the opposite direction from the one I had been expecting – missing my Land Rover by about four-thousandths of an inch as it bounced, and then settled, allowing the silence of the forest to return. I looked around me; no one was watching. The next two came down where they were supposed to.

Our mast was to be 50 ft (15 m) long, and the book *Boatbuilding: A Complete Handbook of Wooden Boat Construction* by Howard I Chapelle recommends a hollow mast to save weight; so I sawed the tree trunks into three lengths of 20-odd ft (6 m) each – that being the longest length Steve Groves can get on the table of his sawmill – and asked him to saw them in half lengthways. My plan was to hollow them out, glue the two halves back together, and then scarf the three lengths together. Steve lent me a hollow-faced adze, with which you can gouge out chips of wood, and which was probably invented for hollowing out trees to make canoes. You couldn't tell it from a sledgehammer except that the addressing face was shaped like a sugar scoop – and was razor sharp. All Steve's tools were razor-sharp – the blades hanging on the wall of his workshop hissed at you as you passed by. He showed me how to use it, swinging it between his legs like a croquet mallet, but doing the work on the backward stroke. As I reached out to take it from him he held on to it for a moment, drew me closer, and raised a cautionary finger between us.

'Mind your ankles,' he said.

I was bad at adzing, but did the job adequately, and it felt great to be using a hand tool in the way that it had been used for hundreds of years. Before gluing the mast back together we took the opportunity to fill the hollow with aluminium takeaway containers, so as to give a better radar echo at sea. We asked everyone to save their containers for us, and pretty soon folk were driving hours out of their way to bring us the remains of their last night's Chinese takeaway, still in white carrier bags dripping with red oil.

'Aren't people funny?' we'd say to each other when they'd gone, and we were wandering around the workshop looking for somewhere to chuck half a container of cold barbecued pork and some chicken chow mein, and for some soapy water to wash the grease from our hands.

With our boat the right way up, we put in the engine (a 50-year-old Perkins P4 bought at a reclamation yard, in gleaming condition – and possibly never used for anything but training mechanics); in went the fuel and water tanks; then the furniture was fitted, and finally we laid the deck – sealing up the boat, as we no longer needed free access to the accommodation area.

Launch day loomed; visitor numbers grew; a film crew arrived to shoot part of a television series called *Dreamboats* for the Discovery channel; people came from miles around to see the final result and pronounced her 'A1', 'Gorgeous' and 'Incredible' – and I suppose she was incredible, when you think who built her. We'd been so busy that it wasn't until we heard the unanimous 'Ooohs!' and 'Aaahs!' of our friends that we stood back and realised we'd done it, we'd been successful – we had built a boat and she was beautiful. John Hesp, the designer, had 'imagined' her of course, and it is to him that all credit is due for her lovely form – but we hadn't *spoiled* his vision. Her lines were soft and sweet, and her varnished wood shimmered like bronze. One night a spirit entered her body and when we arrived for work the following morning she spoke to us, promising lazy sunsets after fast passages.

With a view to lifting our boat out of the barn and transporting her to the sea, a representative arrived from

South West Crane Hire to survey the job. Road access to the barn was by a typically narrow high-sided Devonshire lane. I'd measured it before we moved into the barn and thought we had just 2 inches to spare, so I knew he wouldn't be pleased.

The man who arrived was Ken, whom I had met a few years previously back in Dulverton when we were deciding where to build the boat. Our house was on a hill 70 feet above the road, and I'd been wondering if it would be possible to build the boat in the front garden and then have it craned down. Ken had come along to survey the site at that time and, shaking his head, pointed out that it was just too difficult – because of the height, because of nearby power lines, and because the roads were difficult of access in a long vehicle. So we took his advice and put the boat together in the barn we now occupied, 12 miles away, and with (slightly) better access.

As soon as Ken jumped out of his car I recognised him, and walked over with outstretched hand; but before I could say, 'Hi Ken, how are you?', he huffed off along the lane, hissing and tutting, and began measuring things obstreperously – the width of the road, the height of the hedges. I looked at Linda and frowned – she shrugged her shoulders, and we let him get on with it. Ten minutes later he stormed into our barn and banged his tape measure down on the table.

'Look!' he shouted, 'I think we can do it... but why don't you blokes that build boats think about how you're going to get them out before you start?' I was speechless – but it didn't matter because Ken had more to say.

'Anyway, this is *nothing*,' he softened his voice and beckoned us toward him, as though he were about to let us in on a big joke. 'A few years ago, I went to see a bloke at Dulverton – do you know Dulverton?' We nodded faintly, exchanging glances. 'Well, this bloke lived way up on a hill – you know that road that goes out to the moor?' he asked, describing the road we lived in. 'Well, this bloke lived up that hill – and he only wanted to build a boat in his front garden! Haaaaa!' He banged the table with the flat of his hand, and tears of mirth filled his eyes. '...Yes, in his *front garden*,' he reaffirmed, as though we doubted his word. 'Imagine! And this bloke,' he said, snatching tiny little breaths that let you know the story is about to get even better, 'this bloke thought that we, right? – *we* would come along with our crane...' (here he raised his arm and a limp hand high above his head) '– never mind all the power lines!' he said, wafting them away; '...pick his boat up – and lower it all the way down to the road... and onto a truck!' He lowered his hand slowly to the ground for effect, disappearing behind the bench as he did so. 'God only knows how he expected the truck to get out of Dulverton,' he said, reappearing; 'what with those narrow lanes and blind corners!'

He wept with joy, taking a minute or so to regulate his breathing and dry his cheeks before resuming the dignity of one privileged to view the madness of this world from an elevated position. Aftershocks of mirth still troubled him five minutes later as he handed us our paperwork, and climbed back into his car.

Two years and nine months after we had started building the boat, it was loaded onto a truck by a crane driver who probably used to work in a circus. He wore skintight blue jeans and yellow rigger boots, which clomped hurriedly about the yard, having only two speeds – stand and run. It was as if he were living against the clock; and to add to the sense of urgency, he kept his tongue – which he stuck out of his open mouth – constantly banging from side to side, like the hammer in a fire bell.

Having wound out the hydraulic legs, levelled the crane, tied his strops, and taken the strain, he threw open the door and called me to his cab: 'Justin! Justin!' A crowd of 50 or so friends and neighbours had gathered to watch the boat leave its shed, and I ran from among them, jumping up to the cab to find out what was wrong. He didn't say anything, but took the strain once more, and an alarm went off...

'Hear that alarm?'

'Uh-huh.'

'Well... that tells me the lift is too heavy for the reach.' He waited for my disappointment as the finality of what he said sank in.

'Oh,' I said.

'But I'll tell you how we deal with that...' He lifted his rigger boot high into the air and then stamped it down onto a red button on the floor of the cab; the alarm stopped, and with a revving engine he sent my boat whirring into the air like a sprat on a fishing line.

The transporter that was to take our boat away had not yet arrived, so he swung the boat out over the road and left it hanging 80 feet up, blowing softly in the wind, and read his paper while we all waited. Distantly hearing a car approach along this quiet country road, he threw his paper aside, let the boat stream down on its cable, and placed it gently on the road – entirely blocking it. When the car appeared around the corner you couldn't help but chuckle to see the look on the passengers' faces to find the road blocked by a boat. Up it went once more, and stepping out of his cab with a gallant sweep of his arm the crane driver ushered them through.

The truck arrived at last and the boat was loaded on board. It began its 120-mile journey by crawling away toward the narrowest part of the lane, on a bend, and constricted by an old oak tree growing right at the roadside – it was the part that had been worrying me all these years, and the driver told me to shout if it looked like we wouldn't make it. As the boat approached, I could see that it *wouldn't* make it – I drew a panicked breath and shouted, but no sound came from my mouth. I tried again, but still no sound came. The truck drove on; a metal fitting on the boat plunged deep into the ivy that clung to the oak tree, stripped the trunk bare, and then passed on without incident.

For the first few miles of the journey, a retired farmer who had always been the first to volunteer whenever we needed help rode with me high in the air on the deck of our boat, ducking the branches. After a while he turned to me with a genuine sense of achievement and said, 'I've travelled along this road many times in my life – but this is the first time I've been along here in a boat.'

3 BUMPS AND BREAKAGES

Three years of hard work were over; we slept the sleep of the just and woke from our first night spent on board at the boatyard – still on the trailer – to simply lie there and admire our handiwork. There was a knock on the hull and I was just about to call 'Hello?' when I heard a voice sniffily say, 'Nah... it's ferro-cement.' And walk away.

Linda got up to make a delicious cup of coffee in our new home. The sun shone high in the midsummer sky, while eddies of wind blew to us the unfamiliar smells of the marina.

Later in that disorienting day, as the crane picked our boat up and whirred it to the water's edge, a crowd of invited and uninvited guests (equally welcome) stood on the dockside to watch us launch – among them the designer, nervously waiting to see if she would float.

After waiting for my brother to deliver himself of a speech emotionally praising the craftsmanship and determination of his younger sibling – qualities he had previously entirely overlooked – and then anoint the bow of our boat with some fine *Caol Ila* whisky (after which she is named), amid heartfelt wishes for happy voyages, the crane operator lowered her into the water, stopping just before she floated to suggest I check the bilge for leaks – all dry. In the words of Joshua Slocum, she floated like a swan – and as our boat was launched, so were we, into a new life as live-aboard sailors.

Cornwall's maritime heritage goes back to the year dot and has been passed along intact through the generations, so that even today hard-won knowledge of the sea is safely held in the hands of its fishermen, commercial boat operators, and town-quay prowlers.

'Now then, an old fisherman taught me this,' our sail-maker said, as he grabbed from me the rope that I was coiling – badly. Cornishmen are modest and will always pretend that knowledge they hold themselves is only on loan from someone else – someone more accomplished. They love to lampoon themselves, competing with one another in their claims to be the biggest bungler, even showcasing their art in the Falmouth Marine Band, which lines up in marching formation at important events in the town, immaculately dressed in costume. The bandleader calls order, shouts instructions that don't make sense to anybody, and then starts them off... Not one of them is able to play a note on the instrument he is holding; they have no sense of timing; they don't know how the tune goes (or they all play different ones); and when they sing they don't know the words. On closer examination, their instruments turn out to be bits of old plumbing stylishly formed into the shape of a trombone, plastic toy trumpets, and drums formed from empty paint tins dangling from bits of string; and in any case the band marches off in all directions because no one's told them the route... The only sure thing is that it will both start and end in a pub. All this chaos is received with thunderous approval by the crowd. It goes to the very heart of Cornish playfulness, lack of ostentation, and debunking of formality – three things that *are* taken seriously. Roger Daltrey asked if he could join in for his birthday. 'Listen,' said the bandleader threateningly, 'you might *be* somebody – but you don't hit your drum 'til I tell you... or you're out.'

The sailmaker showed me the way 'an old fisherman' would coil a rope, and I've never coiled one badly since.

By launching our Cornish-styled boat in Cornwall, we received the full benefit of this fund of shoreside knowledge. It was better than a book, it was a degree course, and gradually we learned which ropes went where; why a spar was rigged in this way and not that; how the boat was tidied away for smart appearance – and the advice was always appended with words like: 'That's how they *used* to do it anyway... in the *olden* days.' Or: 'That's how *I* might do it... I don't say it's *right* – but that's how *I* might do it.'

A week or two later, with the mast rigged, a mile of rope rove through half a hundred blocks, and a thousand feet of sail bent on, we began deliriously happy days of sea trials. Again, we were taught by people who knew their subject, among them our good friend Peter Chesworth, a photographer who has travelled the world sailing on and taking shots of classic boats; and in the unlikely event that he didn't know a thing himself, he knew the man who did. Stepping back ashore after a sail, someone we'd met twice would pop by with a gift: 'Now here's a cranse iron belonged to my father – 'twood suit your boat 'ansome... and e's only sittin' in my garage, gettin' in the way.'

We were eager to learn our new boat so that we would be ready for a forthcoming event, which had already been on our minds for three years – a series of races known as the Falmouth Classics, open to all classes of classic and gaff-rigged vessels old and new. During the boat build, when our spirits flagged, we found new energy by dreaming that our vessel would be fair and fast, and that one day we would prove it by entering the Falmouth Classics, race against similar craft, and not disgrace ourselves. With that thought in mind, we'd pick up the sanding pad once more, and continue to smooth her curves.

We entered *Caol Ila* in her event and pretended indifference to whether we won or lost; but speaking for myself, my nerves were unbearable. We had six people on board on the day of the race and left our mooring early to try to form ourselves into a team. Out in the harbour, the water was a foaming frenzy of over-canvassed craft constantly involving themselves in near-collisions. The start of our race was signalled and we got to the line as the gun went off, only to be immediately embayed between two vessels – caught in the lee of one, unable to bear away because of the other, and seemingly unable to pull ahead (which I felt we should be able to) because we were shielded from the wind. Add to that the fact that the three of us were heading in the wrong direction owing to a misunderstanding of the route by the upwind vessel. We were pinned so intimately together, we three ships, that Andy, our well-tanned, muscular foredeck-hand, made a promising start to a relationship with the daughter of our neighbouring skipper. A moment more and we would have lost him... but I noticed that *Caol Ila* was inching ahead; she was getting a sniff of wind into her sails, and the more she got, the more animated she became, like a lioness waking from the effects of a tranquillising dart. Suddenly, we heaved over a wave and she was off! – surging ahead, furious at having been held back, she smashed angrily through the waves, pushing them aside and throwing spray high and wide.

She laid a new course to the first marker buoy a mile or two ahead, strung out in the direction of which were the rest of the fleet in our race. In the lead, *Wylo* – who we had already marked out as our greatest rival – was throwing spray too as she climbed into the Force 6 breeze. We had no hope of catching her, but were pleased to be passing slowly through the fleet, ticking them off one by one – second place would suit us well. After five minutes of this, I noticed almost with disbelief that we were closing with *Wylo*, fast. We settled a course to overhaul her on her windward side, and watched the faces of her crew – now on us, now looking to their rigging to see what changes they could make.

'Shake out your reef!' was their shout as we drew even with them, shadowing them from the wind – their remark aimed to shame us for our lack of courage in not carrying full canvas.

'We don't need to,' was the reply, as we crashed ahead.

Caol Ila, now in the lead, rounded the windward buoy, and scarcely touched the water as she flew home on the downwind leg. She galloped so hard that not only did she win her race, but she came second in the race that preceded it. I was emotional with pride.

At the prize-giving event that evening, the music played, the beer flowed, and the atmosphere was uproarious – it thrilled us to be a part of it all, and owning a boat like *Caol Ila* was the passport to this new and energetic maritime community. I wondered if I would be required to make a speech, and formed some words in my head just in case. The prize for our race was set on a pedestal, the room hushed, third place was announced; then second; and then first prize was awarded to... *Wylo*. We, the crew of *Caol Ila*, stood frozen and looked at one another in non-comprehension. No words came.

Later, I noticed from the race list that we weren't even named among the entrants. By the time I had established with a race official that there had been a clerical error, and that we had indeed won, the race committee's marquee was closed up for the night. But, peeping through a gap in the laced-up door, who should I see standing right there but the race-committee chairwoman? This sudden opportunity to put things right, together with the injustice I felt at not being awarded the cup, brought matters to a head in me and, on the verge of tears, I wailed through the lacing: 'Open up – there has been a terrible mistake! You've given the prize to the wrong person! You failed to enter our name on the entrants' list. You must get the cup back and give it to us – *Wylo* themselves say that we won!'

The chairwoman calmly said they would sort it out in the morning and walked away.

Linda had been standing behind me while all this went on, and when I turned around I was embarrassed to notice her expression was evenly split between pity and mortification.

'Who were you talking to?' she asked, looking thoroughly humiliated.

'The cleaner,' I replied.

Two days later *Wylo* came alongside, and in a little ceremony all their own awarded us the Winners' Cup.

Linda and I now had the boat to ourselves, and had to learn to handle her. With the two exceptions of a ferry crossing to Santander and a pleasure cruise on the paddle steamer *Waverley*, Linda had never set foot on a boat before we launched our own. She was born in Glasgow, moving south to England when she was 6 and living, for the next 30 years, remote from the sea. She trained first of all as a nurse, then a midwife, and at 26 qualified as a health visitor – a community nurse specialising in infant health care. It was shortly after that that she and I met, and her chances of a steady career were ruined.

No amateur handlers of the traditional 'gaff' rig have made more mistakes – and no boat on the water suffered as many teething problems – as we did those first few months.

Hell's bells – within five minutes of starting the engine on the first occasion that *Caol Ila* moved under her own propulsion, I looked into the engine compartment and saw that the gear box oil had entirely emptied itself in our bilge.

Out on open water, Linda and I hoisted sail and pottered about for the day before heading upriver to explore, and to find a quiet spot in which to anchor for the night. Following our progress on the chart, and coming to the navigable limit of the river, it was time to drop the sails and turn around. The river here was narrow, made narrower still by three rows of moored vessels on our port hand. As so often happens when you think of taking sail in, the wind increases, and so it was for us – but to make matters worse, I pulled on the jib reefing line and it jammed. I reached to start the engine – but it wouldn't start. We accelerated toward the mudflats, full sail set, with every expectation of making a public disgrace of ourselves. The only thing that could save us – though it was a danger-ous plan to follow considering that we were sailing at eight knots – was to attempt to turn into and sail among the moored vessels, without sinking one.

We had already noticed, since launching, that our boat turned a lot of heads on account of her old-fashioned good looks. Eyes followed us now, but what had been a point of pride, a moment before, was suddenly an impediment as we bowled along out of control. Add to this a suspicion I have that there is an erroneous assumption among boaters that anyone sailing the gaff rig has salt running through their veins.

Picking one of the moored yachts, we aimed for her stern and in a moment shot past at full speed, lifting her with our surging bow wave; turning further upwind, we slipped just ahead of a boat in the next row, found a gap in the third, and then brought our head up to wind with the sails flogging noisily. As she slowed, in the shade of some trees, I ran forward to throw out the anchor, noticing as I did that the water here was almost shallow enough for wading – at least the anchor would hold. It did, in spite of our boat thrashing about like a bird taken by one wing. A minute or two later we had the sails lowered to the deck.

A long look at how we had arranged our sail-furling and at the engine starting/stopping routine allowed us to make a couple of changes so that those particular problems couldn't arise again.

It was early September and the days now began with cotton-wool fog, which we watched, during breakfast taken in the cockpit, slowly drawing away in veils over the mirrored water until dewy sunlight was revealed in the fields and on the hills, giving us our first clue as to which way the world was facing. By mid morning a light breeze would set in to allow those who go about their business under sail to start work; accordingly we hoisted sail, weighed anchor, and rippled silently away in the direction of Falmouth, increasingly hearing the noises of civilisation – the town, the docks and the people – taking part in the world; to buy groceries, pop into the library, or collect pieces of chandlery. By mid-afternoon we would be ready to catch the tide back upriver to a secret place, and so, weighing anchor once more, we would leave behind the town's busy murmurings, and head along to whichever creek promised us the most restful night among the birds and the trees.

During those early days we had numerous visitors, including my dear friend Steven Thomas – who has stuck by me now, mercilessly, for 30 years. He is a film-maker, and had come to capture the first steps of our infant boat as she pattered across the water, shivering her canvas to a light breeze. Writing in the sixteenth century, the Italian historian Vasari, speaking of one of the brightest lights ever to shine, said, 'Occasionally Heaven bestows upon a single individual beauty, grace and ability, so that, whatever he does, every action is so divine that he distances all other men, and clearly displays how his genius is the gift of God and not an acquirement of human art.' Time had to wait almost 500 years for his antithesis – but the long wait was over when, in 1961, Brian and Barbara Thomas announced the birth of their son, Steven. Having watched him ruin our house by bumping into things, accidental spillages, unwanted matter brought in on the soles of his shoes, taps left on, incandescent material left smouldering on soft furnishings and that kind of thing, we felt obliged to follow him fairly closely on board now that there was the added danger of someone being drowned. With him arrived two friends of his who own a company that makes the world's biggest lights and we were relieved to see that they hadn't brought any with them. For an hour *Caol Ila* thrilled us all with her film-star poses, eventually gaining the harbour entrance.

'Ahhh...! St Mawes!' Steven roared, not missing the photo opportunity as we sailed past St Mawes Castle, the famous landmark of that pretty Cornish fishing village. 'I once spent an absolutely filthy weekend in St Mawes!'

An awkward silence followed, during which we tried to avoid looking at the images offered to us by our minds' eye. 'Were you on your own?' I asked.

Steve

Linda had the boat arranged as comfortably as a country cottage. Fresh fruit and vegetables swung in a net hammock, where they would be airy and stay free from bruising. A convenient home had been found for all the gear we carried, and everything from crockery to cooking oils were secured against breaking or spilling; and in that trim we set off on a voyage 200 miles along the coast to Chichester, Sussex – the county in which I grew up – nibbling away at the miles in day-sized chunks. This was to be our shakedown cruise.

On that first day, of our first voyage away, the sun shone on fields of green and yellow, hedged by hawthorn and sloe on the cliff-tops; and a gentle breeze blew across our beam as we tinkled steadily through the water until 40 miles had ticked away. We entered the River Yealm riding a strong ingoing tide, which threatened to carry us into trouble: the river quickly became narrow, shallow and crowded with moored boats, and we, still green, were somewhat out of control as we swept in. The harbour master happened to pass by just then, so I took the opportunity to hail him for advice about where to moor up.

'Here would be good,' he said, indicating a vacant spot on a pontoon.

'Where will I have room to turn?'

'Go for it now.'

And with that official encouragement to snap me out of my inertia, we swung round to face the stream – narrowly avoiding holing a haughty-looking craft with our bowsprit – and drifted into the vacancy.

The harbour master came alongside us with a smart turn which, taken together with his battleship-grey beard, marked him out as an ex-naval man.

'Nice boat,' he said, laying his hands on the varnished chestnut of our cap rail. I announced that this was our first new port in our new boat, and offered him a nip of whisky to help us mark the moment.

'I shouldn't really, you know.'

'It's a single malt.'

'Ahem. Just a small one, then.' I poured him a drop of Caol Ila, and told him the story behind the name. There wasn't much to tell, really.

'Oh,' he sniffed, when I'd finished, and downed the whisky in a oner, banging his glass on the deck. He gave a little cough, and then choked on his next breath.

'I say – it's got a kick, hasn't it?' he squeaked.

Unmoved by our hospitality, he wrote us out an exorbitantly expensive ticket for the pontoon berth – when we read it, it was our turn to choke.

We saw how our money was being spent later that night when I happened to go on deck for a pee, and found myself illuminated – like a fox in the chicken shed – by the accusatory beam of a spotlight operated by the harbour master and river police, who were silently patrolling the water, and had mistaken me for a thief.

We left first thing the following morning, preferring to take our chances among the bandits, and encountered an unexpectedly steep swell, which alternately threw the bowsprit into the air and then plunged it into the water. Linda let out a scream to see our boat tossed about like a cork and at first refused to allow me to leave the cockpit to attend the sails – which I needed to do. After five minutes she was calmer, we set some sail, and headed more comfortably for Start Point.

When the wind picked up I took in a reef and gathered up the idle sailcloth, which now hung under the mainsail, by tying it with the six reefing pennants built into the cloth, so that it resembled the rolled parchment of a Dead Sea scroll; later, as the wind fell lighter again, I shook out the reef, but forgot to untie the last pennant; it alone held the sail, which filled suddenly to a straggling squall of wind, and the sailcloth ripped itself free from its binding, causing the first damage to our brand new sail.

We entered the River Dart that evening, where a range of cannon from the battlements of Dartmouth Castle has guarded the entrance for 600 years – but by maintaining an audacious front we slipped through. The old town, with its medieval black-and-white half-timbered houses, is quickly followed by the hurly-burly of the new – ferries churn the water; fishing boats arrive with their clouds of screaming gulls; naval vessels slip smartly by; and everyone, it seems, is either in a boat, or waiting for one. Upriver, things quieten down again, and you soon arrive at the village of Dittisham – locally rendered as

'Ditsum'. Intending to anchor at first, we noticed that it was after 5 pm, and the harbour patrols had finished for the day; so we found a vacant mooring buoy, planning to use it free of charge overnight by slipping away before 9 am... yet as we motored slowly up to it and I put the engine astern to bring us to a halt, I heard a 'clonk' from underwater. I confirmed my suspicions by putting the gearbox ahead again, and finding no drive concluded that the propeller had just spun off. Every cloud has a silver lining, and ours was that we had a very entertaining pub – the Ferry Boat Inn – virtually at the end of our bowsprit. It was to here that we repaired to contemplate our next move, and it was to here ten days later that our new propeller was delivered... though we *had* been back on board in the interim, even if only occasionally.

I installed the new propeller – properly this time – and we set off in the drizzle for Weymouth, which we entered with a hot engine at about 7 pm. The harbour was very busy, and if there was a harbour master on duty when we were looking for a berth, he wasn't answering his radio. When we arrived there was some kind of fight going on among the fishermen, accompanied by a good deal of shouting, which gave the harbour an aggressive feel which it may not deserve. But when we rafted up seventh from the quay and a harbour official jumped down and rushed out to us, leaping from boat to boat – like a chimpanzee who has spotted a fallen banana – to collect his £25 for this indifferent berth, I felt *myself* getting a bit hot under the collar. On an alphabetical list of UK harbours, I notice that Weymouth is very nearly the last one you would come to – which *exactly* reflected how we felt about it.

The following day we carried on for Poole. Fifty yards from the town quay there was a violent explosion from our engine compartment, followed by an extravagantly showy cloud of steam billowing out of the companionway hatch. You couldn't see into the accommodation, which looked like a Norwegian bath, and we didn't know if there would be a second explosion, so it was only with difficulty that I persuaded Linda to feel her way down and turn the engine off. Not quite sure what had happened, we continued on our way to the quay, where we were caught by the willing hands of the local steam society who had heard the blast, seen our cloud of steam, and had dropped everything to come and admire us, immediately conferring on us honorary membership. Although disconcerting, we found it a very convivial way to arrive, immediately putting us in touch with all interested parties, among whom we struck up friendships new.

Opening up the engine box, we saw that a cooling water hose had burst when the cooling water in the system had all but boiled off. This alerted us to an overheating problem that was to recur many times over the next year before we traced it to an inoperative heat exchanger.

Next stop was Yarmouth on the Isle of Wight, where our lines were caught by the skipper – Hamish – of a yacht called *Low Profile*. Hamish was a retired English teacher of Scottish descent, who introduced us to the very agreeable habit of taking a wee dram at 6 pm to help swallow the news. Chatting to him, we mentioned that we came from Falmouth... he rolled his eyes.

'God, don't talk to me about Falmouth. I was setting off from there to go to Ireland last year – unusually for me, I had decided to pick up a crew member to make the passage easier; leaving the harbour early in the morning, I left my crew at the helm while I went below to make breakfast and have a wash. Thirty minutes later there was a hell of a crash, and a rush of water. My crew had fallen asleep at the wheel and steered us onto the Manacle Rocks. The boat had to be towed off by the lifeboat, who put a pump on board to keep her afloat. I've only just got her repaired.'

Also in the harbour was Hans, a Dutchman who wore a floppy blue cotton hat with a sweat-stained band, about which something was lost in the translation – it was probably the height of fashion in Holland, but here in England you only ever see them in television comedies, worn by people pretending to be a village idiot. He was on his way to Portugal, waiting for the weather – intending to arrive in time to spend Christmas with his daughter. His boat was small, and it was late in the year to be heading to Portugal, but somehow, looking at him and his quiet manner, you didn't doubt he'd make it.

When we were motoring away from the pontoon a couple of days later, I found the gear lever was snagging, making it difficult to engage gears. We drifted back alongside to investigate, and as we did noticed that plastic-smelling smoke was coming from the engine box, and removing a panel found a flame dancing under the engine, shedding a cheerful light into all its dark corners; fortunately, it was easily put out with an extinguisher. The powder from the extinguisher was not so easily dealt with, and we were weeks clearing it up. In reverse gear, the gear lever cable was able to lie across a huge 400-amp alternator; vibration had worn away the plastic sheath in which the cable travelled, baring the metal and allowing it to spark across the alternator and set light to the plastic sheath. We sat on the pontoon with Hamish and Hans, who had witnessed the event, waiting for the smoke to clear. Hans slowly rolled himself a cigarette, put it in his mouth, and then patted his pockets.

'Duss anyone have fire?' he asked, flashing us a smile.

I replaced the cable and tied it back, well away from moving parts.

We motored out from the harbour a day or two later into the strong tides of the Solent and immediately picked up a ball of floating polypropylene rope in the propeller, which seized. By good chance the strong tide washed us down onto some small craft moorings sited just outside the marina entrance in the Yarmouth Road, and we grabbed one of them with a boat hook as it went past; from there, the marina launch towed us back in. Hans and Hamish were expecting us.

Next stop was Newport. To get to Newport you have to sail past the world-famous harbour of Cowes, and it was here that we passed a wooden replica of Joshua Slocum's boat the *Spray*, which we had considered buying five years previously, before we had struck on the idea of building our own, and were interested to see her still at her mooring. The price had been too high for us, and sailing past now we realised that we had no regrets about the way events had unfolded. Upriver from Cowes we arrived at a low-season pontoon berth opposite the Folly Inn, to be met by the toothless grin of a man in his fifties, bare to the waist, giving himself a haircut as he leaned overboard 'a-groof' to see his reflection in the water... and as he looked up we could see it wasn't going well. From the other side of their boat his stern-faced wife, who had been mechanically tearing off pieces of stale bread and throwing them to some swans she was grooming for the pot, straightened up and stared at us with an expression of mild annoyance.

'Hello!' we called. She tossed her head in acknowledgement and then, having resigned herself to our presence as yet another trifle to be endured, she returned to her husbandry.

We visited the pub, which had the appearance of a tired village hall the morning after a fourteenth birthday party; it smelled of spilled drinks and cooking oil, and had mouldering lavatories. It was run, however, by people who were used to partying, and who consequently were never too tired to be cheerful.

The following day, we had a brisk wind to scoot us along to Chichester Harbour, which I hadn't visited for years. There is a sand bar guarding the entrance, which calls for close attention – particularly when the wind is in the south, as it was today. I got it wrong – I know I did because I could see the sand bar through the turbulent water... but I don't know how wrong, because we didn't have a functioning depth sounder. We creamed along, riding the ingoing tide – helped to even greater speed by having the wind behind us – toward the town of Itchenor, just before which we turned to face the wind and tide and drop the sails, a thing we achieved tidily enough... but as soon as we turned back on course under engine, clouds of steam drifted up the companionway, warning of more overheating, and the engine had to be stopped. Just then a yacht and smiling crew passed by close enough to admire our varnishwork, so we improved on the situation by asking for a tow the few hundred yards to a mooring buoy, hoping to save ourselves the trouble of hoisting sail again. They obliged and manoeuvred us excellently among the crowded boats to leave us quietly moored at Itchenor, before heading off with a cheery wave.

Our persistent engine trouble in those early days whittled away our trust in it, slither by slither, until we were surprised when it started, and never expected it to run for long – not a bad relationship to have with an engine, on reflection. When motoring, we learned always to have sails ready to hoist, and to navigate such that we could *sail* out of trouble, if necessary, at any time – strong tides and flat calm being the greatest danger.

From among the trees a punt set off to meet us, and its skipper introduced himself as the owner of the traditional boatyard – which had stood on that shore for 150 years – out to take a closer look at our boat and its strong resemblance to a local craft known as the Itchen Ferry. He had the hallmarks of a craftsman; his coarse hands bore the legend of a thousand superficial wounds.

'Build her yourself?'

'Yes.'

'Lovely... How long?'

'Three years.'

He was solid in stature and slow of speech, with restlessly searching eyes; his dark hair hung loose below his shoulders; he was clean without being neat, friendly without being polished, and invited us to come and look around his yard. I took him to be a private man, and couldn't have been more honoured.

As he showed us around his yard – a collection of old buildings and historic craft that amounted to a private museum – he treated me as an equal, under the weight of which I staggered. He showed me steam boxes, stocks, frames, moulds, and stacks of sweet-smelling oak. He showed me boats-in-build, boats in for repair, and boats that would never sail again. His yard stood by the shore amid breathtaking natural beauty. Invited into the large shambled house, we were greeted warily by his thriftily dressed wife as she set a kettle on the hob of an old range. We compared notes on our philosophies for living – on simple pleasures enjoyed, on the importance of having enough money, and the ruin brought to those who have too much. After tea, the stove door was swung open, and an unfeasibly large chunk of waste hardwood, sawn from another boat-in-build, was thrown onto a fire which has worked steadily at consuming that diet for a hundred years – a banquet I hope it never finishes.

A day or two later a 'Sunbeam' came alongside. A class of racing dinghy established in 1922, these beautiful historic wooden boats are still made today, ignorant of the plastication of yachting. We'd been told to 'look out' for the owners of this boat by a mutual acquaintance – and they in turn were 'looking out' for us, and generously invited us to dinner the following day, leaving us with a promise to pick us up at 5 pm. Their offer saved us a long walk to the shops. Cooking and eating is a hobby that Linda and I both enjoy. We buy and cook food freshly every day; it's a ceremony that for us replaces television. At 8:30 pm the next day, three and a half hours after they were supposed to pick us up, our would-be hostess telephoned to say they'd been out for the day, were just back, and too tired now to entertain. We were a little surprised to be let go so easily, and went hungry that night; but it brought into focus something that we'd been noticing on our journey, and hadn't been able to put our finger on – as you travel from west to east along the coast, generally speaking, you notice that in the west people have time for people; in the east, they are bored with them and have lost the human touch. It was time to head home. Above us, swallows flew south on the northerly breeze, as if to confirm our decision.

First port of call on the way home was Lymington. Entering the narrow river, crowded with moorings on either hand, a ferry came up fast from behind and made the sound signal: two long blasts, followed by two short. As a result of two years spent minutely studying navigation and seamanship, I felt legitimised suddenly, as part of the 'salty' fraternity, by immediately understanding the secret language of this seldom-heard signal to mean 'I intend to overtake you on your port side', and was dignified by his assumption that I would understand it. I hummed a merry tune, gave way, and was rewarded by a hearty wave from the skipper as he passed ahead, dressed in a peaked cap, and wearing a rampant beard of the finest merino.

The steep wet cobbled streets of the town that dark Sunday evening were deserted, and we cast longing glances at the cosy-looking properties for sale in the estate agent's window. The autumn winds, blowing still from the north, began to chill the damp air, giving the seaside town an out-of-season feel. We heard a forecast of gales for the foreseeable future, and noticed the days were getting shorter. Walking back to the boat we met and spoke dolefully with the owners of a Weimaraner – our dog had been a Weimaraner and had died during our boatbuild. We began to feel far from home. In the rush of events since launching, we had not yet turned our minds to installing our wood-burning stove, and returning to find our boat dark and cold decided that it was time – we needed the homely cheer it would afford us, and it would be the first thing we did when we arrived back in Cornwall.

Before the gales set in late the following day, there was time to get in one more leg on our journey home by sailing to Poole Harbour – 14 square miles of shallow water dotted with islands and channels, which would provide interesting, protected anchorages for the duration of the unsettled weather. At sea that day the masthead drew idle circles in the grey sky as we sailed over agitated water. An exhausted bat, blown offshore, fluttered around the mast, trying to catch it; but the eccentric movements took him by surprise time and again, batting him away each time he thought he was saved. I crossed my fingers for him, but he gave up and flew out to sea – yet returned a minute or two later, more desperate than before. He flew lower and lower until he fell to the deck, where he crawled on all fours to appear around the corner of the coach house, close by where I sat. He used his wings as front legs, the skin of which flopped uselessly onto the deck with every step. A wave splashed on board and washed him away, but he took flight again, headed for the mast, hit it and fell into a gap formed between it and our mast rings. He had found by accident the very cleft he needed, and stayed there to recover, not leaving us until the following day.

Arriving at Poole, we noticed signs reading 'Quiet Area' and followed them. On our last visit we'd been amazed by the number of power craft churning up and down the channel with not a boat's length between them – it was the closest thing in a harbour to a rush-hour motorway – so a 'Quiet Area' was just what we were looking for. We followed the signs to Green Island, where we dropped anchor and settled down among the peewits, while shallow water wavelets, blown by the rising breeze, trilled along the hull. We felt safe and looked forward to our sojourn, riding out heavy weather: we had everything we needed. No one came and no one went; the only activity not suitable for a wildlife documentary that afternoon was from three small landing craft, painted army green, beaching themselves in convoy on the sandy shore nearby and, having done so, refloating and returning from whence they came.

As darkness fell, we were preparing dinner in the kitchen and accompanying a CD of Kasey Chambers as she sang *Not Pretty Enough* when I stuck my head out of the hatch to flick some vegetable peelings overboard and, as I did so, I heard the crack of a rifle shot, and ducked.

'I bet that's a poacher,' I said to Linda, climbing back down. Linda poked her head out. There was another shot, and then a third.

'Quick! You'd better come down,' I said, then popped out again, myself, to see what I could see, hoping that a stray bullet wouldn't find my poor head. As I peered into the darkness, a fourth shot rang out from behind me. I turned and saw flashes as a volley of shots rang out; these were answered by shots away to my left. Then there was a roar of engines, then shouts, followed by explosions, and new gunfire now opened up on my right. With that, the whole area crackled with the sound of gunfire, long volleys forming into continuous action. I slithered back down; war had broken out.

''Spect it's just an exercise...' I said to Linda, but turned the radio on just in case.

Secretly, I couldn't help wondering why we hadn't been asked to move earlier in the day if it was just an exercise, and we'd parked on their exercise ground. On the other hand, I reasoned, they must be firing blanks as we hadn't taken any hits yet. That set me to wondering whether the hull would protect us if we were hit. Battle raged for 20 minutes or so, and with each passing minute that we remained unscathed, we consoled ourselves that, 'war' or 'exercise', they weren't interested in us. Eventually someone won, and the guns fell silent.

'Thank God we're in the quiet area,' Linda said.

The next leg of our cruise took place during the height of the petrol strikes of 2000, and so it was with a good deal of self-satisfaction – having sold the car and left ourselves with our boat as our sole means of transport – that we hoisted sail to reach out of the harbour, fuelled by thin air. We climbed into a gentle breeze with all sail set, including our spanking green and cream topsail, and ploughed a gentle furrow along to Studland Bay, anchoring for the night among a surprisingly large fleet of craft, including a ghost ship from Dieppe, France, which drifted in shortly after us with its huge gaff sails and spars silhouetted against an accumulating bank of sunlit fog.

From there, we set off, I am surprised to notice from my log, to Weymouth again. On a lively sea, and in a brisk wind with Linda at the helm, we experienced an accidental gybe – the boom crashed heavily into a loaded backstay and shattered the block, sending shivers through the rigging, but nothing worse. I went to replace the block with a larger one, then stopped and replaced it with an identical one – it would be better to break another block than lose the mast. I would a thousand times rather that it had been me at the helm at the time of the accident, because Linda's growing confidence was utterly crushed by it. After hours of silent dejection, she yelled: 'There's the *Waverley*!'

'What is?'

'Over there,' she said, pointing to a speck on the horizon. 'It's the *Waverley*, I know it is!'

As far as I could see, at that distance, it could have been a rowing boat, or it could have been the *Queen Elizabeth II*.

The *Waverley* is the last seagoing paddle steamer in the world; Linda's late father had taken her on it as a little girl, when it plied a route from Largs, in Scotland, where her family had a stronghold. It was her father's life's joy to see that boat, she explained, and he once asked to borrow the captain's hat so that he could take a photograph of Linda wearing it – a photograph she still has. Sure enough, she was right – 15 minutes later it splashed past us like a running duck. Linda waved wildly and was as proud as she could be to think of her father on board, in spirit, and to be sailing her own boat now alongside the *Waverley*.

The following day we set off early and arrived late at Dartmouth, where we headed upriver to avoid another season of bad weather, anchoring outside the main channel below the Anchor Stone rock. The following morning we were woken by a clamour in the heronry, which is situated on the shore close by, among the treetops of the Greenway Estate, one-time home of Agatha Christie; blood-curdling screeches presaged aerial bombardment, and a hundred crashes into foliage, only stopping when the airframes of the warring parties were too badly damaged to fly.

An hourly ferry service, courtesy of the vessel *Champion*, runs between Dartmouth and Dittisham, the village near where we lay at anchor; and every hour it passed us at a polite distance on its way. Needing to get to the shops, we raised the ferryman on the radio to find out if he was willing to pick Linda up and set her down from on board our boat, to which he readily agreed. Linda enjoyed the door-to-door service so much that she did it every day for a week, and it helped us to pass another weather-bound detention.

Next we dropped anchor in Tinker's Hole, Plymouth; our anchor went in the hole, but our boat didn't, and we only discovered this near low water when our keel was planted as firmly as the nether millstone – and we heeled over somewhat. It was the first of a thousand similar occasions over the years – deliberately or by accident – and we have seldom minded drying out partially or completely, considering it a small inconvenience to be endured if we wished to explore secret waters where others fear sewing a foot.

Taking advantage of a lull in the weather, we set off early next morning to steal a march on the wind, which was set to blow hard again later in the day. We romped along to complete our cruise, arriving home soon after lunch, and as we creamed past Falmouth Docks, driven from behind by a near-gale of wind, we dunked the buoy bearing the legend 'Speed Limit 5 knots' – just to let it know we were back.

Caol Ila

Arriving at the town, we were bounded on three sides by the dock, a marina, and the stone-built harbour wall. The plan was to make a triumphant and exciting gybe – turn to face the wind, and then drop the anchor. On a gybe, the wind is behind you – in our case it was coming slightly over our left shoulder – and you steer the boat so that the wind passes behind your back and comes from over your right shoulder (or vice versa). As you turn the boat one way, you haul the boom with its mainsail across the other way, so that it remains on the opposite side of the vessel from the wind. Often this can be dramatic, as the mainsail passes through the eye of the wind and slams over, taking the boom (ours weighs 200 lbs) with it. In a gale of wind, drama is assured, yet we'd just completed 500 miles of coastal sailing during which we felt we'd been educated by a lifetime's mishaps, and were feeling confident about handling our boat under any conditions.

As we began our gybe, I hauled on the mainsail – but it wouldn't come across. Suddenly I remembered that I'd deliberately tied the boom to prevent it coming across in another accidental gybe like the one Linda had experienced a few days earlier. It was too late now to stop the boat from turning onto her new course, because the wind had got around to the other side of the huge mainsail and was throwing us round ever further. The boom bent like an archers bow. I only had time to call to Linda, 'It won't take much more of that!', when suddenly there was a 'Crack!' I imagine a tree makes a similar noise when it splits into two, having been struck by lightning. One part of our boom fell to the deck; the other piece was flung through the air and landed in the water. Ho hum.

As I sat that evening with my nip of whisky, listening to the six o'clock news, I was pondering the day's events and wondering how long it was going to be before we could sail again (the workshop was over a hundred miles away and, of course, we had no car), when a thought occurred to me. A few miles upriver I'd noticed a small stand of larch trees, possibly 40. They stood on land owned by Lord Falmouth... surely he wouldn't miss one?

4 HOW TO STEAL A TREE

There are three ways to get to Tesco in Truro: on foot (the store is right in the city centre); by car (overstay penalties apply); or by boat.

At first glance, the chart showing the approaches to Truro doesn't look very promising – on it, the blue area (which very logically indicates the presence of water) doesn't extend so far as the city. The last mile and a half of river dries into hummocks of oozy mud for 8 hours in every 12; but at high water the sea visits the city for a few hours to collect plastic bags, traffic cones and beer cans. We read in a sailing guide that the Harbour Authority welcomes visiting yachtsmen to the town quay, and so, with pictures in our minds of the dignitaries and bunting that awaited our arrival, we set off. We knew we would have to shop either very quickly, or – if the speeches went on a bit – very slowly, stranding ourselves against the wall of the town quay overnight.

The first clue we had as to the wicked sense of humour possessed by the people of Truro came as we blindly felt our way along the convolutional 'deep' water channel, which the Harbour Authority wittily describes as being 'well marked'. We found it to be elusive and narrow; you are either in it, or you are aground. The trouble started at the village of Malpas, where the depth sounder (we had one now) drew our attention hypnotically to the fact that we had only 3 feet of water under the keel; by the time we got to Sunny Corner, we were committed – there was no turning back. The channel (which we couldn't see through the muddy water and polythene bags) was only wide enough to float us lengthways, not sideways. Drawing on slowly past Boscawen Park, perambulatory city folk stood and waved at us, enjoying the novelty of an arrival by boat; some others turned their backs ostentatiously and took great interest in the bins, as if to say, 'You are the 17th sea-going vessel to arrive in the last hour and you bore me'... which is a lie, because the voyage to Tesco in Truro is so hazardous that there aren't 17 arrivals in any one year. We motored for another minute before noticing that the land had stopped moving, and came to the sad conclusion that we must be aground.

So loathe are we to waste anything that when we broke the boom, we turned a part of what remained into a long and clumsy boathook-come-depth sounder, the distant end being marked off in foot measurements. Our thrift came into its own now that we had no clue as to whether the deep water channel lay to the right or left, but our new stick found it, and enabled us to fumble along on our way. Linda manned the foredeck, constantly punting the boathook into the mud on one side, then the other, calling the depths. From ashore, first-time visitors to the city could be forgiven for thinking that Truro and Venice were twinned, and that both had singing gondoliers. Turning gingerly into the channel that leads along the last 100 yards of the journey, we found an old wharf building that rises vertically out of the water on the starboard hand had been turned into posh new balconied apartments. Our mast crosstrees tapped politely on their tinted windows before tipping their potted plants into the water.

Either no one told the harbour master we were coming or he hadn't expected us to make it, because the quay was utterly deserted when we arrived except by one man of about 60 who stood a little back from the edge. He appeared to be waiting for us, and being of a miserable turn of mind I wondered if he was about to tell us we couldn't park there, at which I bristled, and thinking of all we had been through to get this far, carried on defiantly. Securing a rope around a bollard I jumped ashore. He leapt forward. 'Oh, my boat!' he cried, clasping my hand, shaking it, and refusing to let it go as he released a tide of words, which had evidently been building up, held back by his lips like water level with the dam. 'My boat! My boat!... I always call your boat my boat – I get up some mornings and see your boat at anchor outside my house – I have a farm at Calenick – and I call to my wife, 'My boat is back!' I love to see you at anchor there... she is so pretty.'

Ted Grainger loved boats and farmed Charolais cattle – one of which he invited us to come round and eat that Sunday. His old farmhouse has a window offering views of the river, on the pane of which are scratched the initials *A.H. 1862*. His farm is lost between the interlocking folds of a hill and can be accessed from the water via a hidden creek, which was often used for smuggling, he explained; these initials were cut by a smuggler using the diamond of his ring.

We'd come to Truro to buy a carpentry saw – that was top of the list – I have a chainsaw on board, but carpentry saws are quieter. We did our weekly shop, bought the carpentry saw, and then had a pint of HSD at the Old Ale House. We stayed overnight tied against the harbour wall, enjoying the contrast the city noise made with the silence of our usual haunts – skidding traffic; sirens; breaking glass; motorcycle youths in the car park 'burning doughnuts'; the exuberant screams of revellers... that sort of thing.

The following day, when the liberating tide floated us, we felt our way back downriver, scarcely daring to breathe until we got to Malpas, and deeper water; then continued on to that part of the river where the larch trees grow, tying up alongside a pontoon conveniently placed for those who wish to steal one.

That afternoon we slipped ashore to investigate the larch, found our tree, marked it, and then improved upon the occasion by gathering a load of wood for the fire. We were just loading it into 'feed' bags when we noticed a small blue yacht arrive at the pontoon from upriver. A short dark figure got off and knocked on our deck, adding to it a call, which we couldn't make out. There was something strange about the way he walked. I whistled from the shore and indicated for him to wait five minutes and we'd be there, which he acknowledged.

He filled this gift of time by swaggering up and down the boards of the pontoon, blowing a tune through missing teeth.

Arriving at the pontoon, we noticed he was wearing an unusual style of jacket – black, brocaded, with neat rows of buttons – on permanent loan, perhaps, from a nautical costumier. He thrust his chest out and greeted us with his toothless grin.

'Arrhhh!' he said – which I thought he was going to follow up with 'me hearties!', but he didn't… he just said, 'Arrhhh!'

'Nice boat there!' he hissed, when he'd thought of something to add to it, and then he continued swaggering back and forth with a wide-legged gait, as though his reproductive equipment required a *lot* of room and a constant draught. Standing face to face with him was disconcerting. There was an angry-looking scar on his cheek and one-half of his left ear had been bitten off; pendant from the other was a gold ring. Turning to admire his boat, which seemed only polite since we were getting on so famously, I was shocked to see that one side of it was thickly coated with mud – the rest merely smeared. It was tied to the pontoon with knotted lengths of bailer twine, and protected from the danger of chafe by a single deflated fender, which I myself had seen float upriver two days earlier. He was less muddy than his ship, being only daubed on most parts of his body. He didn't explain the mud, seeming to accept it as a hazard of sailing – though not one we'd encountered.

'Could you look after me boat for a few days? I've got to go away.' A sense of relief washed over me.

'How did it get so muddy?' I asked.

'Arrhhh!' he said, swaggering under great flourishes of his sword arm, ' – load of bloody landlubbers on board… we was coming down from Truro when the tide suddenly went out and left me boat on the mud – landlubbers couldn't wait, could they? I told 'em it would come back in – but they got panicky and tried to walk ashore… loada landlubbers, they was.'

I promised him we'd keep an eye on his boat; he expressed his thanks, gave us a toothy grin, and then leapt into an open boat and zoomed away to keep another appointment. As soon as he'd gone, we moved further down the pontoon to disassociate ourselves from his mouldering wreck.

Two days later we read in the local paper that the fire brigade and inshore lifeboat had spent three hours rescuing a couple of men from the mud at Truro after they had become stranded in a boat – both had nearly drowned in mud, one was still in hospital. We couldn't help wondering if the events were connected.

Four months later, the boat was still awaiting his return – looking through its windows to satisfy a nagging doubt, I saw that there was water in the accommodation up to the level of the seats. The Harbour Authority removed it just before it sank.

The river, hereabouts, is thickly wooded with oak, ash, beech and holly, which spread their branches out low over the water so that every spring tide deposits flotsam in their leafy twigs; at low water, dark beards of seaweed hang down to the mud, giving the riverbank an appearance that one urchin described to me as 'well spooky'. Climbing ashore, into the heady aroma of fresh sea smells and moist composting leaves, I was discreetly screened from river traffic. I climbed steeply away from the water's edge until 100 feet up, reaching the small stand of larch trees; I knelt clutching my saw; only the nervous pounding of my heart broke the silence. For ten minutes I looked and listened, trying to see the eyes of keepers or rangers, which I imagined were trained hard on me, watching... And then, when my paranoia subsided, I began sawing, then listening, intermittently for an hour, until with a few sharp 'cracks', which I tried to hush with my jacket, the tree began to fall. It didn't fall very far – it just sort of leaned into its neighbour, then stopped. I couldn't leave the tree like that in case someone walked under it and it chose that moment to fall (and my fingerprints were found on the trunk); so shinning up to the height of about 30 feet, where a slight breeze played among the needles, I began sawing off branches to unsnag them from the neighbouring trees, and with each one I removed, I and my tree fell a little further – like going down in a lift that stopped at every floor. At last, there was a ping, the doors slid open and we arrived at the ground floor – the right department for replacement booms.

I tied a rope round the downhill end of my tree and pulled. This was going to be easier than I had imagined – it slid as though it were on rails. After giving it the first heave to get it moving, I found I had to sprint down the hill in order to keep ahead of it, or risk being skewered like a cocktail sausage. Later, under cover of darkness, I towed it across the river to the floating pontoon.

By lunchtime the following day I had stripped it of its bark, planed it smooth, and was just admiring my handiwork when the harbour master hove in sight. I looked around for somewhere to hide a 25-foot tree, together with a pile of shavings that would have filled the shed of a no-nonsense gardener; but finding nothing, decided to wave benignly as he motored past. He half-raised a hand and screwed up his eyes to see what was going on.

'Jesus… he'll be back,' I muttered, and with that came a change in note from his engine as he turned and motored slowly to the pontoon, drifted the length of my stripped tree, and stopped next to me where I stood knee-deep in bark. Our eyes met.

'Hello!' I said.

'Can I ask what you're doing?'

'Erm, making myself a new boom.'

Fearing that his next question would be, 'Where did you get that tree?', I launched into an elaborate account of the circumstances leading to the breaking of the old one, and left him no time to ask. He listened sour-faced to my tale; his expression told me that he was changing his opinion of me, and not for the better. He pushed his boat back into the flow of the river, engaged a gear, and swept his gaze over the woodland as he left – but he never asked where my tree had come from, and I'll always be grateful to him for that.

Our new boom was slightly on the thin side – aesthetically speaking – and resembled a Twiglet both in shape and colour, but was so serviceable that we employed our giant Twiglet for the next four years.

Winter had now set in. That area of the river was so peaceful that we spent a lot of time there. It was convenient, too, being equidistant between the centres of Falmouth and Truro, and because the river wound back and forth in folds, it was a perfect place to anchor whenever storm-force winds blew through.

We made no attempt to find work that first winter – we'd invested some money from the house, and always lived frugally anyway. We walked a great deal during those days, exploring, Ordnance Survey map in hand, finding out footpaths that hadn't been walked for years; paying lunchtime visits to country pubs with real fires; and it was nothing to walk two hours to the butcher in St Mawes – whose beef was always scrummy – and then two hours home again. We discovered farmers' markets, and prettier ways to get to the shops, returning always – carrier bags cutting into our hands – to find *Caol Ila* lying quietly to her anchor, with blue woodsmoke curling up from the chimney. Home, sweet home – and what a location!

Often, these walks threw up surprises. Just when you imagined you were the first person ever to set foot on that land, we'd find an abandoned piece of history – today it was a limekiln together with its associated quay, and other signs of old industry, now thickly overgrown. We learned from a book that chronicled the history of Cornwall's limekilns that the one ashore from where we were anchored had been the site of a tragedy – three men arriving by sailing coaster a hundred years earlier had unloaded their cargo and gone ashore to an inn at Truro; returning late at night they found they were unable to make it back to their boat. Limekilns – which produce as much carbon dioxide as quicklime, weight for weight – burned overnight, and so the stranded men lay down on the perimeter wall of the kiln to enjoy the warmth. All three were overcome by fumes and fell into the kiln – their charred corpses not being discovered until the following morning.

We found ruined shoreside fishermen's cottages, beautifully situated, hidden among the trees, and impossible to imagine how they were ever 'given up'; abandoned roads cut into the hillside, which used to be main carting routes but were now deeply littered with leaves from the overarching trees, and ran from nowhere to nowhere. Once, when we were walking in a remote spot, a startled puma leapt out from the undergrowth alongside us and disappeared into the woodland. The hairs went up on our necks as we looked at each other, but the sighting would have seemed even stranger to us had we not lived on Exmoor and seen similar wild cats from time to time, including three adolescent lions playing together on a bank in the autumn sun. But – in the words of the 'Four Yorkshiremen' – 'You try telling the young people of today that... and they won't believe you. No.'

On spring tides, at low water, we would forage along those parts of the beach that are seldom exposed. Within a few yards' rowing from our boat there were beds of giant mussels, which had grown large because no one ever picked them; oysters, too; and we would eat one or two of both raw, right there on the beach, before taking the rest home. In a creek nearby there was a brackish field of samphire, which allowed us to create, back on board, the kind of dish you expect to be served when your knees are draped with the starched napery of a posh restaurant owned by a TV chef, and someone else is paying.

We smoked eels in the chimney of our wood-burning stove. We could find eels two or three feet long, hiding under flat rocks or in an old pipe or something similar on the muddy low water shore. Lifting the stone, they remain quite motionless – but the moment you touch them they slip away from your grasp like a balloon you've blown up, but fumbled before you could tie. Linda embarrasses me by screaming and hopping from leg to leg when that happens. Once they have fled a safe distance away, she pretends to follow on usefully – but if by accident they turn back in our direction, she sprints away screaming; leaping boulders in a single bound, she's up the beach in moments, and disappears over the brow of a hill. Let Boudica have her attacks – my wife's place in history is secure for her retreats.

It was a macabre business, killing the eels – they remain mobile for a couple of hours after you've cut their heads off, and we'd hear their dead bodies writhing on a bed of salt crystals in the bucket, transmitting a haunting scratching noise through the deck... so we didn't do it too often; but smoked eel is extraordinarily good to eat. To smoke them, we'd break a chunk from a dry-rotted branch of oak, light it with a blowtorch, and allow it to smoulder in the wood-burning stove for six hours or so, whilst the eel dangled down from the top of the chimney. We smoked mackerel, too, and any roe from the fish we caught, to make Taramasalata. We didn't have a refrigerator on board and whenever we caught more fish than we could eat 'today and tomorrow', smoking was the perfect way for us to extend its shelf life by up to five days.

On rocky beaches we'd pick 'queen' scallops and squat lobsters, too, together with shore or 'green' crabs, which make the most amazing crab broth we've ever eaten – anywhere. We'd boil them for ten minutes, peel off the carapaces, pick out the dead man's fingers – they're not poisonous, but they've got a very unpleasant name – and then put them into the liquidiser attachment of the Kenwood Chef – without which we couldn't have contemplated living on board, even though we had to install a powerful inverter to fire it up. We put all the crunched-up crab back into the saucepan with a pint of milk, some fried onion and garlic, salt, pepper, mace and star anise, then simmered it for a while, salivating continuously with a wooden spoon, then sieved it before serving. You'd hesitate to offer it to guests with fastidious tastes because the colour of it is ever-so-slightly disturbing, being somewhat grey; but for the *bon vivant*, one bowl is never enough.

We made a net and caught shrimps of a good size in the late summer and autumn, while the water was still warm. It consisted of a 'T'-shaped frame – a wooden handle with a bar crossing it at the bottom. We formed a semi-circular hoop from a length of plastic plumbing hose, secured at both ends of the cross member and again a couple of feet up the handle, and strung garden netting from it. Bouncing the bar along the seabed while pushing the net steadily ahead of you causes the shrimps to jump out from the weed in which they hide, and they are gathered into the net which follows. We would pick out the 'whoppers' – about the fatness of your thumb – and return the rest. Back on board, we'd hurl them into a hot wok in which a couple of ounces of butter sizzled with garlic, and quickly clap the lid back on – otherwise they'd ping out of the pan like popcorn, turning up days later in our light fittings, the pockets of our aprons, and the turn-ups of our trousers. After two minutes of cooking, we'd lift the lid to see if they'd turned pink, then – and my mouth waters to think of this – serve them with hot French stick, and a generously filled glass of white wine. Our meal would be punctuated with remarks like: 'There's no one else in *Britain* eating prawns this fresh!', as the butter ran down our chins.

* * *

'I feel sorry for Pete,' Linda said, looking through the porthole toward his boat, which was just arriving. 'He's always on his own.'

Anchored in a leafy creek, the silence was broken when Pete chucked out an anchor – the chain of which clattered over a metal bow-roller – and then yelled: 'My missus says to me – what you gonna do for your fiftieth... d'ya wanna party?' A scandalised raft of ducks banged across the water and shot into the sky. 'I says to her – what do I wanna party for? Fifty years old! What's to celebrate about that? – Nah, I just as well stay on my boat, I says – so here I am!'

'Happy birthday, Pete,' we chimed. His boat has a very small hatch for someone of his girth, and we watched as he lowered himself through it, to go and cook some sausages. He got stuck halfway and shoehorned his belly down to the accommodation, handful by handful.

Back down below, I turned the heat on under a saucepan of seawater in which there were 20 shore crabs, freshly gathered. 'Do you know what Pete eats?' I asked.

'What?'

'Sausages.'

'Oh, come on... he must eat more than that.'

'No, he told me, when he stays on his boat he just brings a few pounds of sausages and a pack of lard,' I told her, as I dropped some shredded ginger into the water and swirled it among the crabs, which spun round in the eddies left by my spoon, '...isn't he funny?'

In the mornings we would take a cup of fresh coffee back to bed and ask each other what we should do with our day. It was luxurious to be able to spend it on seemingly trivial errands: 'The deck needs oiling,' we'd say; or, 'We must get some more firewood today.'

'We need some more chillies,' Linda suggested, intimating a trip to Falmouth.

'...and water, and paraffin.'

We don't have a windlass, so, in order to save myself a hernia every time I haul up the chain, we sail off our anchor. With the anchor still down, we hoist the mainsail and sheet in hard; then we unfurl the jib, which flies from the end of the bowsprit, and allow it to back in the steady breeze, throwing the bow off to port or starboard – as we choose. When *Caol Ila* lies about 45 degrees across the wind, we reset the jib to fill away on a close reach. Within moments we will have sailed the anchor onto our beam and the chain comes taut, pulling the bow onto the next tack, for us. On this new tack, we head straight for our anchor and have only to gather in the slack chain as we overrun it. The only part of the operation that might cost a finger one day – but hasn't yet – is when the bow of the boat reaches that point where it is directly over the anchor, and the chain is short 'straight up and down' – at that very moment I throw a couple of turns of chain around the Samson post to make it fast, and our momentum snubs the chain powerfully, tripping the anchor out of the ground.

We fill away rippling the water, gathering speed, and nod gently to the small waves in the Carrick Roads, where we sail past the professionals who raise a craggy hand in acknowledgement. The Fal Estuary is home to the world's last licensed fishing fleet 'under sail', and the men who operate these classic craft – the 'oyster dredgers' – know how to handle a boat under sail – because they are not allowed to do it any other way. There may be 12 or 20 of these boats on any weekday in the winter – strictly between the hours of 9 am and 3 pm – dredging the banks for oysters, just as they have for hundreds of years; old craft handed down through the family. They have long bowsprits, which arch low over the water, and their tatty appearance, resulting from hard work, seems to add to their charm as they shoulder the heaving waves, hauling their loads behind them. Oft-repaired sails of grubby white or tan flutter in the breeze; and while work goes on on-deck, they sail themselves unattended along their course – like draught horses, they know as well as their drivers which way to go.

Four oyster dredgers

Entering the harbour, I wound in my fishing line, we doused sail, and Roger caught our mooring line as we drifted up to the Falmouth pontoons. Softly, he asked me if I had 'heard the weather'. He worries us a bit – worries some of our friends, too. Falmouth is the last port of call for yachts intending to 'jump off' on a blue-water cruise; they gather in numbers in August and September like migrating birds, to buy last-minute items of chandlery, fuel, water, and provisions. They form themselves into chirruping groups on the pontoon to discuss their forthcoming adventure, make plans to sail 'in company', and exchange weather forecasts. For any number of reasons, when the migratory dawn flight takes to the air some get left behind... perhaps they have an engine fault; a piece of gear has been ordered but has not arrived; they have a health problem, a crew problem; or perhaps nerves cause a fatal hesitation. Roger is among those who got left behind, and he still speaks of leaving, in spite of the fact that at this time of the year, one clear day is followed by a gale the next, and it is cold and exhausting to be on the high seas if you are not prepared.

Roger doesn't seem to be prepared. It is a matter of respect that no yacht skipper enquires too closely about the preparedness of the next, or condemns his plans; and so when Roger tells us that he is planning to sail to the Scillies, or to Madeira – he hasn't decided which – we forbear to ask if he knows that while the Scillies are a day's sail away, Madeira may take three weeks to reach. Or that, at this time of year – owing to its exposed location – every boat owner on the Scilly Isles has brought his craft ashore to avoid storm damage.

Roger is alone – he can't find anyone willing to go with him. His boat is too small to be out in a winter gale, and it looks old and frail. On deck, there is rope everywhere. Coils of different sizes, colours and states of repair litter his deck to knee height – it's impossible to walk on board his boat without getting in a tangle. Privately we questioned his judgement too – he'd bought a piece of thin Perspex describing it as a 'storm door' for his main hatch; yet it was flimsier than a cat flap.

When we saw Roger a week or two earlier he was hanging out of his hatch, choking in black smoke, calling for help.

'Bill! Bill!'

By coincidence, Linda and I were just arriving at the pontoon under sail and Bill appeared on the deck of his boat having heard his name, saw us, waved and went back down again.

'Bill! Bill!' came the call again, more urgently. Bill came back up, saw Roger and his smoke, and rushed to his aid.

We all admired Bill and Jill. They'd returned to Falmouth, ten years into their world cruise, to buy a bigger boat. They'd been pig farmers in Norfolk all their working lives and had worked toward their cruise for 30 years.

'We planned to be garn ten years,' said Bill, when we called at their boat later to hear about Roger's fire (as we arrived they'd just finished drinking 125 ml of water, and Bill was recording the fact in a book); '...but,' he continued, 'we've been garn ten years already and only went 'arf way round!' Jill offered us a cup of tea, and began removing the kettle, the cups and the cutlery from the felt sleeves she had sewn for them ('Stops them rattling at sea,' she explained). Bill fetched some biscuits from the cupboard, put on his glasses, read the 'Nutritional Information' panel, placed four of them on the table, and noted the fact in a book. 'I 'spect it'll take us another ten years to do the other 'arf,' he said.

'What happened with Roger earlier?' I asked. Bill rolled his eyes significantly and pushed his glasses to the top of his head, where they bedded down comfortably in a nest of soft white hair. He folded his arms, neatly.

'He'd garn across to pick up some diesel-fool and his starter motor jammed on – but he didn't notice – not for 15 minutes – and only noticed when he got back here on fire!'

I pulled a face as if to say, '...Strange?'

'I know,' said Bill, 'and what's worse, I was just showing him how to bypass the switch, 'cos it's the switch what's garn, and sayin' to him, "Now, you put the red wire here, and just touch the blue one there..." and when I looks over my shoulder he's sitting with his back to me, watching the telly!'

Only Roger seems unaware of any shortcomings he or his boat might have: 'I'm waiting for a weather window,' he whispered with a smile as I jumped ashore and took back from him the mooring line he caught, but didn't do anything with.

'I've done a silly thing!' John interrupted, cheerfully. He'd followed us downriver and arrived in his boat *Sun Tyne* a moment after us. He is a powerful man of 55 with a grey beard permanently parted at the lips to reveal two neat rows of smiling teeth.

'See that?' He parked a 5-litre container of spirit vinegar under my nose.

'Uh-huh.'

'I bought that yesterday – I only read the word "spirit" – and thought I was buying methylated spirit! – I haven't even been able to have a cup of tea all night because I couldn't light the stove!' He strode away, whistling. He always whistles. I think he does it to show the world he is content, and he probably is content, too, even though he avoids contact with people if he can. He sequesters himself away in quiet spots on the river, waiting for spring when he will begin his voyage to the 'Med'.

'I used to be a fisherman out of Newhaven,' he told us once, 'but I'm retired now; me and my wife always wanted to take a boat to the Med, but sadly she died last year. In a way I'm doing it, now, for her.' We passed his boat often on the river, alone, and from down below would come the sound of sawing, or the gentle tapping of a hammer. As we passed he'd emerge wearing his trademark black woolly hat (the significance of which we were to learn later), throw out a piece of scrap wood, and seeing us would smile and explain: 'I'm building myself a little – Oh, it's just a silly thing – but I've always wanted somewhere to store my CDs; so I'm making myself a little rack from a few bits of cheap pine. It's going OK!' Then back down he'd go, whistling.

When we returned from our shopping trip a few hours later with both red and green chillies, Geoff met us on the pontoon.

'Roger's gone.'

'What – *gone* gone?'

'Yep.'

'Where to?'

'No one knows.'

'When did he set off?'

'James saw him motor out this morning.'

'I thought there was supposed to be a gale this evening?'

'Yep.'

***

'How ya doing, Ian?' I called across the table to a tall, nervy man of about 45 with dreadlocks, who lived on a derelict boat in Penryn Harbour. Penryn is sympathetic to derelict boats in the way that Percuil – on the other side of the estuary – isn't. On the Percuil side, residents have formed a 'Shore Committee', whose patrols regularly find an audacious piece of seaweed that has stranded itself on their beach.

Linda and I had come to listen to the band in a crowded bar and sat ourselves down at a table with 12 or 15 people we knew or half-knew.

Ian had deeply carved features that spoke of a life lived outdoors, and was as brown as an autumn leaf. I'd first noticed him one day in a tatty but well-made rowing boat, lurking around near us, and couldn't make my mind up whether he was admiring our boat, or seeing what bits came off easily; so, having faith – believing where I couldn't prove – I sprang on deck and greeted him. His beard was untidy, his face dirty; and his dreadlocks, which hung down below his arse, were clogged with debris like a nylon scourer that's been used to clean the barbecue. He had told me about his historic Brixham trawler and his long-term plans to restore her; how he had lost heart since his girlfriend left him; and how working at the docks took all his time – but he still 'did a bit'. And I had described to him how we'd built our boat; and ever since that meeting we'd always stop to exchange a few nostalgic words about classic boats.

'Yeah, nice one, mate!' he answered from his side of the table, bursting into a spasm of movement. I'd noticed that whenever we met or parted he couldn't remember whether we high-fived, low-fived, crashed knuckles, thumbs-upped, or just waved... so to be on the safe side, he did all of them at once.

The evening roared away, the bar was packed, the band played; then I noticed – yet again – that half my beer had gone... I'd just been to the bar, but there was my glass – half empty... if it *was* my glass. At the end of the next song, there was the usual riotous applause as everyone who wasn't already standing in the crush jumped to their feet or climbed on chairs to cheer the band; I broke off early to take another swig from my pint before any more of it could evaporate, and as I did so I caught sight of Ian grabbing someone's glass – when he thought no one was looking – and chucking half of it into his.

The following morning, I woke at about 6 am with a throbbing headache and did a double take as I walked past a porthole. What I thought I saw was the lead singer of the band from the night before – a blonde-haired, blue-eyed woman of about 40, with the square jaw of a bounty hunter who lived aboard a patched-up piece of maritime history (which floated nearby), in a close but ill-defined relationship with several people. She seemed to be wearing only a pair of rigger boots and a shirt and to be bending over to examine something on her deck. I went back to the porthole and looked again – I was right. As my blood pressure rocketed, my head clanged like a Tibetan bell... so I made the life-saving decision not to look any more. I had a late start to the day, but when I was out of intensive care, I bumped into Geoff.

'What do you think?' he said.

'About what?'

'About that.' He nodded across the harbour to where, a couple of hundred yards away, rags of sail were whipping noisily in the wind from the mast of a yacht.

'What's going on there?' I asked.

'That's Roger – the lifeboat brought him in last night.'

The wind continued to blow hard and a day later the remains of Roger's sail were still cracking in the wind, echoing across the harbour.

'I wonder he doesn't take it down,' said Geoff, adding with a smile, 'I didn't sleep a wink last night.'

'Perhaps it's stuck up there and he needs a hand.' Ten minutes later I stood next to Roger's boat and the rags of sail above my head waved like a distress signal. 'Here's a casualty!' they seemed to shout. I felt like an intruder in a private matter, but Roger came on deck when I knocked and smiled his greeting.

'Do you want a hand getting that down?' He followed my gaze up his mast as though noticing it for the first time, and shrugged his shoulders. 'It doesn't bother me,' he said.

'How did it get torn?'

'Well, I managed to get round the Lizard,' he said, as though that dealt with the difficulties of the voyage, 'then a gust of wind blew the sail to pieces. So I started the engine – but it was quite rough and some rope got washed overboard and caught round the propeller... I couldn't do anything then.'

We cut and pulled at the twisted, knotted cloth until we were neck deep in terylene and looked like the sole survivors of a fight in a pillow factory, picking ourselves free from bits of fluff. Roger began gently sobbing.

'That's a hundred pounds I paid for that!' he said, between breaths. 'Now look at it! – it didn't last more than a couple of hours.' He'd bought it second-hand from a shop along the street, he told me, just before he left.

I tried to lighten the mood.

'Tell you what you should do, Rog – bundle it all back into the sail bag, take it back to the shop where you got it – then say, "Look! I didn't notice this when I bought it..."'

I was pleased to see him laughing along.

When I saw him a couple of days later, he was installed back in his old spot on the pontoon, and I wondered if he was going to ask me if I'd spotted a 'weather window', or if he'd given up all that and had decided to settle down patiently until next season, like everyone else.

'I took your advice,' he called.

I drew myself up to full height. 'What advice was that?'

'I took that sail back to the shop.'

5 STRANGE FOLK WHO LIVE ON BOATS

'Let's roast a pheasant on Sunday,' Linda said. She'd been staring out through the porthole for ages, to where the noise of barking, shouting and gunshot echoed between the river-banks as a shooting party stumbled its way along the shore, frequently stopping to refresh itself from a hip flask. Every gunshot would be followed a few seconds later by the pattering of lead shot as it landed on deck. All morning they thundered away at wildlife, which remained largely unscathed until, watching them through binoculars it became clear from their own astonishment that they'd hit something and it had landed in the river, bobbed to the surface; and begun to drift away. The picker-upper was pointing to the corpse and shouting himself hoarse in increasingly desperate attempts to encourage his retriever into the icy water: 'Fetch! Fetch! F-E-T-C-H!' he yelled. He leaned down to the dog's ear: 'Fetch-the-bloody-bird!!' But the dog looked at him disdainfully, as if to say, '*You* go.'

While the 'guns' stood sullenly on the bank watching their morning's work drift away, I hopped into the dinghy, took a leisurely row to intercept the plump pheasant, waved my grati-tude and then swept my oars toward home.

We spent some time that first winter finishing off odd carpentry details of our boat, improving the electrical system, and replacing some engine-related components. We'd built our own wet-exhaust box by moulding epoxy-impregnated fibre-glass around a dustbin, and it had worked well except for the sharp angle where the lid was moulded on to it. The constant 'panting' of the box had eventually caused it to fail, and we replaced it with a proprietary model now that the workshop was so far away.

And we spent time preparing for our first summer cruise in a hundred different ways, from recording how quickly we consumed things (water, diesel, paraffin, etc) to applying ourselves to the dutiful study of such nautical publications as *Navigation for the Shipwrecked Mariner* and *The Yachtsman's Guide to Burial at Sea*.

We'd often wondered, when we were boatbuilding and still owned a cosy home, what it would be like living on board in the winter when nothing stirred, our friends were hibernating, and the air was heavy and cold. What would be the worst part? Would it be the cold, the boredom, or the misery of dark days spent in a small cabin? Yet as autumn turned to winter, we found we were still waiting for any signs of hardship – or perhaps there was a degree of hardship but it went unnoticed. We sang softly as we went about our daily routine. In the morning, when we got out of bed we lifted the mattress to air it and rubbed down the cabin walls with a towel to dry them of the fine droplets of condensation which had formed overnight, to keep the boat fresh. We took breakfast, boiled a kettle to make tea, then another to fill a bowl with hot water so that we could bathe in front of the fire, gazing as we did so through the porthole from time to time to watch an oyster dredger on the shore loading his boat for the day. In the background, Radio 4 kept us up to date with what was happening in the real world – how *un*real it sometimes seemed to us.

By nine we'd be ready to walk, sail, shop, gather firewood, or whatever we had chosen for the day, and by late afternoon our thoughts would turn to cooking something we'd bought or caught, and we'd begin elaborate preparations in the galley, starting by opening a bottle of wine to set on a shelf behind the wood-burning stove where it would catch some incidental heat, and breathe. At six we'd listen to the news, make sure the world still revolved, and enjoy a dram in the cockpit in the chill evening air – or by the fire if it was blowy or wet. Then we'd have supper and chat about the day or what we planned to do with the next; wash up (accompanying Great Big Sea as they sang 'Lukey's boat is painted green'); and finally ruin our eyesight by settling down to read under the soft yellow light from our brass-gimballed hurricane lamp. Linda read *War and Peace* until she was too exhausted to hold it up and I heard the soft purring of her snores... similarly, my choice was Gibbons: *Decline and Fall of the Roman Empire* – which never failed me in inducing the decline and fall of my day. We draped our bedding in front of the stove while we read, so that it would be warm to climb into.

We kept our wood-burning stove, an Aarrow Becton 5, burning night and day. We'd bought it two years previously because the literature had described it as being 'ideal for narrowboats and barges'; and we'd had the benefit of it in the workshop/stable while we built the boat; but, when the time came to install it on board, we hesitated amid speculation that it might be 'too hot', and instead installed a different one – a cheap 'pot-bellied' stove of oriental manufacture. It had no fibreglass rope seals; the doors rattled and the gaps around them caused it to over-fire; and we found it impossible to keep 'in' overnight. By inspiration, we filled it with anthracite, which, when it was well alight, glowed like a blacksmith's brazier – it throbbed with heat, but soon set fire to the wooden bulkhead close by. Only by steadily squirting water from a washing-up-liquid bottle onto both the fire and the bulkhead, until the stove cooled down, were we able to prevent it from taking hold. That was the last straw and we installed the Aarrow 5 – it is perfect and we have it on board to this day. Intending to throw the pot-bellied stove away, I forgot it and left it on the pontoon in Falmouth for a fortnight. When we returned we scarcely recognised it for rust. Tiiti and Antti, students from Finland overwintering on their boat in Falmouth, asked if they could have it. We'd noticed that they stayed in bed until midday, and when they got up they looked cold and stiff behind their cheerful smiles – they'd be wearing thickly padded layers of clothes and funny hats, and looked like well-dressed vagrants. It was embarrassing to give the tatty-looking stove away, but never was a gift so gratefully received.

We wanted to do more for them, so we started by offering to show them where they could pick mussels.

'Mar-sools,' said Antti, enjoying mouthing the English words.

'Are there many?' asked Tiiti.

'Tens of thousands,' I said, 'and all huge.' Antti was impressed.

'Dens – off – towsans!' he repeated, throwing his thick eyebrows as he pronounced each word. After that we would often see them picking over the mussel beds, wearing the dazed smiles you expect to see on the faces of shoppers in a super-market where everything is free.

'My mother sends me a parcel of goodies!' Tiiti announced one day, clapping her hands and doing a little dance to express her excitement. 'Come and try!' We climbed aboard and stepped down into accommodation in which there was just room for four people seated. The saloon was long, thin and dimly lit and we sat opposite each other, looking across an old table, which had long since lost its varnish.

'These are Finland sweets – Oh – they are *so* nice!' said Tiiti, holding up a small dark nugget and jabbing it into the air as she spoke to emphasise her words. 'We don't find them here.' She gave us one each. In England... and Europe – well, in the whole world really, except for Finland, it seems – sweets are made from sugar. These, I discovered to my horror, were made from salt and were utterly disgusting, inducing in me a regurgitant effect within a few moments. Although I man-aged to stop myself from gagging, I couldn't hide my alarm. A moment later, when I'd reached the nucleus of the blighter, another flavour violated my senses – it may have been aniseed, but was probably a crumb of rapidly oxidising cobalt. Tiiti, who had been watching my face closely for signs of ecstasy, found she enjoyed my horror better, and for the next few minutes sprayed us with spitty laughter, which escaped from between the fingers of the hand she had clamped tightly over her mouth while convulsed by paroxysms of guilty mirth of the kind you get when you are seated comfortably in an armchair, watching footage shot from a camera that has been turned to show the grotesque facial expressions of children strapped into adventure-park rides with names like Oblivion and Nemesis.

With our wood-burning stove in operation night and day we were always cosy, and so it came as a surprise one morning to find the cause of a scraping noise, which had woken us – it was gentle at first, but gradually increased in volume until it sounded as if Planet Earth were being finely milled. I climbed out of bed to investigate, noticing as I dressed that our thermometer showed the outside temperature to be −7°C. I tapped its glass in disbelief, but being digital it stayed where it was. On deck, the thick frost crunched underfoot and I slid down the camber of the deck to the gunwhales; as far as the eye could see up and downriver, the water was frozen white. There had been a very slack tide during the night – the lack of movement helped ice to form, no doubt, and perhaps increased the proportion of fresh river water to salt. But now that the tide had begun to ebb, a thin sheet of ice, half a mile long to my certain knowledge, was being dragged past our hull with the outgoing tide – breaking itself up on us, piling itself up, and scratching at the hull like a thousand little knives. After that we never wondered again if we'd be warm enough on board in a winter wilderness.

Later that day the river quiet was shattered by the drone of a helicopter hanging motionless above the water a few hundred yards away, the flight deck of which was turned to face the oak-clad hillside. Slowly it tracked side to side, and up and down, like a hoverfly examining a flower. The harbour master passed us at speed, blue light flashing, on his way downriver, hugging the bank, then returned later in the day hugging the other bank. As it grew dark he came over to talk to us.

Nearby, the river accommodates ships of a breathtaking size – especially when viewed in the context of the river's narrowness and steep leafy banks. The Fal Estuary is the third largest natural harbour in the world, and offers relatively cheap moorings to laid-up ships while they await work, or a new owner. A skeleton crew remains on board to carry out maintenance work and keep an eye on her security, and it was from the crew of one of these vessels that a young man had gone ashore on leave the previous night, and not returned; he was now reported as 'missing'. When a taxi driver came forward to say he had dropped the young man off, alone, at one o'clock in the morning, on the stretch of road that runs closest to his ship, a search and rescue operation had been launched. It had been a bitterly cold night, and the helicopter was carrying thermal-imaging equipment, we learned, and was scouring the surrounding hillside looking for any sign of him, while the harbour master inspected the tidal regions of the riverbank. From the road to the riverbank was a distance of 100 yards and from the riverbank to the ship just 20. It was assumed that the man, being unable to raise his fellow crew in the early morning to ferry him on board, had attempted to swim the short distance, where he would have succumbed to the cold in less than a minute and been carried away on the tide. The search continued for a week... but no trace of him was ever found.

It was easy for Linda and me to spend days on end in the reclusion of one another's company with nary a cross word between us – but when tempers got frayed, we suspected cabin fever, and a change of scene, with time spent in the refreshing company of other people, was the balm we needed.

We set off for Falmouth with too much sail set – from our protected upriver anchorage it was difficult to tell how much wind would be blowing further down, where the estuary was wide and more exposed, so I always erred on the side of incaution, to Linda's understandable annoyance, though it never seemed to matter much because the water in the estuary was relatively protected even in a hard blow – and it's generally the sea state that causes trouble.

Bowling along at 8 or 10 knots with the mast bending to some of the squalls that roared up behind us, I was relieved that we didn't have too far to go before we arrived at Falmouth and I could claw down our sails without having to admit that I put too much up in the first place. Linda emerged from down below, passed me a cup of tea, and looked around to get her bearings.

'Will we be all right over this bank?'

'What bank?' I asked, trying not to sound alarmed – though even as I spoke I remembered it. You never had to worry about it at high tide, or even at low water neaps at a pinch – but this was one of the lowest spring tides of the year, and you could virtually smell the bank. It lay dead ahead; the depth sounder was already falling; and the colour began to drain from my face. It wouldn't have been too late to turn to port and avoid it if the mainsail had been set somewhere else, but the boom needed to be gybed and the backstays swapped; and, as things were, the sailcloth was pressed so tightly against the rigging – like a carrier bag blown against station railings – that it would have been difficult to gybe quickly, even if we'd been crewed by six strong men. These thoughts raced through my mind while the depth sounder counted steadily down like the timing device on a bomb, and by the time I'd finished thinking my hopeless thoughts it was too late – it read 1.7 metres, which exactly matched our draught. We saw the bow bump upwards; heard the crunch of our iron shoe climbing onto the shelly bank, and tutted as the tea spilled from my cup. The depth sounder continued to fall to 1.6 then to 1.5…the speed fell from 8 knots to just over 3 and then confused me by staying there. We needed eight more inches of water to float – yet here we were still crunching along at 3 knots. The irresistible force of the wind in our sail was driving the keel on, carving an uncharted channel through the well-charted bank. For half a minute we rumbled onwards in our amphibious vehicle, until at last the depth began to increase, and we rejoined the main channel on the other side. I looked over my shoulder and noticed that the water's surface wore a brown scar – a mixture of rust from our iron shoe and silty deposits stirred up from the bank. I looked at Linda.

'*That* bank,' she said.

Back in Falmouth, Roger had taken off again. 'Aren't some people reckless?' I said to Linda. She held my gaze for an unnecessarily long time.

Roger had found a couple in their late twenties with no sailing experience who were willing to go with him, and had left in the company of another boat of our acquaintance – a 25-footer, home to Terry and Liz. Leaving 'in company' with another boat innervates you to get out of the harbour – which can be very useful sometimes – but within six hours or so you are rarely in sight of them, and after a day or two, you probably won't get them on the radio, which has a nominal range of 40 miles. This time it was Terry and Liz who were brought back by the coastguard – Geoff told us he'd seen them on the telly.

Terry and Liz are larger than life and it is a miracle – particularly on their tiny boat, aboard which there was only room to lie down – that they were still on speaking terms... and Terry with his exuberant flatulence. But if ever we heard the cheerful sound of mirth tinkling across the water, the odds were that it would be coming from their boat, and that Terry had just farted. They were always laughing, always socialising, always broke, always in the pub.

They'd been desperate to get away to warmer climes and had sailed away, despite it being late November, in fair weather to try to cross the Bay of Biscay.

'We started off in a force 5,' said Terry, laughing like a troll through his red beard, 'and for every day we were out there the wind increased by 'one' on the Beaufort scale. When it reached gale force 8, right in our face, we took the sails down, lay on our bunks and just waited – but the next day it was force 9; and the one after that it was storm force 10!'

'Crikey!' we said. 'It must have been terrifying.'

'Funnily enough, it wasn't too bad. Well, we didn't eat for two days, I couldn't have stood much more of that! Anyway, after that, when the wind dropped it disappeared completely, so we decided to motor back to Falmouth. After a couple of days we ran out of fuel just off the Lizard, flat calm, not a breath of wind, and there we were just lolling about waiting for enough wind to blow us the last 12 miles home. A lifeboat, which was out on exercise, came by and asked if we were all right. "Yeah, fine," we said. We told them our story and they asked, did we want a tow back to Falmouth? Er – yeah, all right! So we get back here and the next thing we know the TV 'ave come out to interview us – and when we saw the news, they made out as though we were irresponsible, and were in trouble or something... which we weren't.'

'What happened to Roger?'

'Er, dunno!' he said, adding with a chuckle, 'but I expect he found it a bit bouncy!'

Linda and I were pondering our own cruise for the following spring. For years I'd thought of sailing to Greenland, but all these stories of wild weather and cold – together with Linda, who petitioned for heading south – moderated my own ambitions, until we both agreed that in the spring we'd like to set off for Scotland, our trivial purpose being to visit the Caol Ila Distillery – a pilgrimage. We knew nothing about whisky and didn't even know where the distillery was until we looked at the map. When we were boatbuilding and casting about for a name for our vessel – coming up with lots of witty gems, which would have amused us for a week and been a burden to us thereafter – Linda hit on *Caol Ila* simply because it sounded pretty.

A welcome in the Highlands

My first introduction to Caol Ila had been in 1988 when I drove from London to attend a meeting in Inverness, after which I popped into a wine merchant.

'I'd like to take an interesting bottle of whisky home – what would you recommend?'

The merchant was about 30, short, and had an immaculately trimmed beard of speckled colour, which complemented the natural dyes of his Harris tweed jacket and tie. He reached for a bottle on the shelf behind him and began wrapping it in a self-assured way.

'Try this,' he said, simply – and as he twisted the crêpe around its neck and clumped it down in front of me, it was as if he knew he had just completed an action that would change my life.

When I'd got a moment, I unwrapped it. 'Caol Ila' said the label – I couldn't even pronounce it, and read on. 'Pronounced: Cull – eela' it continued, helpfully, 'Port Askaig, Isle of Islay'.

Having settled on the romantic purpose of a sailing pilgrimage to the Caol Ila Distillery, we began to organise and equip ourselves for a summer cruise to Scotland. At the library we read the sailing accounts of Frank Cowper – in whose wake we would be following – in his *Sailing Tours*, written more than a hundred years ago. We admired him, and felt a strange affiliation because he sailed a gaff-rigged boat, had been about our age and had just two people on board – him and a 'boy'. The difference was that in 1895, of course, he had no engine – whereas we never knew if we had one or not.

Our trip would take us to the Scilly Isles, Ireland and Scotland, and so we began 'picking the brains' of other yachtsmen who'd been cruising in any of those places and who could pass on some useful advice. Geoff and Nikki passed on their entire Scottish chart collection for a small consideration.

Our enquiries opened up a new avenue of entertainment for our winter's evenings as we visited other live-aboard yachts to nose about and see how they lived, swap stories, laugh, and try to swallow some surprisingly bad food. Shore folk who enjoy holding dinner parties outdo each other with the exotic sumptuosity of their board. The practical folk who live on yachts worship at the altar of 'speed' and 'economy' when it comes to mealtimes, and fill their cupboards with the meanest convenience foods in the belief that every meal will be taken trying to weather the Bishop Rock in a storm, and they'll be grateful for what they get. We had advanced warning of this delusion back in the days when we still lived in a house, but didn't pick up on it at the time. We'd cooked for friends who were yacht owners and our preparations began early one morning, marinating meat, making a fish stock and so forth. When we brought the dishes to the table that evening, our friends fell on them, splashing about like unseated riders at the water jump and weeping tears of gratitude – as though they hadn't eaten for three months and this had come just in time to save them.

'You must come to our boat,' they said when they'd licked the patterns off their plates, and were still shivering with gratitude, 'and let us cook for you on board.' Linda was thrilled with the opportunity to taste early the life that would soon be ours; but, arriving at their boat, no welcoming smell of cooking assailed our nostrils; the galley was sparkling clean; and our hostess was remarkably composed as she sipped her pre-dinner gin and tonic from a plastic bottle labelled 'Gin and Tonic'. Our eyes scanned surreptitiously for any sign that we might be offered something in addition to the limp crisps before us, until at last, turning to her husband – who grunted his approval – our hostess declared with theatrical reluctance, 'Well, I s'pose I'd better start cooking,' at which she dragged herself up from the table, opened two tins, splodged the contents into what looked like a bedpan, and heated it until the first laval pops could be heard above the sputtering flame, so that within four minutes it was dumped in front of us on melamine plates with an aluminium spoon sticking out from its turdy mound, to the triumphant announcement: 'This is what we call our Can't-Be-Bothered meal!'

She stood back, her pride welled up and her cheeks glowed as though she had just discovered a new isotope, and was waiting to be carried on our shoulders through the streets of Plymouth, while saved nations shouted 'Hurrah!'

In appearance it was indistinguishable from pet food, but differed in that you occasionally find pet food you're tempted to try. After an emotional struggle I put a little into my mouth – it was by far the worst, least-inspired, most miserable food I have ever tasted. I begged our hostess for the recipe, so that we would know in future what to avoid, and her hand, fluttering with success, recorded for future generations the low-water mark of world cuisine.

* * *

On our next visit to Falmouth our attention was drawn to a tormented-looking soul who paced up and down the pontoon as though revisiting the scene of an abhorrence.

'This is one of Roger's crew,' Geoff said, introducing me to him, '...sounds like they had a bad time.' He gave me a knowing look and turned to face a dark-haired, wiry man in his mid twenties; he looked streetwise and a bit 'tasty' – I wouldn't like to meet him on a dark night – but he sounded traumatised.

'We dunno nothin' about sailing, and we just thought he did – why didn't anyone tell us what he was like?' he demanded, gently.

I asked him what had happened.

'When we was off France, the wind started blowing a gale and all the sails ripped. So we put the engine on, but after about four hours, that packed up... so then we had nuthink. The sea was, like, really *rough*... we kept asking him, when are you going to call the coastguard? But he dint want to – he just started drinking.' He curled his lip as though that was the moment they lost respect for him. 'After about a day – when he was pissed out of his head – he wasn't even answering when we called him – we called the Coastguard ourselves... The lifeboat came, and we got in it – but Roger wouldn't leave his boat; he was just lying there with all these tins. They had to carry him off in the end.'

'What happened to the boat?'

'Sunk I 'spect... they just left it behind.'

We heard what happened to the boat a couple of weeks after that. It had survived the storm and was adrift near rocks when a French fisherman spotted it and took it in tow. Roger heard it had been saved and travelled out to pick it up and to thank the fisherman – but he wanted salvage money, which Roger refused to pay. Last we heard Roger was living in India, having flown out.

* * *

'It's some blowy!' said Knud as he wandered along the pontoon playing his accordion, and stopped for a moment to see what I was up to.

'At least it helps dry this oil!'

'Oh – you oyling you deck?' Knud and his wife had arrived from Denmark to overwinter, and planned to set off in the spring for the Med. He picked up the tin I was using and studied it with interest.

'Danish Oil,' he read aloud. 'I nebber heard about that.' He handed the tin back. 'What do you find on the beach?'

'Oh – we were just gathering some oysters,' I said.

'Ahh,' he said knowingly. Then, 'What is orster?'

'Gosh – have you never seen an oyster, Knud? – Let me get one to show you.' When I came back it was with our bucket of oysters and a strong knife. I prised open a shell with the usual difficulty and showed him what lay inside… frills of thin white flesh surrounded a snotty lump of grey meat.

'How you cook this thing?'

'No, Knud,' I said, beginning to enjoy myself, 'you don't cook them – look.' And with that I swallowed it whole. Knud's jaw fell open and he stared at me; he was quiet for a long time; his skin was always white, so it was hard to tell, but he may have been feeling a bit nauseous. 'Would you like to try one yourself?'

There was a long pause. 'Mebbe later.'

'OK, I'll give you one to take back – you could have it for tea.'

'Yes,' he said automatically. 'I give it to Elsa.'

'Have one each.'

'One is OK.' I handed him an oyster from the bucket, and he walked away along the pontoon, carrying it like an unexploded bomb.

* * *

Standing among the Christmas shopping crowds I caught a glimpse of a face I recognised – at his feet a fertiliser bag, neatly turned down at the top, was bulging with mistletoe. It in turn sat in a cardboard box with '£1' scrawled on it with a blue indelible marker.

'Mistletoe!' he called, self-consciously, in between prissily rearranging his sprigs, and swinging his dreadlocks with an exaggerated sway from his upper torso to rehang them tidily behind his back.

'Mistletoe!' Curly had a broad face, as brown as a berry, and high cheekbones, giving him an American-Indian appearance – though his father was an Englishman and had been a commander in the Royal Navy. He lived aboard a boat, but it was a very different command from his father's – its chipped blue paint reminded me of a canoe I'd once bought for a tenner. He was a traveller, and had moved to Cornwall to live on the only boat he could afford – we'd often see him alone on the water, teaching himself to sail in the soft evening breeze. On board his boat there was very little – a bunk, a blanket, and a kettle on an inadequate stove; a small table which hinged against the wall was supported by a single leg – on it were a book, a ring-bound 'secretarial' notepad, a biro, and a night-light candle. There was no heating. Curly was a 'freegan', and fed himself by going through the out-of-date bin at the back of supermarkets.

'Yeah – I'm selling loads,' he said, in answer to my question. 'Some of the girls are kissing me, too!'

He'd hired a van and driven all the way to Gloucestershire to gather his mistletoe – where it 'literally grows on trees', he joked. At a pound I was surprised that it paid him to go all that way.

'It doesn't cost much to hire a van for a couple of days.'

'What about all the fuel?'

'When I bring the van back I just fill it with red diesel,' he said, obviously.

A couple of days before Christmas he popped by with a big box of chocolates and gave them to Linda.

'Happy Christmas!'

'Gosh, Curly – that's very generous of you.'

'Not at all – I saw them in the bin and was wondering who would like them.'

* * *

On Christmas Eve, Linda's friend Fausty, who doesn't like boats, arrived to share the festivities with us. We worry most about those folk who step on board and whose first words are: 'I'm sure I'll be fine.'

We wanted to make her stay on board so solid underfoot that, except for the smell of paraffin, she wouldn't know her holiday accommodation from a posh waterfront apartment with eye-level sea views. It was very brave of her to come at all, and we thought it might make her stay a bit less nautical if we moored close to the shops and pubs so that we could slip ashore whenever the on-board entertainment palled. That proved to be a mistake, because the inshore forecast warned of an easterly gale or severe gale, which in the quiet upriver creeks would have passed overhead unnoticed; but in Falmouth, east is the worst direction. At first our boat lifted and fell as gently as a fairground carousel, and our ropes creaked satisfyingly just as they do in cinematographic portrayals of galleons in the calm before the storm – but before long we were heaving over incoming waves while Linda attempted heroically to prepare Christmas dinner, and Fausty looked on, wondering if she could manage any.

There was a knock on the hull, and standing on the deck of the boat next to us was a man throwing his arms about wildly – his words were torn away by the wind, but the ones that reached me conveyed the impression that he owned the boat to which we were tied, and was demanding that we move in case we damaged the transfers on his hull for which he had just paid – was it £2,000? – but surely no one in their right mind would pay £2,000 for a piece of nonsense like that? Cursing him roundly – once he'd gone – I started the engine, untied the mooring lines, and pulled clear to head out into the darkness and look for somewhere else to moor.

Two minutes later I could have fallen on his neck and kissed it, for no sooner had we left our berth than the wind suddenly increased to a storm and white-capped waves marched into the harbour like gangs of youths looking for trouble. We struggled against the wind and water so that at half-engine speed we managed a quarter of a knot. We found a lee close by the lifeboat slip, alongside the docks – it wasn't quite the scenery we'd planned for our festive meal, but here the water scarcely moved; Fausty settled down with a contented expression, which spoke for all of us; and any nervousness we might have had about fulfilling our elaborate plans for a Christmas day meal were soon dispelled by the delicious smells oozing from the oven. Soon glasses chinked cheerfully amid wishes for a Merry Christmas; and we addressed ourselves to the mouth-watering and colourful feast before us. The wind singing in the rigging, and the occasional heel to port as the mast was caught by a particularly strong squall, only added atmosphere to a happily memorable occasion enjoyed on all sides.

Unbeknown to us, back at the pontoon things were turning bad. Tiiti and Antti stayed up all night lashing rope after rope to the pontoon in the horizontal rain; others bucked about at the full extent of their mooring lines and their crews, we later learned, were unable to jump ashore for almost two days – but, worst of all, a boat that had been left unattended while the owner was away for a week broke free at the bow and slewed round, forcing her stern against the steel-reinforced corner of the pontoon; and her movement, at odds with the movement of the pontoon, made short work of holing her, after which she sank. No one even noticed she'd gone, though an emergency light was strobing eerily underwater, and the tops of the masts which broke the surface of the water at an odd angle had no boat under them.

'Is it always like this?' Fausty asked.

* * *

During the early months of the following year no one came, and no one went. We spent days together floating silently in a quiet backwater, until it seemed strange to go to town and fall into conversation with another human being – to hear a new voice, to listen to new thoughts. John from *Sun Tyne* felt the strangeness of it too and his isolation was complete. When we saw him he had 100 metres of chain laid out on a silent upriver pontoon, and was examining it thoughtfully when we startled him with our approach. He shuffled, composed himself, and then smiled coyly. 'I've done a silly thing,' he said, 'I've bought 100 metres of uncalibrated chain for my windlass – but it only works with calibrated chain.'

'We'll buy it from you,' I suggested, 'we need a second chain – and we don't use a windlass.' We agreed a price and loaded it into our chain locker there and then. Our thank yous were interrupted by the distant roar of an engine, the rapid approach and ever-changing note of which told us that we were about to see a helicopter, and moments later it throbbed into view, banking so steeply as it cornered into our stretch of the river that it looked like a fallen windmill. It levelled out, passed overhead – then it shot up and looped back in a circle to pass over our heads once again, waggling as it came, so low this time that we all ducked. The word 'POLICE' was the last thing I saw.

'Crikey! That was low!' I said, embarrassed to find myself lying face down on the boards. When I got up I noticed that Linda was wearing a different hairstyle.

'I think that was for me,' said John, the only one of us to remain upright. The thought went through my mind that he was becoming a bit deranged and I must have looked at him doubtfully, because he went on, 'Yeah, I think they're telling me I've got post at the harbour master's office.' He threw me a look after he'd said it, and held my gaze for just a moment too long. He was on a different wavelength – so I invented something new to say.

'It makes me feel guilty when they come to see what we're up to!'

John looked away. 'That's not how it makes me feel,' he said, watching wistfully as it disappeared over the trees, 'it... it just reminds me.' He turned to face me – that same look again – for a long time; then he said, 'There's something I haven't told you. Have you got time for a cup of tea?' We nodded. 'Come on board – let me show you something...'

We climbed aboard his boat for the first time, our curiosity ignited, and settled ourselves down at a neat, plain table. It was pleasantly warm, everything was ordered and tidy, and on a shelf was a photograph of his wife. He put the kettle on the stove, calling out some pleasantries as he did so; and then went to a bookshelf under the cabin windows, where he dragged his finger along a row of books. 'Now, let me see...' He pulled a dark cardboard slip from between two books, unfastened the cord that bound them, and opened it onto the table. Inside were some large-format monochrome photographs, which he spread in front of us; they were of an ordinary high street, deserted except for a handful of armed police officers, crouching behind cover, their weapons trained on a building; and all wearing the same black woolly hat that John wore now. 'That's me,' he said, tapping one of the figures.

'I did used to be a fisherman; I wasn't lying to you about that, I grew up in an orphanage and went straight into fishing after that. But one day someone suggested I train to be a policeman – and it was the best piece of advice I've ever had. After the bombing of the Grand Hotel in 1984, when Maggie Thatcher was staying there, they decided to train up a special armed service unit within the police force. I was one of the first recruits for that training.' He went on to describe the training – how he had fallen from a helicopter once, injuring his leg; and some of the actions in which he was involved. We listened to him, enthralled, and when he had finished he said, with more than a hint, 'When I retired they told me I could talk about my life if I wanted to – though I should choose who I told... as a rule I prefer not to tell anyone.' We felt honoured that John, who kept himself so much to himself, had let us get closer to him, and learn so much about his life. Although he and we, living aboard boats as we did, shared a lot of mutual acquaintances, we never mentioned his story to any of them; I've told the story here, but in respect to John, I've changed both his name, and the name of his boat.

As the days lengthened, so the waterborne activity increased. One of the first to make an appearance was Pete, out for another sausage weekend. We hadn't seen him for about three months, and now that he had turned up he looked different, sadder. He draped himself pathetically against his rigging and his boat heeled in sympathy. His hairy navel peeped out from between a white T-shirt that wouldn't pull down and black jogging bottoms that wouldn't stay up.

'You know my missus, Sue?' We didn't, but because it wouldn't stretch credulity too far to imagine that he was married to someone called Sue, we nodded.

'Well, she gone leff me.'

'Aaaahhhhhooww!' we harmonised.

'Yeah!' He nodded emphatically. 'She just turn round one day she says I don't love you no more.' Then in imitation of her final words he ended with a cheerful, 'Bye-eee!'

Pity choked us, and we found we didn't have anything to add, so he filled the silence.

'Anyway... look on the bright side, I always says; I'm in the market for a noo one now.' And with that he gave an involuntary thrust from his groin, which yearned for the future and sent shockwaves of excitement through his belly. Then he raised his head feigning interest in something that was happening downriver, but stole glances back at Linda to see how she was taking the news that he was a single man.

* * *

Before leaving for our summer cruise we owed a big debt of gratitude to some friends of ours, which we attempted to repay in a small way.

'This is going to knock their socks off!' Linda said, as she opened *Prue Leith's Cookery Bible* to follow the recipe blow by blow. 'Now then, page 319, whiskied pheasant...'; and she began to set out all the ingredients we'd need.

John and Pam, who spent summers on board their boat, had offered us the use of their house for the whole winter while they were away caravanning in Crete, and although we hadn't taken up the offer because we were enjoying life aboard so much, it had been a comfort to know that the offer was there. We'd arrived at their house to cook a meal for them in their own kitchen.

I browned the pheasant in a casserole dish and whilst it sizzled I turned on the extractor fan on the cooker hood, lighting the area and 'whooshing' in a business-like manner – adding a touch of professionalism to our kitchen-craft. Linda called the next instruction, which was to pour two ounces of whisky into the hot pan and flame it. I measured the whisky into a tumbler – it didn't look much, so I filled it and was about to chuck it in the pan when it occurred to me that John and Pam might enjoy the theatre of this next step, so I called them into their kitchen.

'John! Pam! – don't miss this bit!' They hurried in to join us and assembled themselves as spectators.

'The recipe calls for the whisky to be flambéed – so don't worry! – everything is under control, but I thought you might like to watch. Have you got any matches, Pam?'

'Yes – in the drawer on your right.'

I chucked the whisky into the hot pan where it hissed angrily, and the alcohol evaporated to form itself into a nuclear-shaped cloud... and before it could get away, I lit my match. There was an explosion, followed by a surprisingly vigorous fire which engulfed my head, singeing my eyebrows and burning my forelock on its way to the extractor fan, which swallowed it whole, shuddered – as though it had eaten something it didn't like – and then stopped. A moment later it started again, tinnily, before bursting into flames above me and sending a cloud of black smoke billowing across the (formerly) white ceiling.

Instinctively, I turned the fan off, at which thousands of tiny balls of molten foam rubber (which had been held aloft by the vortex) began parachuting down, each hanging from a sooty flame, to land over a wide area – the work surfaces, in open drawers, in bags of flour, and in the casserole. I sensed that it had all gone rather quiet behind me, and turned to gauge the mood. Looking first at John's face, and then at Pam, it would be fair to say that shock was one of the emotions they were experiencing, but they hung on resolutely to their smiles.

John was the first to speak. 'That's it, Justin,' he said, soothingly.

'Go on!' said Pam, as though that was just a minor prelude, and she was now ready for the main performance.

'I am *so* sorry!' I began, but John overspoke me, raising a hand.

'Justin – you've done me a favour there – I've been meaning to change that bloody filter for years...'

'Do you think they enjoyed their meal?' I asked Linda when we got back to our boat.

'Well...' she said, trailing off thoughtfully. She never did finish her sentence, but her tone implied doubt.

6 AN AGGRESSIVE LOBSTER

'What time are you setting off tomorrow?' Bill asked. He pushed the glasses to the top of his head, folded his arms, and sat back to scrutinise me like the headmaster of a private school. We both intended to start our voyages by calling at the Scilly Isles the following day, 70 miles away; after that he would be cruising west to the Americas, we, more modestly, to Scotland. Because Bill had been sailing for ten years without hitting anything, and because he had been helping me with my astro-navigation, I hoped my answer would impress him; I'd done my homework. Citing the tidal stream at Lizard Point and at Wolf Rock, the forecast wind strength and direction, and our expected boat speed as a result, I concluded by telling him that we'd be leaving at 4 am. He closed his eyes tightly and shook his head with disbelief.

'Amazing! – I absolutely agree... that's *exactly* what we've decided.' He even managed to make it sound as though it were *he* who had been vindicated.

My watch is radio-controlled by the atomic clock at Rugby and consequently is accurate to one second in 30 million years; so it was without surprise that, when its digits blinked to 0400 the following morning and I heard links of chain rattle over a bow-roller somewhere in the darkness, I concluded that Bill and Jill – the most punctual people alive – were getting underway.

It had been a busy winter for them – sticklers for accuracy, they had had boatbuilders back on board for months rebuilding their new boat wherever it differed by more than a few millimetres from the agreed specification.

'My motor/sailing signal is four hundered mil long and I always keep it in the forward locker – I told them that, but they've garn and built one of their standard lockers at three-fifty – it's hopeless,' Bill had complained, shaking his head and tugging at his beard in frustration, while in the background the builders set about the four-day job of altering it. We grudgingly admired them for their accurate record-keeping and lack of compromise, and how they used it to bring order to all things around them – a two-man Roman invasion – and as they left that morning the only piece of business that remained outstanding was the litigation their daughter had lodged against them. Having looked after their affairs in the UK – the letting of their farm and so forth – for the last ten years, she'd finally astonished them with a bill, which they had refused to pay – so she was suing them. She is a solicitor.

We, too, had frustrations in the final days and weeks before departure – gear that hadn't arrived, an overheating problem we still hadn't solved; yet as we motored out of harbour – while the coast was still no more than a few hundred yards behind us – we could feel all the cares and worries of shoreside life fall away to dissipate over the sea into a long sigh. Our minds cleared; focus returned; we felt tranquil. All who venture out to sea notice the phenomenon. It may be that we merely swap one set of problems for another – but the new set, the challenges of voyaging under sail, are all within our control; they are practical rather than political, relying on self-dependence rather than the vagaries of others; and one can see immediate results from one's efforts, giving rise to that elusive feeling of being in control in an environment – come hell or high water – that means no harm.

Linda sat mute in the cockpit, yawning occasionally – she hadn't slept a wink, turning over her hopes and fears for the new adventures ahead. As we motored past the Manacles Rocks, she blinked dreamily at the horizon while golden light flooded onto it, illuminating a dark sleeping sea gently heaving in the morning breeze, and promising a fine day – a day to be on the water... nowhere better in the world. We hoisted sail, the engine fell silent, and we rolled along at 3 knots, merry water tinkling at our bow – the sound of freedom. No authority can tell you where you should point your bow or limit how far you should go in the soft wind that blows across the deck.

We oiled our arms and legs, filling the air with the exotic smell of coconut, in preparation for the day ahead, and the long summer beyond that. We took interest in every sunny headland as we passed by, found some point to remark on, and then noted it in our log – our voyage was young and we thrilled at each new evidence that we were at last underway.

Off the swirling waters of Lizard Point – the grave of so many mariners, owing to its violent overfalls when the tidal stream flows against a gale of wind – the fishing rod jumped in its grip, then bent to the strain of two good mackerel, which we brought aboard, unhooked, knocked on the head, dressed, and placed under the grill with a drizzle of olive oil and freshly ground black pepper. Ten minutes later they bubbled and steamed on our plates as we sat down in the cockpit to eat them with a fork; they tasted like nothing on earth – moist, creamy, and fragrant. They satisfied both a hunger and a longing.

In the afternoon the wind died and the sea became glassy; the swell – moderated by its 3,000-mile journey into long, lazy waves – lifted and rolled us, causing the idle boom to crash back and forth annoyingly. Four hundred yards away Bill and Jill sat in their cockpit, reading. It was hot and we two were becalmed – 'painted ships upon a painted ocean'. In the mirror face of the sea, tiny creatures floating at the surface whirred away as we drifted toward them – noticed only because of the little bow wave they made in their flight. A curious splish-splash from a limp fin ahead as it fell first to the left and then to the right turned out to be a sunfish swimming by in its odd way. At seven that evening I radioed Bill to tell him that we were going to motor in to anchor under St Michaels Mount for the night – I expected that he would say they'd do the same, but he shamed me by saying they would stay at sea and wait for wind.

'That's OK,' I joked to Linda, 'when we come out tomorrow we'll find them in the same place.' We threw out our anchor under the mount among the petrified trunks of trees said to lie on the sea bed – saw the flash of a camera from the castle, imagined that we were posing for Baron John, Lord St Levan, and then turned in for a blissful sleep.

We continued on our way the following morning – Bill and Jill were gone and we never saw them again; we spoke to them on the radio the following day… the wind had picked up in the night, allowing them to make the Scillies; we followed on, but landed in a different port.

The thrill of sighting land from seaward never diminishes. From first smudges on the horizon – when the argument about whether you are looking at clouds or land has been settled – excitement grows as the islands swell; gradually details can be made out – an airport, houses, a tractor ploughing a field, a van driving along a road, all taking on new significance as they form the first impressions of their community. Romping toward New Grimsby Sound, between the islands of Tresco and Bryher, with the 'strong wind' of which the Coastguard had warned filling our canvas from behind, we tore spray off deep blue water and rushed dramatically at rocks that rose sheer out of the agitated sea. The Scillies motor vessel *Firebrand* roared out to welcome us and to allow the sightseers they had aboard to take photographs.

We shot into the sound – a flooded causeway between two stacks – scarcely in control, and gratefully gained shelter from both the wind and the sea, which spent itself in foam at the rocky entrance. Island smells reached us as we drifted along past Cromwell's castle, felt our way down a line of moored vessels to 'get the lie', and then threw our anchor onto a patch of white sand peeping from among the kelp, close by the shore.

Our first impression of the Scillies was one of tranquillity and colour – flowers peep from behind pink rocks attended by bees; walkers on the hill amble; and boats in the harbour doze at their moorings under dazzling sunlight.

We waved down the harbour master as he passed to know if we had anchored near any hazards, and if our spot suited him.

'You'll be just fine where you are,' he said as though he couldn't be more pleased to have us in his port, talking in that laid-back tone you associate with sun-drenched paradises. He handed us a printed guide to Tresco Island and the breeze toyed with his sun-bleached hair while he patiently answered our hundred questions.

'What's it like here in a blow?' we wondered, knowing already that we planned to stay a while, and having heard that the waters around the Scilly Isles can be rough.

'If it blows, pick up one of these mooring buoys – you may not always be comfortable, but you'll always be safe.'

The following morning, *Firebrand* came alongside to say hello. The skipper and his mate leaned over the gunwhale and wanted to know all about our boat, what she was, and where built. They didn't smile overmuch – theirs was the companionability of 'old friends', seeing that we had met once before. As soon as Linda enquired about the shops on the neighbouring island of St Mary's, it was, 'Jump aboard – we're just going there ourselves.'

Off we raced, now fast, now slow, as they picked their way knowledgeably through the rocks and shoals, while we sheltered ourselves behind the wheel house from the cooling effect of the apparent wind. The young deckhand – dressed only in a pair of shorts, T-shirt and a hat, which flapped in the breeze – sat sunning his brown legs and bare feet over the rail, like a Mexican on a verandah.

Hugh Town was cheerful, small and busy, as was the supermarket – middle-aged men holding places in long queues wore thin-lipped smiles of tolerance while their wives continued to shop, returning periodically to add armfuls of tins and bottles to already full baskets. Shelves were bare in the greengrocery department; in answer to any request, staff were 'just waiting on the next ferry'.

Firebrand came to pick us up at lunchtime, together with five well-heeled pensioners who wanted to spend a few hours on the uninhabited island of Samson. Arriving shortly at that island at low water, the boat couldn't reach the pier.

'OK – roll up your trousers,' the deckhand told them as he lowered the gangway into the water with a splash. They roared with laughter.

'I'm serious!' he barked. 'You've got to wade ashore.' Incredulous looks suggested this was more adventure than they had in mind, and they now weighed their desert island dreams against the necessity of getting wet to realise them. Three reluctantly complied; two mutinied. Without a word the deckhand picked up one of the mutineers, put her on his back, and carried her ashore. Peals of laughter rang out at his audacity until tears rolled down their faces – he returned for the other, who threw herself across his back like a princess in distress; their adventure was underway.

When Linda mentioned how much she was hoping to see a puffin while we were in the Scillies, the skipper sheered away to take us to the outer islands for an hour's wildlife spotting.

Prawns thrive in the warm-water pools at the end of the pier on Tresco. Wading up to our thighs, and with our ankles sinking into the silty sand, we walked along at low water banging our prawn net on the ground ahead of us, inspecting it every minute or so to see if we had any big ones to throw into our bucket. After half an hour we had enough for dinner and took the opportunity to sink a pre-dinner pint in the New Inn, where the beer is fantastic and the staff are imported from all over the world on the basis of irrepressible good nature – a discordant word can ruin a holiday; the island estate knows this and staff are informal and mannerly – and then went home to gorge ourselves on garlic prawns.

We explored Tresco. There are pedestrians, cyclists and golf-carters – then there is a yawning gap in the transport system until you get to helicopters, which fly in four times a day to a well-manicured lawn protected from terrorist attack by a chain nailed to some sticks. A flashing light warned us not to cross the heliport when an arrival was imminent, and a large notice explained the legal consequences if we chose to do so. The only other area with limited access was the abbey and gardens, for which an entrance fee was due – they were wonderful. Elsewhere on the island, exotic plants of every colour cling to the walls and crowd around well-maintained holiday-let stone cottages; noisy birds wade in silent pools; and the island has a collection of pieces of maritime history – figureheads washed ashore from sailing ships wrecked on the archipelago over the centuries, cannon and cannonballs lifted from the seabed, together with ancient glass bottles, cutlery and crockery, and the personal effects of sailors.

We anchored for one night on an exposed stretch of coast on the north side of St Martin's Island and rolled like bitches to the Atlantic swell. Unable to sleep, I dressed at five to walk around the pastoral coast and found, in the middle of nowhere, an unmanned 'internet point' open to all comers with its machines quietly humming; I popped in to send an unnecessary email. On the way back along the beach I noticed, among rotting heaps of kelp, a storm-damaged lobster pot with no floor in it; and lying near by some trawler netting – seeing possibilities for both, I picked them up, and carried them home. Back on board I sat on deck and was halfway through knotting a makeshift floor for the pot using the trawler netting when a fishing boat motored around the corner. We'd anchored near to some pot buoys, and I wondered if he was on his way to trip them. He was; arriving close by, he stepped out from his wheel house and squinted at me narrowly.

'Where did you get that pot?' he demanded.

'Along the beach, over there.' I tried not to sound too guilty.

'That's one of mine.'

'Oh.'

'Has it got a floor in it?'

'No.' I held it up for him to see. 'I'm just tying on this netting for a floor.'

He tossed his head and began to return to the wheel house, calling back over his shoulder, 'Ah well – you might as well keep it...'

I'd often wondered if fishermen who set pots for a living get irritated with yachtsmen who set pots for pleasure, but took this gift of a damaged pot as tacit permission to use it. We moved to a different anchorage on the other side of the islands, a journey of only six or seven miles, but requiring close attention in these rocky shoals. There are five populated islands, together with hundreds of uninhabited ones and rocky islets, all low-lying – and with many more obstructions submerged just below the surface of the water. As newcomers we struggled to verify the chart with what we saw around us; all the rocks and islets looked the same, and in any case they all merged into one. The tide runs swiftly, too, threatening to sweep onto unseen rocks – named after the men or ships that had accidentally discovered them – all who lose their bearings.

At the height of our concentration, the fishing rod, which was trailing a lure through the turbulent water, leapt to life as we passed through a rocky canyon; I snatched the rod up just in time to stop it going over the side and felt something kicking wildly – I tried to wind it in while steering with my foot, but it was too big for our tackle and got away.

We sailed for 'The Cove' on St Agnes Island and were sure we had made a mistake, finding no gap in the rocks where an entrance to the anchorage should be – but at a range of a couple of hundred yards the camouflage failed and we saw the hint of an opening. Once it had given up the secret of its location, it proved not only shy but pretty, with colourful slopes climbing away on both sides and a white sandy bar at the head of the cove. The scent of flowers hung in the air, and the sound of screaming gulls whirled around it.

Setting off from there to go fishing – hoping to catch some bait for my new pot – I loaded the fishing rod into the dinghy and the bail arm accidentally flicked open, allowing the weighted line to run out to the seabed twenty feet below. Through the water I could clearly see the margin between white sand and rocky weed; I settled myself into the dinghy and found that the line, when I tried to retrieve it, resisted – having snagged on some weed, I supposed. I pulled hard and it answered by pulling back... on the hook was a 6-pound pollack. I remember Linda's face when I stood again in the hatchway, less than a minute after leaving it, and her eye fell to the huge dripping fish in my hand.

I filleted and salted the fish in preparation for smoking it the following day, then hung the head, bones and guts messily in the new lobster pot as bait – how could we fail to catch something with it? I rowed away to drop the pot into a gulley where the water was 100 feet deep at the foot of a stack, and buoyed the pot with a fender.

Having survived their long sea voyage, seeds wash ashore and flourish in the microclimate of the Scillies. The sun-dazzled white sand pathways are strewn with bird of paradise flowers, agapanthus, and triffids – it's hard to believe you are still in Britain. Speaking personally, sitting outside the Turk's Head pub on St Agnes Island, looking over the archipelago on a sunny evening with a pint of HSD, is as 'abroad' as I ever need to go. In contrast with the rolling of the night before, we slept that night aboard a boat set in a limpid stone of blue crystal.

Only the gulls had urgent business the following morning. I lay in bed listening to their calls as they criss-crossed overhead to the breeding colony on Gugh with scraps for their young, before remembering that I too had urgent business, and got up to inspect my pot. I'm always mindful of how easily I could become a casualty when I stand in my puny dinghy with fathoms of wet rope pulled up from the deep lying in coils around my ankles; it snakes back and forth with the working end still attached to a weighted pot, which wants to plunge back down to the depths and wouldn't hesitate to take me with it. The pot, when it came up, snagged under the transom as it always does, and I leaned over precariously to free it. When it broke the surface there was an almighty thrashing from inside, which sent foaming water in all directions.

'Jesus Christ! I've caught a whopper!' I said aloud, falling onto my seat to get away from it. 'Would you look at the size of that?' The clunking armour of a lobster – which must have been nearly 2 feet long – rattled menacingly inside the pot. 'Wait til Linda sees this!' Back at the boat, I could hear her on the phone to Pam. I climbed aboard, opened the lobster pot and carefully took out my prize, which by now was torpid. Stepping down the companionway with my back toward Linda to shield her view from the lobster and save the surprise until the last moment, I turned.

'CRIKEY! Oh my God!' she yelled down the phone; eyeing the exits. 'PAM! Justin's caught a lobster... and it's bloody huge!' she said, gasping for breath. 'Oh, I wish you could see it!'

'How big is it?' I heard Pam shriek, tinnily.

'Tell her to hang on a minute, and I'll weigh it.' I put the lobster down and rummaged through the cupboard for the kitchen scales; they seemed very small suddenly, and it was a bit of a fiddle to know how I was going to weigh it. In all the excitement I forgot the claws – but the lobster must have been waiting for his chance, because as I went to grab him a giant claw rose from the table, swiped at my hand, and caught me by the thumb, closing on it like a pair of industrial scissors.

'AHHH!!! The bugger's got me!' I screamed, and grabbed at the pincer with my other hand.

Whenever I get hurt in amusing circumstances, Linda's enjoyment soars. She howls with delight to see me dangling from a bridge by my fingernails, or up to my neck in a bog; and she collapsed onto the companionway steps now, gasping for breath to see me fighting to release my thumb from the lobster's shears. Tears of mirth rolled down her cheeks as she struggled to convey the scene to Pam.

'It's... it's got him!' she stammered into the phone. 'Oh, Pam! – it's got him by the thumb!' Fully six hours later, whenever there was a quiet moment, or Linda caught sight of my bandaged thumb, she would rush away to shut herself in the cabin, from where I could hear the half-suppressed snorts of her chuckling.

Our crossing to Ireland would take up to 36 hours; it was to be Linda's first overnight passage and she was getting nervous. She bought sacks of lemons, barrels of salt beef, pots of grow-your-own herbs, and all necessary requisites for a passage to India, until at last I was able to steer her into the Mermaid Inn where she could meet happy folk who didn't give a hoot for the morrow. Standing shoulder to shoulder at the crowded bar amid the merry din, we were just ordering our drinks when the chap next to me turned and said, 'I think I've seen your house...'

Not quite sure how to respond, I looked at him to see if his eyes were in focus, or if he had learning difficulties – or whether this was the punchline of a joke I vaguely remembered hearing about Jesus calling to Paul from the cross. He looked sober and earnest.

'How do you mean?' I asked.

'Did you live at Dulverton?' He was 50, short, slightly built, and wore a tracksuit. I'd never seen him before in my life. He explained that he had viewed our house with an estate agent a couple of years previously, and had noticed, pinned to the wall of our workshop, a line drawing of our boat... and recognised it now that we were anchored in the bay.

He himself was here on a boat with two friends, both of whom stood with him at the bar – the first was quietly confident, and Yul Brynner bald; he smiled a lot and spoke with a Lancashire accent. The second was intense, silent and dishevelled. Linda invited them back to the boat that evening to have a look around, and share a meal.

The laughter, stories of people and places we held in common, and quirky Exmoor reminiscences went on until late in the night; yet ever the third man sat quietly watching from his corner. He had intelligent eyes and a tolerant smile and it struck me that he might have been finding this all a bit frivolous – I asked him how long he'd been sailing.

'I was born sailing. And when I saw these two reprobates trying to drown themselves in the harbour I thought I'd better come along.'

'We were all right until you came along – trying to drown us! We thought you were suicidal.'

'I've tried suicide and I've tried sailing – I'm better at sailing.'

'Obviously!'

'Have you really tried suicide?'

It was his failure to answer that question that caught everyone's attention. As his chin rested on his chest, he flashed bright-eyed glances at us through bushy eyebrows – watching our curiosity, and slightly amused by it.

'A couple of years ago my girlfriend left me and I was feeling a bit down...' he began – his words were evenly spoken, but you could see that it still hurt. 'First I lost my job, then my flat. I lived on the streets for a while before arriving very logically at the conclusion that there wasn't anything to live for.' He was so plain in what he said, with his soft Irish accent, that there was no awkwardness as we listened. The rapt attention of his two friends suggested that they, too, were hearing this story for the first time.

'I decided I'd kill myself by jumping off the cliff at Tregowan beach, but in spite of taking a really good run-up, I landed on a ledge about 50 feet down... I didn't know it was there... I hadn't really researched it properly,' he joked. 'I'm afraid of heights so I hadn't gone close enough to the edge to have a good look down. I lay there with me two broken legs and a broken arm thinking, "Jesus Christ, I can't even get that right." I was lying there for hours, thinking – then I saw someone walking along the beach with a dog and I managed to attract their attention – and they waved back, like, "Hello, how you doin'?" "Well, not too good, actually"; but they must have thought I was pissing about because they just walked on. Some more people came and I managed to attract their attention, too, but – Jesus – could I get anyone to understand that I needed help? I don't know what it was. After a while as I lay there I realised that I didn't want to die, so I tried climbing back up – or down, but I couldn't really move to get off the ledge. Do you know how long I was there? Do ya?'

'Go on.'

'Three days! Three days before I got anyone to help.' There was a chorus of disbelief.

'In hospital the doctor was like, "Ach – you'll be fine"; he patched me up and sent me home to stay with my mum – but for two weeks I got steadily worse with chest pains, vomiting and dizzy spells and coughing – every time she phoned the hospital they told her it was bruising. After a fortnight I was rushed back to hospital where I nearly *did* die, and then they discovered I had a punctured lung.'

* * *

Linda checked the contents of the survival 'grab bag' a hundred times: chocolate, water, first aid kit, out-of-date flares, and some lavender-scented soap was all it contained. We tied our six-man liferaft, which we'd bought second-hand and which hadn't been serviced for 17 years, to a secure point on deck, and hoped that we wouldn't have to find out if it worked. Then we tied our cockleshell of a dinghy – which we pretended was a second liferaft – on top of the coach-house roof. Early the next morning, before any of the comfortably housed holidaymakers had woken to another day in paradise, we hoisted sail and set out onto the heaving bosom of the Atlantic, bound for Ireland. The rising swell caressed the rocks before falling and spitting foam through jagged black teeth. A south-westerly breeze filled our sails from the port quarter, thrummed through the rigging, and as we cleared the sound *Caol Ila* leaned her shoulder into the sea and surged away to the north, leaving a trail of hissing foam in her wake.

Fifteen miles out to sea, Round Island Lighthouse dropped below the horizon, leaving us alone with the wind and the water. The sun flashed on the dazzling white caps of the waves, and we had all the breeze we needed for a speedy passage. Hour succeeded hour as we rolled on our way, and the passing of time was marked only by the changing arc of the sun and the slow accumulation of miles on the log. Between Linda and I there was no conversation save the words that dealt with the management of the boat.

Supper was more than usually welcome, and the restoring food we ate as the evening wind fell light was in no way diminished by the fact that we were at sea; we sat in the cockpit with plates of lamb chops, creamed potato and steaming green vegetables; washed it down with a glass of wine, and watched the sun melt into a pool of red wax on the horizon. Our speed slowed to 3 knots, and we were left in silence except for the rhythmical creak from a block; the slop from an occasional wave bigger than the rest as it fell on the hull; and, from time to time, a startling slat of protest from the mainsail as a pair of waves with perfect timing rolled us from ear to ear and then passed onwards to end their journey with a roar on some distant beach.

Linda took the helm for a couple of hours. *Caol Ila* needs to be steered every inch of her way, and helming is one of Linda's least favourite jobs. From where I lay in my bunk, I could look out through a porthole in the wall of the cockpit well and watch her paying her tithe to the gods through diligent attention to duty – she scanned the horizon, eyed her course against the compass, and glanced over the sails, always suspecting them of being in surfeit. Like a sentry who knows the enemy cannot be far and trusts quietness least, her eyes never rested. Darkness gathered and, for company – a crowd, as stars sprang out in their millions and our masthead light intruded among them, drawing figures of eight. The Plough pointed out the North Star right above the bow; satellites rode across the sky; and at our stern a green bonfire of phosphorescence sparkled in the water, all else was black.

I took the helm back soon after midnight and saw Linda again through the porthole, but now quietly dozing in bed as we rolled on toward Ireland. Gradually my apprehension of a night watch subsided – a bad experience, years earlier, still haunted me. Leaving Gibraltar one evening in November 1987, bound for the Canary Isles with a glowing forecast, I and three friends, on a 33-foot Westerly Discus, found the wind outside the harbour was already blowing a gale from behind as we pointed the bow out into the Atlantic. Undecided whether this was a 'local effect' or the forecast was wrong, we motored on, making no clear decision about turning back. By nine o'clock the decision was made for us – the wind suddenly picked up, flinging the cockpit cushions so far forward of the boat that we didn't see them land; and the sea behind us grew steep. Committed, we turned the engine off, and found that the wind acting on the bare mast alone gave us 4 knots.

By one o'clock the following morning the wind was blowing with storm force and the water was wild; on watch alone, I suddenly became aware that we had been rising to the same wave for what seemed like ages and so turned to look behind me to see how big it was – but saw only blackness over the stern. Just as I was about to turn to face forward, a tinkling sound far above my head made me look up and there, towering over me, was the unbalanced crest of the huge wave. Fear pumped through my veins; 'Steer straight' was all I could think as I turned to face forward. A few seconds later we were at the summit of a wave so big it had given us a lee from the wind when we had been in its trough – spray fired through the air and pounded onto my back like wet bullets; the mast shuddered; the rigging wire screamed; and idle ropes suddenly leapt off the deck in a maniacal dance, cracking in the wind. I don't pretend to have felt anything other than terror – yet strangely, in spite of my fear, I could only admire the grand scene from up there; all around I saw waves heaving themselves westward like an army of wet mountains advancing on some foreign shore, and from where I sat I could survey from the highest peak the whole mountain range, and feel how insignificant we were amongst them – like the curling streaks of simmering foam they left in their wake.

I felt the boat begin to bounce lightly and knew instinctively that it was significant – but didn't know of what. With that we lurched forward and there was a great 'hushing' sound as we began surfing down the wave with spray cannoning off the bow in great arcs, to left and right. I braced myself as we neared the trough, expecting that we would plunge below the surface and it would be all over. The bow bit deep into the water, burying the foredeck up to the mast; and there we stranded for a moment, threatening to pitchpole. I felt some mute kicks of protest from under me, then we settled back and the foredeck burst up through the surface throwing water like a submarine. Relief was short-lived – the stern lifted again, the huge wave had caught up with us once more, and it had yet to get past.

Back up at the crest after another stomach-sickening climb, I noticed again how completely the wild chaos contrasted with the tranquillity of the trough. This time the wave seemed to dispense with us more decisively – we overbalanced backwards, the bow was thrown into the sky, and we slipped down the wave's back as it tossed us into its wake.

I sat in shock for a while, I believe, and didn't notice at first the figure sitting on my left; I turned and found that it was my father. He had been a Commander R.N. (Retired) and had seen action serving on board, among other vessels, HMS *Ajax*, which had achieved heroic fame in the Battle of the River Plate during the Second World War, and as such this would scarcely be his first heart-stirring moment at sea. He didn't look at me, but sat staring across me, over the waves and into the darkness. His face was stoic, he didn't speak; it was enough that he was there.

He sat with me for an hour or two during the worst of the weather, but by daybreak I could sense he'd gone, and that our danger had passed. During the morning a French cable-laying ship came out of her way to see that we were OK – we gave them a cheery wave, which they returned from their flying bridge – and late that afternoon we set our first rag of sail, the wind having moderated to an ordinary gale, which blew us into Porto Santo, an island off Madeira, six days later. Speaking to my father about the incident months later, he listened with growing amazement as I described to him a dream he remembered having at about that time.

Tired at first in the wee hours of our passage to Ireland, the cool air soon refreshed me, and I let Linda sleep until five.

The hours had passed with nothing to see as we lifted over lonely waves – and I was just wondering if life on earth had ceased to exist, and only we remained, when, in the gloom of the new dawn, I saw a masthead light twitching close ahead... then another – and altered course just in time to avoid hitting a yacht. Styled on an ocean-going racing yacht, they were tiny – only 10-feet-long 'pocket racers' – and because of that turned out to be much closer than they at first appeared. I watched them sail by on automatic pilot, French flags fluttering at the backstay, but no sign of life on board. Turning one last time to watch them sail into our wake, I saw a figure jump up and stand blinking in his companionway hatch. Because his boat and he were nearly the same size, he looked like a sea creature emerging from his shell, eyes out on stalks. We remained staring at one another, coming to terms with the improbability of a near miss in that wilderness. He turned urgently to look ahead, once, to see if we, too, had a companion who was about to mow him down; and then we watched each other become mutual specks.

An hour after we had changed watch, I was dozing back in the warm bunk Linda had left when she called me urgently on deck – I could tell from her tone that she wasn't alarmed, and a moment later heard a high-pitched squeal of bubbles through the hull, and knew what she wanted me to see.

'Look, Alfie! Dolphins!'

We were surrounded by fins broaching the surface, and every few moments a dolphin would launch himself to become frivolously airborne, before diving back in. A surge of gratitude and love overwhelmed us... I think a lot of people have the same longing when they see dolphins. They danced for us – and if we leaned over the side to watch one, he would turn onto his side and watch us with his upturned eye, the shape of his mouth naturally suggesting a smile – and the fact that we were 30 miles from land made the visit more personal. Delirious with joy, I climbed down onto the rigging underneath the bowsprit, still naked, to trail my foot in the water; I slipped, and only just saved myself from falling overboard. I secured myself, trailed my foot, and the dolphins rose to nudge it with their backs.

After ten minutes of this it dawned on us that they were part of a huge pod. Looking through binoculars, we saw that they were heading north-west, and could see fins breaking the surface or unaccounted splashes stretching out of sight, and toward the south-east, the splashes of those that had yet to reach us. It was useless to try to guess how many there were – but that didn't stop us from agreeing that it would easily be 400... or a thousand. Half an hour later, when new arrivals were still dropping by to greet us, we had long since become speechless to express our excitement.

By late morning we glimpsed the coast of Ireland through haze that thickened and thinned, but stubbornly refused to lift. Somewhere in the vicinity of Coningbeg light vessel, a few miles from Waterford Harbour, the water was still, and the wind died completely. Making a quarter knot, we faced another night at sea, but were reluctant to start the engine to finish off our journey because it was still prone to overheating. We sat and waited. A fin came in sight, heading toward us, which at first we hailed as another dolphin – but soon realised that it moved in an entirely different way. The forward fin cut the water menacingly, and a tail fin followed, slicing its way through the water from side to side with the regular sweep of a pendulum. It passed slowly alongside; it was large, white and had no fear of us as it turned to circle. The hairs stood up on the back of my neck. There have been sightings of great white sharks in the Celtic Sea, and we wondered if we were 'sighting' one now. Having circled the boat once, it lost interest and finned casually away, rippling the mirror surface of the water. Coming so close alongside, laying itself length for length with our boat, we could guess that it was 12 or 14 feet long.

As evening drew on, we anchored just outside the fishing harbour at Dunmore East, forbearing to go *into* the harbour having read some coded language in one of the Almanacs that yachts weren't welcome. We rolled miserably for two hours, looking mournfully firstly at the welcoming lights of a pub and then at the deserted harbour with its idle fishing vessels snuggled up cosily against the wall. Yielding to temptation, we went in and tied alongside an industrial-looking trawler the size of a floating factory.

Everything smelled of diesel and fish as we stepped ashore, tripping over broken debris strewn about the oil-blackened quay, to look for a harbour official to ask if we were all right where we were, and to pay harbour dues. We didn't find anyone that day and so walked into the pub, where two old fishermen were talking in the short, grave sentences of wise men as they looked out through the window at our boat. They turned to consult us: 'I says to my friend here – now that's a very old boat ya man has der – you can tell it, you see, because de mast is slightly leanin' to the forward, and that's how you can tell it... But he is for sayin' she's a new boat. Would she be at least a hundred years old?'

These were the first steps we'd ever taken on Irish soil – guests newly arrived at the party, and keen not to offend anyone. We explained that she was a replica of a boat more than a hundred years old, and that we had built her ourselves.

Irish harbour

The following morning, our efforts to find the harbour master produced a man who reluctantly admitted to being 'in charge' as he hurried away.

'What was it you was wantin'?' he called back over his shoulder, while slowing to a halt.

'It's us that's got the yacht in the harbour – are we all right tied where we are?'

'Ach – You'll be just fine,' he said, starting off again to attend to something more relevant.

'And what are the harbour dues?'

'Eh?'

'How much is it to stay here?'

'Listen, if you're happy – we're happy.' And with that music to our ears, he left us.

Later that day, as we fiddled about with domestic chores, someone knocked on our deck; I stuck my head out.

'Ah, well – she's a fine boat you have there!' came the cheerful greeting from a short stocky fella on the trawler, which he followed with other pleasantries. In answer to our question, he assured us that he wouldn't be moving for at least four days. 'I'm a pair trawler, do you see? And the udder half of me has trouble wid his engine, so you'll get plenty o' peace and quiet. Now, I didn't want to trouble you,' he said, raising his palm, 'but I was just wondering would it be OK if I hosed me decks? It's just that you may get a wee splashy water on your deck – though I'll be as careful as I can, like.'

'Please don't worry about us at all,' I said.

In the background for the next 20 minutes we were only occasionally aware of the spraying of a hose as it drummed on sheets of metal; then there was a curious squeaking noise from just above our heads. Looking obliquely through the porthole, we could see that the trawlerman was drying our deck with a newly laundered cloth.

* * *

There were no shelves in the chandlery. Piles of merchandise were stacked in rows directly on the floor – there was no need to impress – and every heap had its place.

'Is it you's got the yacht in the harbour?' the owner greeted me. He was about 30, bespectacled, wiry, and deferential.

'Yes.'

'Well, she's lovely, so she is.' He asked how long it had taken to build her, what sort of boat she was, and what materials she was built from. When I finished telling him, he suggested coyly, 'I'm building a boat myself... will I show her to you?'

A moment later we were climbing a rickety old ladder leading to a solidly welded mezzanine floor above the shop and there, chocked up among dusty boxes, was a lightweight rowing gig with smart lines, under construction – about a quarter complete.

'I've been at her six years,' he told me – which looked to be about a plank a year; and I wondered how long it would take before she saw the water. Reading my thoughts, he said, 'It's not going as fast as I would like – but the next one will be quicker… then perhaps there'll be a living in it for me.' What he had done was well done, and put our rough-hewing to shame.

Back on the shop floor, I picked up some sealant.

'That'll be €13.80.' I gave him a 20. He fiddled around in the till for a long time, eventually counting me €13.80 in change. Our schoolboy jokes about the Irish made me reluctant to point out his mistake, so I left the shop… but because he was such a lovely chap, I turned around and went back in. He looked surprised to see me.

'Forgotten something?'

'I think you've given me too much change.'

'What did I give you?'

'€13.80.'

'And how much did I say the sealant was?'

'€13.80.'

There was a pause. 'Well, what's wrong with that?'

'…Well, I make the change €6.20.'

'Hang on there a second…' He grabbed a calculator and tapped away at its keys, rehearsing the calculation several times before doing it for real.

'No, €13.80 is right,' he said, showing me the screen.

'But if the sealant is €13.80, that's *most* of the €20 I gave you – surely I would expect a smaller amount back?'

He tapped some more numbers into his calculator, trying the sum several ways before laying it aside and asking me what I made it again. Reluctantly he took back some of my change – but his eyes told me he suspected me of fraud.

We caught a bus to Waterford where we were out-dressed by the wealthy Americans who patronised smart waterfront department stores, stocking up on lead crystal cut glass and Irish tartan. Waterford isn't a big city, but wandering dazed through its shocking clamour, leaping backwards onto pavements to avoid cars and buses that had been half a mile away only a moment before, we realised that it was the busiest place we had visited for years; and, small though it was, it made us feel like rustics – fresh from our river creek. In a harbour, we could stand beaming aboard our highly varnished classic boat and enjoy the heroic admiration heaped on us by onlookers; here, we were objects of unspoken derision. The clothes we wore – clean, but un-ironed, and smelling heavily of woodsmoke – made us outcasts in the city, and we caught people looking at us askance before avoiding us altogether.

***

The fast-running tide around Carnsore Point – the south-east corner of Ireland – and thence up the east coast is a white-knuckle ride if taken close inshore, but – if you're up for it – it'll take you a long way in a six-hour tide. We launched ourselves onto the magic carpet, swerving left and right to avoid a thousand pot buoys like floating mines. They threatened to tangle our propeller, which would certainly ruin our day... as would a close encounter with the underwater ledges, sandbanks, counter currents, and 40-knot ferries with which we had to contend. It was brisk work to identify the navigation marks that zoomed by, and to keep ourselves within the narrow channels they marked in spite of a crossing tidal stream that wanted to take us onto the shoals.

Late in the afternoon we dropped our thrashing sails by the pier head at Arklow, to the annoyance of some rod fishermen who wound their lines in rather than lose their tackle. After our economical success at Dunmore East, we had no hesitation in spurning the yachting facilities in the River Avoca in favour of the fishing dock. The water there was bounded on four sides with only a narrow entrance, in which the oily calm – they use real oil – promised us a good night's sleep. We were just tying up alongside a wooden trawler that looked and smelled as though it had recently had a fire, when we noticed the harbour master running towards us waving his hands.

'Tie up to the one behind!' he yelled, 'We've only just put her out and we don't know if she'll flare up again.'

He helped us move, then stepped on board whistling calmly through his missing tooth; he sat himself down in the cockpit, and began leafing through a book of cloakroom tickets.

'Were you serious about that boat?'

'Yes,' he said, without looking up. 'Graham was just takin' de family and a cuppla friends out to see dem new turbines on the bank – just a pleasure cruise, like – when her engine caught afire. She was well alight when the lifeboat got to her. It's ten Ooros for tree nights – whether you stay one night or tree doesn't matter, but if you only stay one night, or two nights, and you're ever back this way again – even next year – hang on to your ticket 'cos your stay will be free. Don't lose it now.' And with that he handed me ticket number 67, on the purple. I asked him what the prize was.

'Eh?'

'On the raffle.'

'Ders no raffle... but if you like the raffle, you're in luck – ders a festival on dis weekend with live music and ozzer sings going on. Ders bound to be a raffle somewheres. To get to town turn right past the lifeboat, follow on to the end, turn left at the junction, bear right at the next, straight on up the hill, over the roundabout, and you'll see it straight in front of you. You can't miss it. Or just ask.'

We were protected from the wind by the dirty-grey industrial building of a porcelain factory; but ignoring that, and the empty oil drums, the smell of fish and newly charred wood, the rusting hulks, and the lack of facilities ('There's showers in the lifeboat station – but you'll need to get the key from the harbour office which is round the ozzer side – it's open between...'; we didn't bother with the showers), the place seemed quiet and friendly. And James the harbour master was an asset.

We heard some music and followed our ears to a lorry trailer, which had its curtain sides tied back, Punch-and-Judy style. The band started their next number in front of a crowd of about a hundred, who leaned fecklessly against the warehouse walls in family groups, or sat on the curb with ice creams bought from a van with a flat tyre; it was the Beatles song 'Yellow Submarine' – it was late in the day and, we surmised, they'd been through all their good songs. It was the worst version of a bad song I'd ever heard, and Linda hissed at me when

I told her so. The lead singer gave it everything he'd got, you couldn't ask for more – not that anyone did – and it would be fatuous to hold him responsible for God's own oversight in withholding the gift of a voice from someone he purposed to be a lead singer. The rest of the band were scrupulous, and shared equally among themselves what strings they had.

There were some sorry-looking wooden yachts propped up in a yard where, years earlier, Sir Francis Chichester's boat *Gipsy Moth III* was built. Occasionally someone could be heard tinkering on one of the hulks. I loved him with all my heart for taking on the Herculean task of returning one of the charming wrecks to its former beauty – until it occurred to me that he was probably cannibalising bits off it. The grass, nettle and gorse that threw tendrils out from between the boards of the decaying boats would one day consume them and return them to the earth. Like the rest of Arklow, the site offered 'extensive opportunities for redevelopment' – and we didn't like it any the less for that.

We motored out of Arklow's fishing dock, back down the River Avoca and along the concrete arm of the harbour wall, at the head of which the fishermen were once again casting, like us, for deeper water. A solitary fisherman will greet you cheerfully; two or more will pretend they haven't seen you.

Next stop was a cultural visit to Dublin, where our luck with fishing harbours ran out and we were asked to leave. We were crestfallen, having read the promotional literature for nearby Dun Laoghaire Marina, which claimed to be either the biggest marina in Ireland, or the most expensive – I can't remember which. As we breathed in our last regretful whiffs of ripe fish, a man introducing himself as Mick de Hoog popped by to say hello, and to tell us how much he liked our boat; he invited us to come and see some of his own craftsmanship at his violin-making workshop. Did he make violins? Linda cooed, fell in love with him, and immediately offered to swap our boat for one.

At Mick's workshop, I watched from under a heavy brow as Linda flitted gay as a butterfly from the workbench – with its thumb planes, backs and bellies of sycamore and spruce – to

Top: The house fire

Bottom: The morning after

Top left: Steve Groves and his sawmill

Top right: Planking the hull

Bottom: Turning the hull

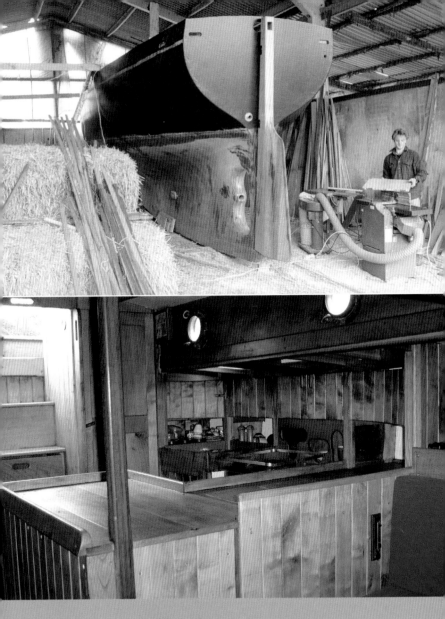

Top: Work begins on fitting out the accommodation

Bottom: The galley complete

Top: Typically narrow Devon lanes

Bottom: Launch party, Mylor harbour, Cornwall

Top: She sails like a dream
Bottom: Justin and Linda *(copyright 2011 Piers Murray Hill)*

Top: Racing to win

Bottom left: The Scilly Isles, seen from Agnes

Bottom right: Summer storm in St Mary's, Scilly Isles... this is what it was like in the *harbour*

Top left: Coastguard helicopter practice – the best breeze we'd had all day

Top right: A casual approach to careening

Bottom: Secret Scottish anchorage – we're hiding on the right

Top: The film set for *Ocean Odyssey*, Isle of Jura beyond
Bottom left: Justin and Linda in Ruan Creek, Cornwall
Bottom right: Romping 'home' into Falmouth harbour

display cabinets of stocks and moulds, and to the shining examples of completed fiddles. I've seen glummer children in a sweetshop with a fiver. The phone rang and Mick listened to the voice on the other end for about two minutes before saying, 'Well, you would expect to pay from about €2,000.' He listened for another two minutes, then, with exaggerated patience: 'I don't know where you would find one for €100 – you could try the local paper.'

I left Linda admiring the fiddles and slipped out to look for a newsagent.

We left Dun Laoghaire, economically cleansed, and sailed the short distance to Ireland's eye. As we neared the Ben of Howth – the headland on the north side of Dublin Bay – the water was surprisingly lively. We ran the gauntlet of more high-speed ferries, and of cargo vessels constrained by their draught, and bounced our way around the Ben – which is surrounded by deep water and can be approached to within arm's length – until we found calm water in the vicinity of Ireland's eye. Our anchor chain clattered down into 16 feet of water among a flotilla of pleasure craft, drowning for a moment the merry laughter of a thousand children drifting to us from the beach.

Spotting us as new arrivals, a swarm of about 50 water-bike enthusiasts buzzed out from Howth Marina to have a really close look at our boat, blissfully ignorant of the fact that they were a bloody nuisance, and reminding me of a time when I was on a woodland walk and accidentally kicked a hornets' nest, attracting to myself a buzz of similarly unwanted attention. Each in turn they sprayed us with cooling water, which pissed into the air like Essex garden fountains... but they kept civil hours, and by six o'clock all of them had returned to the hive. (It is worth noting, en passant, that having inadvertently kicked that hornets' nest, and subsequently received sting after merciless sting, the sight of me emerging from the woods with swellings under every red-headed eruption on my face is another of Linda's most treasured memories, and still produces peals of happy laughter in her after all these years.)

When the water-bikes had settled down for the night, and all the beach families had returned to their boats and motored in between the protective arms of Howth Marina, we were left entirely alone in our anchorage with only the company of an aircraft swooping low overhead every five minutes or so, veiling us in an evening mist of unburned fuel before landing at Dublin Airport – yet even they seemed to operate a curfew, and by mid-evening the creeping night silenced all. We lit our hurricane lamp for an anchor light, hung it from the rigging, and settled down to read until our own bed beckoned us with soft feathers.

We left early the following day to try to reach Carlingford Lough – the entrance to which has strong tides and shoals – in daylight. It was a distance of only 40 miles, but the wind was light. All day we struggled to make the boat 'go', and all day she dragged along like the tantrum-child of frustrated parents. It was like sailing a waffle through syrup. I could have scuppered her later that afternoon when, for no obvious reason, she lowered her foresail unexpectedly to the deck, and we slowed still further. Looking at the shackle, I could see that a split pin had sheared, so I climbed the mast like a native gathering coconuts, using the mast hoops as steps. Although we dawdled over a mute sea, the movement up there was exaggerated and I had to cling on tight – one moment the mast would try to pull away from my grasp, the next it lurched back to biff my schnozz – and all the while I fumbled to house the shackle to its fitting with one hand, screw it closed, and secure it with a split pin. When I got back to the deck, having had a success, I was as weak as a kitten.

There was a distant growl and I looked toward the shore to see a coastguard helicopter striking out in our direction. It slowed as it passed overhead, and – wondering how on earth they could have spotted me up the mast at a distance of several miles – I waved as much as to say, 'Everything OK here.' It circled and followed at a distance of a couple of hundred yards. I waved my reassurance again, at which it circled with exaggerated slowness and once more settled in to follow us – clearly trying to communicate something.

'Turn the radio on – I think they want to have speaks,' I called to Linda.

'OK. Yes! – they're calling us now!'

'Mike Charlie Alpha... We're just out here on exercise, and we was wondering – would it be OK if we followed you for a while at a distance of about 10 metres – just to give us a bit of practice at close-flying?'

'It would make our day,' I told them.

They gave us a course to steer, asked us to keep a steady speed, closed in and hung above us for fully 20 minutes – it was the first decent breeze we'd had all day.

'They're calling us again!' said Linda.

'We were just wondering – could we land a man on your deck?'

'Of course, I'll get the kettle on,' I joked. They gave me some instructions about how to get their man aboard.

The helicopter pulled alongside and a figure appeared at the door, from which he slipped to dangle ever lower over the water like a spider on a thread... and then began to shy us with a ball and line. His first shot caught the wind and fell astern; he retrieved it and threw it again to twang off some rigging and wrap itself three times around everything it met. I untangled it, having read somewhere that helicopter pilots don't like it when their craft is tethered by a falconer's knot.

It was odd to suddenly have a third person on board our boat, out here far from the coast – made the more alien by the way he was dressed in his black survival suit and bog-eyed helmet. He must have sensed our apprehension.

'How ya doin'?' he greeted us, and shook each of us by the hand.

'Do you have a lifejacket?' he asked.

I nodded, thinking: Jesus – what's going to happen next?

'Could you go and put it on?'

I went below, hunted everywhere, but couldn't find the lifejackets – they weren't in their usual spot, I was sure. I looked everywhere for a second time, and eventually managed to catch Linda's eye through the companionway as she helmed the boat. Seeing me frantically waving at her, she frowned.

'Where the f—k are the lifejackets?' I mouthed.

She indicated the wet locker, which I had already searched twice, and sure enough, there they were. Within five minutes I was back on deck, hoping I hadn't been missed.

'Have you got any gloves?' he asked. I vaguely remembered having seen some, but decided that they probably didn't have enough fuel to allow me to find them.

'No,' I said.

He explained that the helicopter would pluck him from the deck, at which he would swing out well clear to port, and my job was to hold the guy rope to stop him from swinging like a pendulum.

'OK?' he asked. I nodded. He gave the command word and a moment later the helicopter plucked him into the air like a sandhopper springing from our deck. I hadn't quite understood the plan, and almost followed him; then let the rope stream through my hands until my skin smoked and the air smelled of barbecue. Noticing my discomfort, the crewman called, 'You're all right now.' And away he went.

We waved them goodbye; the helicopter bowed to us, then turned for home. Back on the radio, they thanked us and mentioned that they had noticed us taking photos of them during the exercise… could they have copies? – They too had taken photos of us, and would send them if we got in touch. Fantastic! We'd taken loads, but on checking our camera found a solitary image – the memory stick was full and we hadn't heard the camera 'pinging' its protest amid all the noise.

7 A PILGRIMAGE TO THE HEBRIDES

'For natural beauty,' said Frank Cowper, writing a hundred years ago, 'the Mourne Mountains, with the splendid facilities for sailing afforded by Carlingford Lough, can compare with any part I know, and will not suffer by the comparison.' We marvelled at his courage to go into Carlingford Lough at all, engineless, because at the entrance – which is mostly obstructed by rocks and shoals – the tide runs at up to 5 knots. If the wind had failed, he and his ship would have been lost.

We prepared our engine for starting – it's not very technical: I open the seacock to allow a flow of cooling water, and Linda says: 'If that engine doesn't start, we'll take the bastard out and scrap it.' We'd sighted the navigational aids to the lough easily enough, visible as they are from miles away – but instead of reassuring us, they struck us more in the way of an early warning. Our nerves were jangling with the numerous cautions that the Nautical Almanac had fired across our bow, finally putting us on notice that 'Yachts may be stopped by naval vessels'. We looked about for gunboats as we passed close by the Hellyhunter Buoy a mile from the entrance, but, seeing none, took this as permission to come in, and threw ourselves into the rapids on a course of 310°, to be sucked into the lough like a leaf floating on a river in spate.

We had intended to strike off to the starboard side once we were past the worst of the maelstrom marked by the

Haulbowline Light and the gloomy ruined blockhouse – which remains, despite being ruined in Cowper's day – but everything was happening so quickly that we lost our bearings for a moment and decided to let the tide sweep us on through the main channel. A container ship bound for Warrenpoint at the head of the lough, approaching us fast from behind and intending to overtake, gave two blasts on his horn, with the meaning 'I am altering course to port' – which came as no surprise, since the deep-water channel, too, intended to alter course to port within a couple of hundred yards – his idea, very sensibly, was to ensure that we were aware of his presence and kept out of his way. He removed his cap and waved it cheerfully from the bridge as he passed us; we waved back – steadying our mugs of tea, steering with a hip jutted against the tiller, and trying desperately to remain smiling and standing as we rolled over his bow wave. Six miles later, near the head of the lough, long after calm had been restored, *Caol Ila* blew like a feather on a duck pond amid towering green hills – for which Ireland is famous – and dropped her anchor nearly a mile offshore from Rosstrevor. We would have approached more closely, but for the shallow waters in which we could almost wade ashore.

Arriving at any new harbour we steal in like uninvited guests, unsure of our reception, and are always apprehensive when a boat alters course to come out to us. Have we moored in the wrong place; have we done something we shouldn't; are we unwelcome? we wonder. A yacht flying no ensign approached us and then circled like a shark around an injured swimmer. 'That's a lovely boat ya have there!' came the tones of a man who didn't have an enemy in the world.

'Thanks!'

'And where is it you've come from?'

'Falmouth, Cornwall.'

He smiled, knowingly, as though reminded of an old friend.

'Well now – I could have guessed that by the type of boat you have. You're very welcome here, and I hope you'll stay a long time and enjoy yourselves...' And with that he turned to leave, sweeping his hand in a generous arc above his head as an adieu.

With his invitation in mind, we set out the following afternoon to row an unconscionably long way to the shore in our
cockleshell dinghy. I irritate myself on these long rowing trips
by counting oar-strokes – I can't help it; by the time I get to
100 I'm pleading with myself to shut up; at 400 the sweat
flows down my back and I look hopelessly over my shoulder
for signs of land. It's at times like these that I quietly resent
Linda – we sit face to face as I row; I, red-cheeked and blowing
at each stroke, cast envious glances at her as, lying back, she
trails fingers dreamily through the water.

'Point to where we are going,' I say. Having my back
toward our destination, I can't see it, and don't know when
I've gone off course. If she points more than 10° off the bow,
I snap, 'Why didn't you tell me earlier? It's all right for you
just sitting there, loafing around.'

She is offended and offers to row – whereupon I see the
sense in the current arrangement, and watch her, exonerated,
as she loafs with more deliberate luxuriance.

The truculent shaven-headed men of Rosstrevor simmered
in the afternoon heat, pint in hand, buttressing themselves
against pub walls, yelling intermittently across the street at
people they knew.

'Focken – Focken – Focken –' they'd call, scarcely looking up.

'Focken – Focken – Focken –' came the sullen reply.

Any other words they might have said were given less
emphasis, and remained unheard by all parties. While Linda
bought some bacon and some bread, I hung back in the closely
manicured and extensive park where it seemed safer, and I
wasn't subject to their brooding scowls of unrecognition.

Across the other side of the lough – the 'Eire' side – a day
later, we dried out on a tide against a concrete slipway to clean
the hull with a nylon scouring cloth. Few people came to visit,
which was unusual – people are fascinated to see a boat high
and dry, and like to pop down to enquire whether they are wit-
nessing a shipping disaster, how many souls have perished, or
to scour the beach for salvage. Eventually, a man in his thirties
drove onto the quay, looked over his boat for a minute or two
while his wife and children stayed in the car, and then, casting

a careless glance in our direction, headed away again. Linda ran to ask him if there was a supermarket in town; during the ten-minute conversation that followed, a warm conviviality grew up between them. As he left, he suggested, 'You might like to take that ensign down – some folks hereabouts get twitchy seein' it.'

We thanked him for his hint and took down our British flag. Remembering that our visitor the day before hadn't flown one, we didn't fly it again in Carlingford after that. Neither had we realised until then the significance of Carlingford Lough forming the boundary between Eire and Northern Ireland, or that any flag flying might be interpreted as a statement rather than a courtesy.

By inspiration, we stayed a night at Greenore Point, a privately run port for coasters near the entrance to the lough, which we mistakenly assumed was disused. Thankfully, no coaster arrived while we were there to multiply the misery that followed. At Greenore we sheltered from the moderate rollers kicked up by a north-west wind by slipping into a narrow gap between the breakwater and the dock, the breakwater providing millpond shelter in comparison to the uncomfortable chop outside. It was a piece of genius on my part because, noting some of the features of Carlingford Lough, the Almanac says: '...due to the funnelling effect of the mountains NW winds cause a worse sea state within the Lough than outside it.'

At 10 pm, just as I was yawning for bed and congratulating myself on finding this unlikely anchorage, the tide rose above the breakwater that sheltered us and allowed white horses to overleap it, rolling us on their way to the harbour wall where they bounced off and fought with the incoming waves to get back out. Caught in the middle of this confusion, *Caol Ila* leaped like a bucking bronco at a wild west party which no one could remember how to switch off, and all the while, trapped inside like a couple of eco-balls in a washing machine, Linda's tormented face and mine bounced against the porthole glass, imploring it to stop. At 2 am, after four miserable hours, the tide fell below the breakwater again, and instantly the sea fell calm – we watched the last few bubbles of foam rise to the surface, and staggered to bed.

The following day we emptied out of Carlingford Lough with the swill of the tide and sailed smartly over a lively sea – the wind having turned directly about – to Ardglass, where we motored in, dead slow, past superfluous navigational marks, planted as they were among the jagged teeth of rocks that required no marking. The harbour was tiny and called for a sharp turn to starboard – which isn't our best side – and it seemed unlikely we could make it, so I threw the engine astern to take off our way, and awaited developments. The stiff breeze rescued us by blowing us sideways between two rows of pontoons, and allowed us to slip into a berth astern as we drifted past it, by judicious use of astern propulsion applied at what turned out to be just the right moment. Spectators on the pontoons standing ready to catch our lines, and save us from ourselves, now wondered at our helmsmanship.

Friends of ours arriving at Ardglass a year or two later in a somewhat larger boat weren't so lucky – they took the services of a pilot and, having been encouraged to navigate outside the track where their instinct would have led them, spent several hours on a rock at low water, and required remedial work to a cracked frame the following winter.

The 7-knot tide in the entrance to Strangford Lough is even swifter than that at Carlingford and mariners only intending to pass by are impelled through the entrance to the lough – in spite of all attempts at resistance – in exactly the same way as they would be impelled through the entrance to an off-licence advertising a half-price sale. Once in, they are swept four miles into the main gut of the lough... where they must wait six hours to be regurgitated.

Being impelled ourselves through the entrance, we prepared to 'get off' the conveyor belt just before the main gut of the lough at the little town of Strangford, and so turned our boat around to face the way we'd come half a mile before we reached the town – not a moment too soon, as it happened. We gunned the engine to slow ourselves and crept toward the west bank just in time to catch an eddy, which washed us up to the quay. Strangford sits on a quiet backwater separated from the main stream by an islet with swans nesting on it (though that may be a seasonal landmark), and is choked with moorings in its relative quietness, together with the towering hulk of the off-duty ferry, kept there on standby. Among all these, we cast our anchor in a doubtful-looking but successful spot, forbearing to pick up a buoy that was vacant in case its owner came back. The following morning it was still vacant, so we picked it up... and an hour later he came back.

'That's my mooring you're on,' he called. He and his yacht were rigged for long distances – the yacht with its wind-steering gear and wind-generator, he with his whiskers. The pair of them were skilfully helmed by his wife, who brought them quietly alongside. We apologised and begged them to give us five minutes to prepare to get underway; but now, after only a moment's acquaintance, they wouldn't hear of us leaving and insisted we stay put and use the mooring for as long as we wished it – they'd take their boat to another mooring they owned a few miles further into the lough. They came on board for tea, a chat and a tour before leaving for their 'other mooring'. They were wildlife film-makers and regularly took their boat to the Arctic (hence the whiskers) to use it as a base. He named several films he'd made that we should have heard of, but hadn't: the fault was on our side. Linda and I haven't owned a television for 20 years and are clueless numpties from the backwoods about even the most commonplace everyday familiarities of popular culture; we only recently learned that *Big Brother* is a television series documenting the lives of people who want to work for Sir Alan Sugar – an unlikely and irascible character invented by George Orwell. Years earlier, a promising new friendship with a very successful model-maker-for-film was ruined before it began by his failure to ignite a spark of recognition in us as he reeled off the names of a dozen blockbusters he'd worked on – until he got to *Star Wars*, when our extravagant recognition of that film only brought down on us looks of contemptuous pity. Still, we are as happy as we are ignorant. Before the wildlife film-makers left, his wife confessed that they'd decided before they arrived that the people on their mooring could 'stay if they were nice'.

Strangford is intimate with its small waterfront. Ashore we met Joe, who wanted to tell us what a lovely boat graced his harbour, and how pleased he was that we planned to stay for a few days. When he learned that we lived on board, he returned sympathetically with a lottery ticket.

'This is for you... and I'm hoping you'll win the jackpot so you can buy yourselves a nice house somewhere.' His sentiment touched us deeply.

'My friend Charles wants to know: d'ya have time for a cup of coffee?' he asked us the following day. 'He's been a navy man all his days, and I know he'd love to meet you... and doesn't have too many visitors these days.'

Short, slight and poised, Charles looked about 75. For our interview he sat erect, holding us in the steady gaze of eyes that matched the colour of the cigarette smoke curling up from the ashtray between us. Each cigarette was lit from the stub of the last, which he crushed out and emptied into a metal bin by his feet – wiping the ashtray clean, and returning it gleaming to the table for its next performance. A gentle smile played about his lips as he told us stories of his life from all corners of the earth, as seen from the bridges of warships.

'The Sound of Islay,' he volunteered, when we told him we were going to the Caol Ila Distillery. 'I once crashed into the seabed in the Sound of Islay – on a submarine being towed at 20 knots.'

And again when I mentioned that I lived in Hong Kong for a while: 'Hong Kong? I once chucked an American warship off a pier in Hong Kong.' His stories were made all the more exotic by the parochial view from his window, across the grass to the stone quay, against which his last command – a flaking blue plywood catamaran – was tied.

When we told him that we were in need of some charts, he herded us immediately into his little car, lit another cigarette, and drove us to Todd's Chart Agency in Bangor, claiming that he was about to go there anyway.

The next day, while Linda enjoyed her first bath for months – Charles's hospitality – I popped into a beauty salon for a haircut, where the proprietress was surprised, but unabashed, to see a man, and sat me down between a blue rinse and a body-wave perm. Everyone agreed, shouting above the whirr of the dryers, that there was a very pretty boat in the harbour. And when we had exhausted that topic, and the shop was empty, the proprietress told me of all the circumstances surrounding her separation from her husband, just as though we had been childhood friends and confidants.

We walked past a gatehouse and into the mature National Trust woodlands of Castle Ward, where we filled our lungs with the healthy, damp, woody smells of summer. Happening upon a pair of arched ornamental gates set extravagantly in an old stone wall, and finding them open, we walked through onto an historic stone quay carefully restored and secured with lead staples – now grassy with disuse – and the lough beyond. It tinkled with the sound of wavelets falling on the carefully laid granite, just as they had for hundreds of years. Further along the shore we found the 15th-century fortification of Audley's Castle, with its stunning views onto the lough, and lazed in the long grass amid the buzz of insects; dazzled by the sun sparkling off the water; if we had been allowed to build a house on a plot of land on those shores, we would never have left.

Around a little headland to the north of our mooring we glimpsed another wooden boat, its brightwork sparkling in the sun, moored all by itself outside an historic-looking house, and watched as a man in a punt put off from there one evening to row himself alongside for a chat. He was preparing for a classic boat rally at Carrickfergus, which he urged us to attend. He, too, told us how welcome we were at Strangford – and since, as we later learned, he was titled to one of the oldest baronetcies, we needed no more proof of it.

We were fearful of leaving Strangford on a day with a strong wind if there was any 'south' named in it, because the sea would be rough at the entrance from the effects of 'wind against tide'; and so consequently we chose a flat-calm day to glide out from our quiet backwater onto the fast-flowing ebb. It swept us out of the lough and into the kind of fog you see at rock concerts, in which we could dimly make out each other, but nothing else. There was no question of turning back, so we felt our way around the coast toward Belfast Lough. Six miles later we had hoped to raise the South Rock light vessel – by the sound of its fog horn (which the chart told us blasted every 45 seconds in these conditions), if not by sight – yet we had neither seen nor heard anything since leaving Strangford, and began to doubt our position. Satellite navigation – which I had never entirely trusted since an early 'valve' model I owned a couple of decades earlier had calculated my boat's position as being among the megaliths of Stonehenge – showed us to be so close to the lightship that we should be able to climb aboard. Fog 'throws the voice' of sound, making it seem to come from elsewhere – but surely it couldn't silence it altogether? A feeling of gloom settled over our little ship. We were lost in fog. 'Perhaps it's off station,' Linda suggested.

In baffling circumstances, even the most unlikely suggestion is seized on as the probable explanation, and we gave up on the lightship as we rolled along through the eerie quiet – save for the drip, drip, drip of moisture running off the mainsail and onto the deck.

Suddenly, right alongside, came a blast loud enough to prolapse a rectum, and the red hull of the lightship thrust itself at us through the fog – we leapt into the air, screaming, and began wrenching the tiller this way and that – even with our hands over our ears, the vibration from it throbbed through us like electricity. No sooner had the ship shown itself than it dissolved back into the fog and we never heard it again. I think we were deaf for a while.

Soon the fog began to thin and allowed us, 16 miles further on, to find a lonely anchorage at Copeland Island, from where we peered across flat water whose surface was broken by the snaking animations of fronds of kelp. Our chain rattled down into the silent water, leaving us feeling friendless and quarantined from the world – even the island was deserted, and no vessel sailed by. Sometimes we wished we were rich, and could afford to mothball ourselves away in the conviviality of a marina berth amid the tinkling aluminium masts, row after reassuring row of bobbing white hulls snatching at their lines, and the smell of aftershave drifting from the silver-haired chest of an owner who's taken time off work to see how his secretary gets on with the rudiments of frapping.

But we weren't friendless and alone for long. We first met Mr Chesworth in the days when we were still dreaming of building our boat. Looking around the Boat Building Academy in Lyme Regis, Dorset, with a view to building *Caol Ila* there,

Peter Chesworth introduced himself with the mysterious words, 'I'm not here, really...', and then went on to play a more senior role in the construction of our boat than anyone else in the room, with the possible exception of ourselves. We chose to build our boat at home in the stable, of course, and it was Mr Chesworth who turned up once again at our place six months later with a carload of glue we'd unknowingly ordered from him. Having been a maritime photographer all his life, he'd seen more boats than most and was a mine of information; when we needed to know what a Highfield lever did, or parrel balls, or a timinoggy, he would tell us, supplementing the information with details of where to buy one new, and a list of people who might have one in their garage. It was fitting that the Chesworths should be our first cruising guests, and they joined us after our lonely night at Copeland Island, flying into Belfast Airport the following day. How cheering it was, just then, to see familiar faces.

With the boom let well off and the wind on the quarter, we skipped over a lively sea across Belfast Lough, laughing as the wind tore the filling out of our sandwiches. We joyfully turned the boat into a gasket factory when the cooker fuel pump failed and our steaks were not yet cooked. And we congratulated ourselves at how content we were to stay on board when we anchored in Red Bay, only to discover that the nearest pub was seven miles away and only opened on a Thursday.

Waking the next morning with the kind of headache you get when your blood/alcohol level is dangerously low, we timed our departure from Red Bay through the North Channel to make best use of the tides, which swept us away from Ireland and on toward our first Scottish destination – the Isle of Gigha – where we anchored in the clear sandy water of Ardminish Bay, smelled the clean air, and heard the call of gulls as they wheeled overhead.

At that time, the residents of the island were just in the throes of liberating themselves from the suffocating grasp of their under-investing laird and, with the help of some lottery funding, into their own hands as a community by buying their own island... but hadn't yet done so. Facilities that we found tired and tarnished then have since been buffed to a new lustre by the enthusiastic island owners. We hired matching cycles – a penny-farthing, tricycle, monocycle, together with what can best be described as a pushbike – and set off to explore the island. The gardens are well worth a visit; I pass that titbit on straight from the brochure – I didn't actually go there myself, preferring the old mill on the west coast and its private lagoon formed by off-lying rocks. I could live somewhere like that for the rest of my days and never feel the need to walk over the nearest hill for variety.

Next from Gigha was the object of our voyage – to bring *Caol Ila* 'home' to the Caol Ila Distillery; and so it was amid growing excitement that we ran up the narrow Sound of Islay toward the distillery, helped along by a 4-knot tide, admiring the lofty scree-topped hills on either side. On the port hand was the island of Islay, to starboard the island of Jura, and buildings were scarce on either – on Islay, the remote McArthur's Head lighthouse, with its white-walled garden, marks the southern end of the sound; the first solitary building appears 2 miles further along the shore. It's a lonely bothy – a one-roomed house in a state of semi-dereliction, formerly used by shepherds but now in service as emergency accommodation for walkers caught out by a change in the weather. It sits on the shore, dwarfed by the green hill towering above it, white-spotted with sheep, its top lost in the clouds. Four miles after that comes Port Askaig with its pier, lifeboat station, hotel and shop... and, in the next bay, the distillery we sought. The Jura coast, as we passed by, didn't seem nearly so cluttered.

Because of its remoteness, this seemed a strange place to be looking for an industrial building producing 100,000 litres of whisky per week for export all over the world, so Caol Ila came as a surprise. Hidden in a cove was a collection of well-maintained buildings dating from the 1970s, standing with their toes in the sea almost, facing across the sound toward the towering Paps of Jura. 'Sunrise over the Paps of Jura' is listed by the *Sunday Times* as 'one of the hundred things to see before you die'. Contrary to what their name implies, there are actually three paps – smooth-walled and rising dramatically – they're impressive at any time of the day. It was mid afternoon when we threw our anchor into the shallow water of Caol Ila Bay and rowed ashore, giggling at our success. We weren't surprised by how quiet it all seemed, because hereabouts *everything* was quiet... but at the entrance to the distillery a notice informed us that it was closed for annual maintenance. No steam rose from the chimney, the car park was empty, and the only sound came from lonely wavelets chattering through the boulders at the water's edge.

Caol Ila distillery

'Oh,' was all anyone could think to say. This wasn't exactly as we imagined it. Gone were the dreams of being greeted by distillery staff like long-lost brothers, while cartloads of the stuff were transferred to our cargo deck. We made a note to return in a few weeks' time on our way home and try our luck again.

We put into Port Askaig next, retracing our steps down the sound by about 200 yards. Mr and Mrs Chesworth were very much looking forward to this part of the voyage – it was, by an extraordinary coincidence, their own pilgrimage, having spent their honeymoon in the Port Askaig Hotel 30 years previously. We went into the bar for a drink and Linda and I sat down at one of the tables and admired the length of traced barometric graph paper that ran round the room in lieu of a wallpaper border, while the Chesworths wandered around in the semi-darkness, running their fingers over the bar-room paraphernalia – old photographs, maps, world currency.

Mr Chesworth rejoined us, smiling broadly. 'Do you know, it hasn't changed a bit!'

Early the next morning we were woken by a couple of minor bumps, then we hit the pier so hard that the mast reverberated like an arrow... a swell was surging up the sound, helped by a change in the direction of the tide, and was dashing our hull into the wooden legs of the pier, against which we were unable to fend ourselves because we didn't carry a fender board. I was relieved to see that Port Askaig was deserted as I climbed onto the deck, because I hadn't had time to dress. Mr C. – for whom it was never too early for a joke – emerged from the accommodation at ankle height to find me stark naked, bent double, heaving on a mooring line, and greeted the vision with: 'Am I interrupting anything?'

We decided to cast off our lines and press on for Loch Tarbert on Jura – as remote a sea loch as can be found anywhere along the west coast, and the shores of which are completely uninhabited except near the entrance, where there is a rather grand summer residence, accessible only on foot or by boat, and owned by an illustrious family.

It began to rain, hard. In fact, as we sailed into the loch it rained so hard that the hills, shores and rocky hazards disappeared from view, and even the boundary between sea and air became indistinct – though the water at around the height of our respiratory equipment was quite well aerated, thanks to which our lives were prolonged. Mr Chesworth and I discovered that we had mutually long-dreamed of sailing into Loch Tarbert, having spotted it on the chart independently of one another, and were thrilled that our dreams had at last come true – though in our dreams the weather had been blazing.

When the Pilot says: 'This is as precarious a piece of rock-hopping as you will find anywhere', it only serves as a red rag to a bull, and whets our appetite to drive on to the very head of the loch – parts of which were so choked by rocks that our attention was diverted from whether we would have sufficient depth to get through – which was always doubtful – to the entirely new occupation of whether there was sufficient width. We picked our way using cruising charts of unknown antiquity, produced by the Clyde Cruising Club, which Mr Chesworth had bought out of retirement from a second-hand bookshop in Hereford, where they had been enjoying a long holiday away from the sea. He had added them to the fund of reference material, declaring: 'Rocks don't move.' Amazing my detractors, who rightly doubt me with regard to navigation, I pointed out that the charts could be dated by comparing the magnetic compass variation printed on them with the present-day variation. After a little calculation I announced that they were published in 1960; the bright sun of my nautical knowledge emerged from behind its cloud and dazzled everyone who tried to look upon me.

We stayed three days in the inner loch, where the weather changed so rapidly from sun to drizzle and back again as it scudded over the bens that surrounded our quiet pool that we were left permanently in doubt about whether it was to be a fair day or foul. So we chose to stay put, not yet having dried out from our last soaking, and instead had a thrilling time walking in this, our first-ever wilderness. Among the heather of those vagrant hills, you could believe your foot to be the first to fall where it did in a thousand years – in ten thousand years!

And by crawling on our bellies through the fern, bilberries and ticks, we could silently crest hills to watch red deer only feet away, unaware of our presence. Jura has a population of 8,000 deer; it's impossible to scan the hills and not see a dozen of them together, topped by a proud stag – trees for antlers – silhouetted on a ridge.

This would be a dangerous place to be out walking in October, we agreed, when the hills echo to the rut, and stags become aggressive. I couldn't help thinking of a story I had read in one of Lillian Beckwith's books about an event that occurred on the Isle of Skye. A crofter, feeling his way as he walked along a remote narrow mountain pass, came around a spur of rock to be confronted by a monarch of a stag coming the other way. They stopped. The stag couldn't turn around – and showed no sign of wishing to do so; the crofter feared to turn or to back away in case it encouraged the stag to charge... On one hand was a sheer drop, on the other a cliff too steep to climb. For a while, the crofter and the stag faced each other, motionless; the crofter could hear the stag's steady breathing, as his mind raced. Then he had an idea and sank slowly to the ground, arranging himself full length on the narrow pass. After a pause the stag came on and, arriving where the crofter lay, sniffed him breathily then, placing his feet carefully, stepped over him and continued on his way.

Mr and Mrs Chesworth left us and began their 600-mile journey home to Cornwall by walking along the rutted track that leads away from where we lay at anchor to the island's only road, and then hitched a lift. In addition to the car which picked them up, their journey was made on four buses, two ferries, a plane and a train; and they never missed a connection.

Venturing out from the pool that evening to re-join the world and get on with our lives, we discovered that the sun shone outside – as it probably had for the last three days. We anchored further down the loch, close by the shore – under a raised beach – to watch a spectacular high-latitude sunset, away in the north-west.

The geological curiosity of a raised beach differs from, say, Brighton beach in only three ways – firstly, it has not tasted salt water for ten thousand years, having been marooned by falling sea levels, or lifted perhaps 15 m (50 ft) above sea level by heave; secondly, the flint pebbles are rugby-ball sized, and covered with pink lichen; and, finally, there are no deckchairs. In the gathering dusk we sat in the cockpit, watching herds of deer wander along the low-water shore, browsing on kelp abandoned by the tide.

The following day, heading north on the open water, we gave the Gulf of Corryvreckan a wide berth for fear of its world-infamous whirlpool – which, if ability matches reputation, would spin us senseless before swallowing us like a toy boat – and entered Loch Spelve on the south-east corner of Mull. We picked our way through the narrow entrance and anchored as the setting sun silhouetted the peaks of Ben More in the west. At the foot of one of those peaks, a little further to the west, there is an unusual grave – newly-weds lie buried, together with the cottage in which they were to live, underneath a huge boulder which rolled down from the summit on their wedding night.

That night the empty loch, together with the silent miles of hills that fringed it, belonged to us. The phone rang – it hadn't for a fortnight – it was the landlord of the Royal Oak in Knowstone, Devon, and the sound of his voice, with which I was so familiar as I sipped ale in front of his flaming inglenook (chatting with difficulty to a local woodsman and chainsaw-user in his seventies who didn't believe in ear-defenders and consequently was stone deaf), seemed incongruous in the wilds of Caledonia; he seemed to be phoning us from a previous life.

'I was just talking about you to someone in the bar and thought I'd give you a call. Where are you?'

I described the scene as graphically as my oracular tongue would allow (borrowing from Mrs Malaprop), but knew I'd failed when I heard him say to whoever it was: 'They're in Scotland.' Then back to us: 'Are you coming down for Cowes Week?'

'When is it?'

'This weekend.'

'No.'

Early the following morning a fishing boat came through the narrows and began tipping sacks of feed pellets into the salmon cages that floated in rows along the shore. I always imagined that people who work in the midst of outrageous beauty – farmers, gillies, fishermen – either worked in silence, hummed quietly to themselves, or suffered a little violin concerto to play in the background as they went about their chores; so it came as a shock to my naivety to be blasted by the 'Wah! Wah! Wah!' of techno-beat pounding out from his boat to echo distantly around the hills, punctuated every three minutes by a DJ informing the wildlife – in tones that implied it was to be congratulated on its choice – that it was listening to 'Rad-i-o One'.

From Loch Spelve we sailed up the Sound of Mull and saw the phenomenon known as mare's tails – black cliffs on the approach to the Sound are punctuated by white threads as cataracts of water fall hundreds of feet to the sea. Referring to these waterfalls, the name describes the effect when strong winds hit the cliffs and lift the falling water back up and away until undulations of streaming water can be seen riding the wind in a silvery ribbon.

Next *Caol Ila* romped past Lady's Rock, upon which Lachlan Cattanach, the chief of Clan MacLean, had his wife tied, 500 years earlier, so that she would drown on the next high water (having survived an earlier attempt on *his* life by *her*). Unbeknown to him, she was rescued by a passing fisherman just before high water, and only when he attended a wake supper hosted by his brother-in-law some months later and saw his wife – whom he supposed dead – sitting with her brother at the head of the table did he realise that his attempted murder was known. By way of torture, nothing was said about the incident that evening – his in-laws were relaxed, merry and attentive hosts – but many years of hand-wringing uncertainty followed, until at last he was murdered by way of revenge.

We tacked up the Sound of Mull, frequently taking water on deck as we climbed against a strong headwind; the luxury cruise ship *Lady of the Glen* came out of her way to give us an encouraging blast on her whistle, which cheered us more than a little as we were getting a pasting.

Tobermory, Mull's principal town, was busy on the water with yachts, which might otherwise have been enjoying the islands, but were here to take shelter from the forecast gale. Only after passing through the harbour on our third scout did we find a hole among more than a hundred moored and anchored craft into which we would just fit. We threw out our anchor, stretched the chain to set it, and cheerfully acknowledged our new neighbours; they in turn waved back their satisfaction with the arrangement.

Ashore we bought some well-made cheese in a deli – just because you can in Tobermory – and then went on a whale-spotting trip hosted by Alison Gill, whale biologist and daughter of our nearest neighbour at the boatbuilding shed in Devon. There wasn't too much activity the day we went out, though we did have a distant sighting of a minke whale. We were jealous of how quickly her boat gets around.

The wind began to build with the promise of a gale the following day, so *Caol Ila* set out to find better shelter in Loch Sunart, and improved on what she found there by threading through to an inner loch – Loch Teacuis – via a tiny channel that separates the Isle of Carna from the mainland. It was in the endless forest in this part of Scotland that the body of a man was found in his tent three years after he had been reported missing – it was supposed he had gone into the forest without a compass and had been unable to find his way out, eventually starving to death.

Having survived the hazards at the entrance, I let my concentration slip and was gazing up the tree-clad hillside trying to catch a glimpse of the vitrified fort on top when I grounded *Caol Ila* on a sandbank, which is clearly marked on the chart. Linda's face appeared in the hatchway, wearing her 'Are we aground again?' look. Her eyes searched all around the boat.

'Are we aground again?' she asked.

Low water was just half an hour away, so it wasn't long before we floated free and dropped our anchor on the south side of the Isle of Carna. The protection in Loch Teacuis is perfect, and if the expected gale arrived we knew nothing about it.

The Isle of Carna is uninhabited. It does have a couple of habitable houses, but the island is so remote from anywhere by road (or sea for that matter) – no electricity, telephone or running water – that it would take a very different sort of 'customer' to live there full time. A hundred years ago it had a population of ten, but improved road and sea transport has allowed them to get off.

With hopes of supplementing our fresh food store, I rowed off in the dinghy with my fishing rod – an almost daily and endlessly interesting diversion for me – and caught a pollack for supper. It thrills every fibre of my body to be in a wildly remote anchorage, catch food for the table, and close the day cosily sheltered from peril.

We surged along toward Oban under reduced sail, with a press of wind, and a foaming bow wave ahead of us – heaving on the tiller to maintain a straight course as we rolled in the troughs of a short sea. Arriving at our destination, we gybed into the shelter of Ardantrive Bay on Kerrera Island, slipped through the narrow gaps between closely moored craft, and found a spot to drop our anchor close under a single storey timber-framed house with a grass roof, home to another recent arrival from Cornwall, famous for writing cruising guides for yachtsmen. Having disclosed the location of every secret anchorage in the south-west of England, he found he could no longer get into any of them and was obliged to journey further afield for his solitude.

***

Our old friend JFW had arrived by train from Devon with his new girlfriend Jenny, and was raving about the scenery through which they had just rolled. The West Highland Line from Glasgow goes on to Mallaig – almost at the north-western limit of British habitation – and is ranked by those who know what they're talking about as one of the top ten rail journeys in the world, way up there with the Trans-Siberian and Orient Express.

JFW helped us build our boat for three months – and as a sheep farmer was eminently qualified to do so – but eventually he became so appalled by the way we husbanded our vessel's timbers that he left to enrol at the Lowestoft Boatbuilding College to learn how to do it properly, graduating with honours just too late to save us.

They joined us as *we* were joining a Classic Boat Rally, which featured sumptuous hospitality at three distilleries, spread over a fortnight – presumably in order to give participants' livers time to recover – and which began right here at Oban. With participation in the rally came the unspoken promise that fine single-malt whisky would flow freely and without charge – an inducement that proved irresistible to the crews of two 'classic' boats that had arrived in a sinking condition from Ireland and which looked, judging by the magnolia emulsion painted directly over barnacles, as though they had been salvaged from the bottom of a harbour especially for the trip. They drifted into Oban as buoyantly as a digestive biscuit in a mug of tea and tied gratefully to the quay like exhausted swimmers reaching the shallow end. An able-bodied seaman wouldn't have risked his life in either of them, and so their trip owed its success to the fact that they weren't crewed by sailors at all, but by wags from a bar at the foot of the Black Mountain.

'How long did it take you to get here?' Linda asked.

'Dunno – we lost track o' time after the third bottle o' Jameson's.'

We were invited on board to have a look around; water squeezed from underfoot as we stepped onto a deck that tilted uncertainly with our weight. Down below we were shown around enthusiastically by the vessel's curators – mushrooms made the most of the ideal conditions; verdigris covered the brass paraffin lamp and portholes; and bedding was strung from the deckhead in plastic bags to keep it dry.

On a tour of the distillery, standing in a line next to a copper still, I took the yard glass that was handed to me and took a sip – it was as warm as milk straight from the udder and as fiery as petrol. JFW, next in line, held out his cupped hands for a gowpenful when I turned to pass it to him – but I refused him on health grounds. He put the glass defiantly to his lips and filled his mouth until his cheeks were puffed out like a gerbil providing itself against future want. At this stage in the distillation process the alcohol is industrial strength, and strongly anaesthetic. JFW turned puce and his eyes filled with tears of regret; too polite to spit it back, he swallowed it in tiny amounts over the next few minutes. He spoke – but his lips were as limp as the balloons left over from last night's party, and it was impossible to make out what he said; you could have pulled all his teeth and he wouldn't have felt a thing.

The following day we spun through Cuan Sound, which separates the islands of Seil and Luing, spotting the obstructions only just in time to avoid them; and then found our way into Ardinamir Bay, the dog-leg entrance to which is guarded by two submerged rocks – the first was marked with a beacon, the second *Caol Ila* found by touch. Twenty years ago, our fumbling entrance would have attracted the helpful attention of Irene McLachlin, who had a house by the shore; she would look out for errant yachts from the window of her cottage and bellow advice in a voice that folklore has it 'could be heard on the mainland'.

Years later, we would nearly move into Irene's cottage ourselves – anchored there for a fortnight on a second visit to Scotland while Linda did some temporary work at Oban (she describes her 'commute' as beginning with a row ashore in the rain, followed by a mile walk along a muddy track; then hitch-hiking along the main/only road to the ferry, where the first vehicle to discover you will stop; and finally taking the world's shortest ferry ride, less than 200 m/220 yd, to her car, and a scenic drive amid riotously wild country to arrive in the Victorian modernity of Oban 40 minutes later). One morning we'd watched from on board as a notice was nailed to the front door of Irene's cottage. Nosiness compelled us to row ashore and read it. It announced to God-knows-who – there *were* no passers-by – that it was to be let. The laird and his wife showed us round, and we liked what we saw; the location was without equal, and we could imagine looking out of our cosy bedroom window on to the bay and our safely moored boat. Linda was all for accepting the cottage and taking over Irene's job; but I didn't have work, and feared we would be exchanging penury aboard for starvation with a centrally heated view.

But back to the present voyage – rowing ashore, we spotted a woman taking photographs of our boat, at which JFW amazed both us and Kathy Mansfield by asking her, 'Are you Kathy Mansfield?' It remains one of life's unexplained mysteries, how JFW knew that. All we could do was to stand there and look at him admiringly. Kathy – a photographer for a yachting magazine – was so astonished that she had to be helped on board, and revived with most of the contents of one of my finest bottles of whisky.

* * *

One still morning, when neither beast nor fowl had stirred, a small herd of Luing cattle, marooned on the island of Torsa – which formed part of our bay – suddenly stampeded toward an empty feeder, and stood there, blinking. Moments later, with a whoosh, the feeders were filled by a timed-release mechanism into the trough. They must have heard some preliminary whirrings of machinery. JFW turned to me: 'Does the name "Pavlov" ring a bell?' he asked.

Such technology seemed incongruous on a remote, uninhabited, 80 ha (200 acre) island.

No trip to Scotland would be complete without attending a ceilidh – and so we did in Toberonochy, a settlement to the south of Luing. It was the perfect last night, too, for JFW and Jenny. Linda throws herself into these occasions with the gayest abandon and, as a noted authority on the Kilconquhar reel, mesmerises audiences with her dainty footwork as she skips around the place as light as a hand puppet. I can't dance, but as my contribution to the evening's entertainment I partner Linda for the first tune only – the band strikes up and we alone take to the floor while everyone looks on, not having 'warmed-up' to the evening. And what do they look on to? – one accomplished dancer, who glides around like a swan on a lake in springtime, and her partner, who stamps his feet as though he's trying to keep warm at a bus stop. When I catch someone's eye they flash me the warmest smile, accompanied by a long nod – as if to say, 'Go on – you enjoy yourself when you're allowed out.'

At last, the accordion stretches out the final note of the tune, everyone breathes a sigh of relief, and when the band have seen me safely sitting down, they strike up again – dancers flood onto the floor, desperate to raise the standard from where I left it, and fling themselves about as though they were 170 years younger.

Our last appointment in Scotland was with Caol Ila Distillery – our fame had by now reached their door, and they themselves invited us to attend a lunch, private tour and presentation hosted by the distillery manager Billy Stitchell, with a photographer on hand to record the day for succeeding generations. Actually, it doesn't quite cover it to say that Billy Stitchell is the manager – his father was manager before him, and *he* was preceded by both Billy's grandfathers, and his great grandfather... so we felt honoured to be fussed over by a man of such long heritage when we ourselves had come so recently to the name. Lunch was good, too – prawns in Scotland are related to lobsters on their fathers' side and we gorged our way through a good many of them while admiring the distillery's collection of black and white photographs from among which the impudent face of a child stared out at us, challengingly, from the bench on which he sat, hands stuffed in jacket pockets, and great clouds of smoke billowing from the cigarette he was smoking hands-free... Written underneath was the legend: Dolly Campbell, aged 6.

Our own portraits were captured for posterity, and a few days later we beamed out from the centre pages of the local paper, the *Ileach*, clutching bottles of whisky.

Our purpose fulfilled, and the wind settled in the north, we set off for Cornwall with an offer of work set to last the whole winter, where we arrived – via Arklow to see if our cloakroom ticket was still good – some ten days later.

Creaming into harbour, we happened to tack just in front of a boat on a mooring that we recognised as being built on similar lines to ours – she was *Hope*, owned by John Hesp, the designer of our boat, and he himself was on board. It gave us an extra thrill to bump into him on our triumphant return back south, because he had warned us in the latter days of the build that we wouldn't be able to sail our boat, just the two of us – her 1,100 square feet of sailcloth would be too much to handle. Linda, who wasn't a sailor in any of her previous lives, said she now felt like one, and surged triumphantly into harbour having earned her stripes.

* * *

'Are you Chustin?' was one of our first hails as we lay to our anchor back in Falmouth. Yarn was in his late twenties, tall, gangling, and had a great sense of humour – though, like most Dutchmen, wasn't aware of it. How he would keep us amused over the next couple of weeks as he stumbled from one calamity to the next, '*po-faced, and piss-wind with importance*' as my grandmother used to say when she was describing anyone overbearing and haughty, and who held everyone else to be vaguely ridiculous. Come to think of it, my grandmother had quite a number of sayings, but that's the only one that's printable. He bumped alongside.

'Are you Chustin?'

'I am,' I said (sounding a bit like a Neil Diamond song).

He greeted me like his long lost brother – 'Ahhh! Chustin, I find you! – I'm a friend of John!'

The blameless faces of the 60 or so Johns I know presented themselves, slide-show style, to my mind's eye – but each in turn denied knowing him.

'Which John?'

'Bazically we were at Lowestoft Boatbuilding College together,' he said, impatiently.

'Oh, JFW – yes, we've just seen him in Scotland with his new girlfriend.'

'John has a new girlfriend!' said Yarn, stepping aboard without waiting for an invitation. 'Wait!' he ordered, 'I tie up… then tell me about it.' At which he helped himself to the use of my Samson posts, cleats, mooring lines, fenders, tea and biscuits.

Politely ignoring the invasion of my sovereign territory, I asked him what kind of a boat his was, and over the next few hours received as full an answer as anyone could hope for. He drew my attention particularly to the decks, which had a cork covering – an innovation all his own, he assured me, and one bound to set new standards in shipbuilding; but which to my untrained eye appeared to be made from cork noticeboards which had had their frames removed. And their notices.

That evening he received some distressing news, and I was the one who unwittingly delivered it. He joined us on board for drinks (actually, he hadn't left), along with some other friends who had come to catch up with the gossip. I was holding forth – exaggerating as usual – and JFW and Jenny weren't spared my slanderous wit.

'...I say we saw them in Scotland – we scarcely saw them at all,' I rambled, '...they were like a couple of bunny rabbits, and had had three litters by the time they left.'

'Wait! John's new girlfriend – what is the name?' asked Yarn, cocking his eyebrow like a TV detective letting you know he's on to something.

'Jennifer,' I said. He nodded, slowly.

'Do you know her?' I asked.

'Bazically she was one of the people we used to drink with – she lives near the college.'

The following morning I was up at five to answer a call of nature, and crept quietly out on deck so as not to disturb our new neighbour, still tied alongside; but was amazed to find that he was already up, dressed, and staring broodingly at his cork deck.

'Morning, Yarn,' I said, unable to hide my surprise. There was a long pause.

'Morning,' he answered, suicidally.

'Gosh – is everything OK?' He drew a long breath and dragged his gaze along the horizon without interest.

'Ahhhh well... you don't want to hear all about my troubles...'

'Right-o!' I wanted to say, but instead heard myself soothe, 'Not at all, Yarn – what's on your mind?'

'Well – it's John's new girlfriend, Jenny... bazically, I thought she was my girlfriend – we have tickets to fly to Canada next month.'

My stomach churned over my bunny-rabbit witticism, and my mind raced to ameliorate what I had said, but found nothing. I deserved punishment, and he wasn't long in giving it. 'But anyway – I decide, "No", I don't get depress, I enjoy the next few weeks sailing with you; you can show me all around the place,' (he indicated the shore and its environs with a dismissive flutter of his hand) '...*and* I decide I will cook for you my special dish!'

'Well – obviously he won't literally follow us around for four weeks,' I tried to reassure Linda when Yarn had gone shopping, '...not *literally*.' And I was right – sometimes he would allow us to detach him from the mother ship if we first put a cross on the chart to say where we were going. And how cheering it was to see him hove into sight each evening and tie up once more, brimming with forgiveness. Sometimes when we wanted to go ashore we would find that, like a mischievous puppy, he had already 'borrowed' our dinghy, marooning us. We would scan the shore through the binoculars and our first sign of him would be a sprawling body inverted on dangerously slippery rocks, or a figure hanging by its fingernails from cliffs, peddling the air; or we might hear the crisp snap of a breaking branch as he dropped waist-deep into soft mud, crawling out like a swamp creature and eventually returning our dinghy to us with the imprint of his muddy buttocks on the seat. Our only regret on these joyful occasions was that we didn't have *two* pairs of binoculars – particularly on the day we saw him sunbathing naked on a private beach while the rising tide made off with our dinghy, together with the clothes he'd piled into it.

After days of gastronomic suspense, Yarn announced that he had been able to assemble all the ingredients he needed for his 'special dish', in tones that implied that he himself didn't know how he had achieved it in a country of such culinary poverty – and that he would prepare it for us that evening. He instructed me to build him a campfire on the beach and then row him and his ingredients, together with our pots and pans, ashore. He began stirring the cauldron at four in the afternoon under a crackling fire, and was still stirring it at ten at night. If great food depended only on diligent stirring, the world would beat a path to his door; but our suspicions arose when at six o'clock we joined him and found ourselves surrounded by the empty tins familiar from any scout camp. We sat around staring into the fire like three wise men waiting for a miracle and watched with dwindling appetites as every few minutes he took a slobbery lick at the spoon, before returning mechanically to his stirring.

At ten he woke us from our trance by shouting 'Perfect!' with euphoric excitement intended to dupe us, licked the spoon again, and then dolloped sticky mounds on to three separate plates, where they steamed off the little moisture that remained. 'Absolutely perfect!'

We thanked him, 'Mmmm'd' enthusiastically when we put it into our mouths, and awarded it position three in our 'worst food' chart. By withdrawing ourselves from the fire a little, we found we were able to whizz it spoon by spoon over our shoulders into the sleeping bushes, which complained by shaking it from their branches.

'What sound is making in the bush?' asked Yarn. We all stopped and listened... nothing.

'Well, whatever it was, it's gone now,' we said.

Stretching out in front of the fire, kicking our plates away and groaning with satisfaction, we heard another noise – a calamitous crash from the direction of our boats in the darkness on the water. We wondered if someone had hit us. The beam from our torch illumined Yarn's boat sprawled high and dry in the mud – which had so often given him a soft landing – and its mast pointing down toward the low water. Having anchored too close to the shore, the outgoing tide had abandoned his boat – the keel had evidently stuck in the soft mud for a while to allow his boat to stand like a stork on one leg, before eventually falling. Yarn slept on board with us until three in the morning when he shook us awake, demanding to be rowed over to his boat so that he could investigate.

I dragged myself up, dressed, rowed him over to find his boat floating quietly on the new tide, and waited in the dinghy while he climbed about, pushing my paraffin lamp into all the boat's dark corners.

'How does it look?' I asked eventually.

The yellow light and his long limbs gave him a cartoon appearance. Without turning to me, he answered slowly, 'Well, everything seems OK... but there is a strong smell...' (he gave a couple of exaggerated sniffs) 'of petrol... coming from...' And with that he and his lamp dived deep under the foredeck.

'Well, I should get that f—king lamp out of there!' I yelled. I had resigned myself to the fact that one day Yarn's antics would kill him – in fact Linda and I had already discovered that we shared a disbelief he could have survived this long – but it was my good lamp, and if there was to be an explosion, who knows where I might find it?

He stood bolt upright, and his eyes swivelled as he waited for the bang – when it didn't come he assumed a blasé pose, but on second thoughts sprung back on deck.

He never seemed to be enjoying himself so much after that and one day announced that he was booked to travel back to Holland, having arranged road transport for his boat.

* * *

Sailing out for what was to be our last jolly of the year in the company of friends on their boats – John and Pam, whose kitchen I had destroyed, and Marc and Anne, who were still nervously waiting to pay the price for being acquainted with me – we decided to anchor for a beach barbeque near Looe, Cornwall, in Whitesand Bay, which is exposed to the weather in almost any conditions but the very settled ones we now enjoyed. Evidence of the dangers of these shores lay all around us in the form of a mountain of planked timber having slipped from the deck of a Maltese registered cargo vessel – the *Kodima* – which had run aground seven months earlier in a February storm, thereby creating a bonanza for every joiner in the south-west of England, who came to fill white vans from

'Oh, come on, Fausty,' I soothed; 'don't be so hard on yourself.'

I was only joking about the brothel, by the way.

Fausty

Standing on the church roof, prising off rafters and chucking them to the ground, I had a panic attack and almost fell to my death.

'What on earth are *we* doing on this roof?' I asked Linda when I'd steadied myself – she was working as my labourer, and was levering the feet of the rafters off the wall plate with a wrecking bar. 'I haven't got a clue how it all goes back together.' She looked at me in surprise, but I was ready to run.

'Come on – let's leg it before Fausty gets back.'

'It'll be fine, Alfie,' she said calmly.

It was October, and I leaned against the bell tower, snatching deep breaths of despair. I gawped across the five interlocking roofs of the vestry, nave, chancel and other bits which I couldn't name – on which there were almost 10,000 slates – and let my eyes drift away longingly to the distant hills of autumn brown, which were settling down for a hard winter.

Climbing back down to the ground I went to fetch a tape measure and began to take notes about the length, angle, number, distance apart and size of the timbers.

If it hadn't been for John Locke, a highly regarded builder in the area, coming onto the roof in the early days (after watching my painfully slow progress) and coaching me, I'd still be up there now. He would flutter the fingers of both hands, like a cartoon dog about to crack a safe in which he knows there is a bone.

'Let me show you how *we* do that...' he'd say – and slash off 20 slates with a trowel in the time it took me to grind off one.

His generosity was all the more remarkable as he'd lost the roofing job to me on price – but he *had* got the job of building the extension, which was handy because he was never far away when I needed advice. I held John in reverence – drawn to him by his charm, but always on guard because of his excoriating wit. The stories he told every coffee break, as we and his workforce sat around on crates or piles of bricks under the dripping roof, had us wiping away tears of laughter... unless, of course, you happened to be the butt of the joke.

Linda and I had long since fallen into that cringing middleclass habit of calling each other 'darling' – I think it started as joke, but now we didn't even notice we did it. Thus, Roofer would call down to Roofer's Mate, booted against the site mud and muffled against the cold: 'Darling, could you bring me up the cropper, and another bag of nails?'

From where I tapped away on the roof I could overhear snippets of conversation between John and his gang, and it wasn't long before their conversations took on a new tone.

'So – just to be clear, John,' I'd hear his joiner ask, 'what you're saying is you want me to set the whole frame back one more inch?'

'Yes please, darling.'

At the beginning of the job I suffered embarrassing bouts of vertigo as I clambered up to the ridge; but within a couple of weeks my confidence grew, so that when the rotten batten I was standing on snapped, quickly followed by five more like it, and sent me skiing down the roof sideways – only stopping when the seventh one held – I didn't even falter my sentence, or feel the need to take my eyes off the person I was talking to as I shot past him. By the end of the job I felt a spiritual companionship with the roofer whose work I was replacing: *John Taylor*. I knew that it was he who had clambered all over this roof more than a hundred years before me, because I found his beautifully etched name on an underlap of lead I was removing – together with the date *1892*.

John Locke returned in February to look over the finished job, and I could tell he was impressed – but the credit was all his.

As we worked on the roof that winter, our boat was laid up at Gweek Quay at the navigable limit of the Helford River in Cornwall. Without an engine, our only means of propulsion had been by sail – and we'd spent an educational fortnight, before laying the boat up for the winter, learning to handle *Caol Ila* under sail alone while getting into, and back out of, the tightest nooks and crannies of the town harbour – even using a bucket thrown over the stern and tied on with rope to help slow us at critical moments. It was a masterclass, culminating in the near-catastrophic practical examination of our arrival at Gweek. We'd had a propitious wind blowing steadily from behind as we sailed up the winding river on a big tide. Two yachts overtook us in the lower reaches, belching black smoke from their exhausts as they hammered past – but they slowed when the navigation became more intricate, and we, having no brakes, now threatened to overtake them back. We could see by their half-turned faces that they thought we were just being 'difficult'.

Not knowing the river that far up, we arrived at Gweek quite suddenly as we rounded a bend, threatening to make matchwood of every boat on the quay. I rushed forward to drop the sail in an effort to slow her down, but the mainsail jammed in the spreaders, making it impossible to lower it, and it continued to drive us on. The channel in which we sailed was narrow and didn't permit us turning round so we were running out of choices, having no brakes and no steering. To add to our confusion, a launching party was underway – we could already hear the satisfied hum of conversation from a large crowd composed of old salts and hedge-fund managers as they smiled down on the gleaming restoration of an historic Bristol Channel pilot cutter, which one of the yard's boatbuilders had just completed at a cost of hundreds of thousands of pounds. She glowed with newness in her berth alongside the quay, and the assembled well-wishers were just thinking that the day's excitement was over when we appeared.

Amid my growing alarm, I suddenly remembered a trick employed by the Thames bargemen of antiquity, before marine engines were even invented… they would *dredge* their anchor. I noticed that the depth was just 2 m (6 ft), and so sprang up forward to let the anchor down on 4 m (13 ft) of chain, where it would *dredge* along the bottom – slowing us down, but failing to catch hold. Our speed fell immediately from 4 knots to about a quarter of a knot, allowing us time to untangle the mainsail, which we got down on deck without a moment to spare. As we drifted silently alongside the quay, our deck was a pleasingly chaotic mess of rope and canvas; we let out a few more metres of chain so that the anchor would bite, came to a stop, and threw our lines ashore with pretended calm – though we dare not speak, lest our voices betray us. The old salts who lined the quay to look us over sent plumes of appreciative smoke into the air from their pipes.

To those whose boats are harboured in a modern, slick marina, Gweek Quay will come as a refreshing change. Tall thistles grow between boats still awaiting the refit for which they were hauled ashore 20 years earlier; oddly shaped men stand in rheumatic poses discussing the merits of rigging her as a gunter; and the air smells of mildewed cotton and Stockholm tar.

The forefoot

George Bernard Shaw once said: *The true artist would rather see his wife in rags, his children go barefoot, and his mother begging on the streets, than give up his art...* At Gweek we found the maritime equivalent – old sea dogs long-since abandoned by their families, living alone on boats that no longer rose with the tide.

'I'm going to sail her to the Pacific next year – get a bit more sun!' Peter was our nearest neighbour and he smiled at us, revealing how many teeth he'd lost during his 65 years of malnutrition. He stood on board his large wooden yacht, which had been built 80 years earlier and was now driven hard into the mud of the water margins 'twixt sea and shore, protected under a patchwork of green tarpaulins heavy-bellied with rainwater.

The rain was easing at last and had given way to the sudden squalls of wind that a passing front heralds; to add emphasis to his words, he tossed his head significantly at the water that hung above his head – and with that a squall of wind got under one of the tarps and emptied a bathful of cold water down the back of his neck. He had hoped to remain unflinching for our benefit – but his eyes grew round with shock as the cold water ran down his back, and he allowed himself a little 'Brrrr!' followed by a doggy shake.

He invited us aboard and we sat chatting whilst his bilges popped and sucked, draining with the falling tide. Through the gloom the accommodation seemed unchanged since the day she was built – oak boards, grey with age, formed the cabin seating on either side of a brass-hinged saloon table, which was stranded remotely on the floor between them; there was a threadbare gold cushion for furnishings; and on the wall a faded print of a Tall Ships race.

Peter made us tea by boiling a canteen kettle on a chipped enamel stove, which flickered toothless flames of irregular length from its burner; and pulled rusting biscuit tins from dark cupboards which contained milk, tea bags, and sugar. He opened them, and finding everything in order, let out a triumphant little, 'Ha!'

'The rats take everything that's not in a tin!' he said.

Every day he worked toward his planned voyage. One day he begged from me a piece of wood, which I was just throwing out – and a few days later showed me the carving he had made from it, an ornamental trim for the poop-rail... while twice a day the low tide revealed which planks were missing from her hull.

Having had time on my hands the previous winter, I had discovered to my surprise that I could draw, and had found half a dozen galleries who were willing to show my maritime work; and as a fledgling artist here at Gweek, I sought out a man I'd noticed who frequently wandered around the yard wearing an artist's smock daubed with oil paint, to see what I could learn. By way of opening the conversation I asked him if he was an artist.

'I went to an art gallery once,' he told me, 'and two women at the till said to me, "You look like a St Ives artist." I am a St Ives artist!' he said, stamping his foot.

That seemed to be my answer; as he stood staring at me disconcertingly through glasses in which one lens was smeared with grease, and the other was missing entirely. 'Wait there...' he commanded, and left to collect some evidence. He didn't invite me on board – it may have been that he felt ashamed of his 'boat', which was actually an old caravan parked on a raft of steel drums, and fringed by fencing posts in the style of a Victorian railway station; it was gated by a tired rose trellis, part of which had collapsed, and under that he bobbed, bouncing a strawberry-roan ponytail which had been tied up with a green scrunchie.

'Here we are,' he said, returning and handing me two brown envelopes, on the back of which were two miniatures executed in oil. One of them was lovely – really lovely – and I told him so. He came to stand shoulder to shoulder with me to admire them with his good eye. Yes,' he agreed. 'I don't paint as often as I should, you know.'

Clive, who owned the yard, ran his business with the thinnest veil of tolerance for his customers; he was a big-limbed farmer-turned-boatyard owner, who withered you into an apology whenever yard services were requested. We begged him to give us a date for craning our engine out and another back in, so that we could arrange its delivery;

'Oh – I can't do it yet... too busy.' After several days of harassment he agreed to Thursday afternoon; and then turned up alongside our boat on Wednesday morning, threw down the window of his crane, and yelled: 'Do you want this bloody engine taken out or not?'

We connected the new engine to its cables, fuel lines and propeller shaft, and a few days later were ready to motor away from the quirky camaraderie of Gweek, in which it would have been so easy to stay for the rest of our lives. There seemed to be only one other escapee that year, and his freedom was short-lived. Carl's early glass-fibre boat was stronger than a bomb shelter, having been built when they were still experimenting with the material. He had spent the winter in quiet solitude, strolling around the yard for an hour in the morning and an hour in the afternoon for exercise, with one arm folded behind his back and the other brandishing a silver-pommelled cane with which he cleared chippings from his path with a golfer's swing.

'Lovely – I like that...' he would call into the boatbuilding sheds, pointing at something with his cane whenever he passed by and noticed someone at work. His own work was finished – he was retired and his boat was shipshape, ready for sailing 'off to the Med' with the first high tides of spring.

On the day of his departure he stood in front of a small farewell committee, dressed in a jerkin that glittered with badges collected from steam rallies and looking like a man about to step out on to the gallows.

'Well, I'm off,' he sniffed, 'and there's no point in any of you trying to stop me.' He looked from one person to another, imploringly. No one spoke. 'And you – I expect you'll miss the income?' he suggested to Clive. But Clive only raised his eyebrows and allowed them to fall slowly, as much as to say 'We'll get over it.' Ten minutes later Carl motored reluctantly away from the quay, one arm stuck behind his back in the manner of an Edwardian explorer, the other pushing and pulling at the tiller to discover which made it go left; and with that he disappeared around the corner.

Half an hour later he was on the radio to Clive. 'Clive! Come and get me! I've run aground... my mast is tangled in a tree... and the tide's going out fast!'

'I'm going to leave him down there for a tide,' Clive told me later that morning, 'give him a chance to have a think about things.'

For a couple of days we anchored a mile or two away in the quiet of the Helford River close to Frenchman's Creek of Daphne du Maurier fame, amid which romantic history we brushed off the dust and cobwebs of our winter retreat before rejoining the throbbing hub of the world in Falmouth.

'How's the new crew?' I called to Neil as we arrived at Falmouth town quay. Neil had one of everything on board his blokily untidy steel boat, and none of it worked, as I'd discovered when he lent me a super-magnet in an attempt to help find a £500 wind generator I'd dropped overboard in a moment of supreme ineptitude, in 8 m (26 ft) of water. For three hours, during which I refused to lose hope, I cast his magnet into the water secured to a line, expecting it would clamp itself to my generator... and for three hours nothing happened. Then it occurred to me that it was strange that it hadn't picked up *anything* – not even a rusting bolt – particularly as there was the wreck of a steel barge only 30 m (100 ft) away, sunk by the Luftwaffe during the Second World War. Bringing the magnet back ashore, by way of an experiment I placed a paper clip on it, and watched it slide off.

During the previous summer Neil, who despite being 35 years of age still looked like a boy scout, had set out from Southampton for an extended cruise with his brother, but only got as far as Plymouth before they fell out; his brother had abandoned the voyage and Neil came on to Falmouth to look for crew. We'd seen the notices he'd placed in the launderette, the women's shower block and the hairdressers advertising for female crew (without success); then he'd had a brainwave and advertised on an internet noticeboard, and had been inundated with offers. Having whittled them down to the most interesting sounding girl, he'd managed to agree a trial weekend.

'No good,' he said, dismissively.

'What was the hitch?' He glanced about to see if we were being overheard.

'I suspected it all along, to be honest – she turned out to be a bloke,' he half whispered as if to preserve the privacy of her secret.

'A bloke?'

'Yeah – you know... dressed like a girl and everything, but...' He dropped his head onto one shoulder and held his arm as though it were injured in an attempt to mime something that wasn't quite right.

'When did you discover that?' There was a long pause during which he began to show signs of traumatic stress.

* * *

Our plan was to spend the coming summer in Brittany, enjoy lazy days in the hot sun, and thrive on the sumptuous farm produce for which France is so dearly loved. In preparation, having laid in a store of boat husbandry consumables, hard-to-find pieces of chandlery and a wad of Euros, we took our boat upriver for a day or two, where we threw out our anchor and settled down to stow all the dry stores and spares in their allotted places.

Late the following afternoon a commotion from the pontoon a few hundred yards away, where a small rally of day-boats had just arrived and were busy putting up awnings and boom tents for the night, made me peer out to see what was going on – raised voices became shouts, followed by whining engines and thrashing water. Three of the boats had splintered away from the main group and were rushing heroically through the water toward us, filling buckets with water. The first man to arrive was just about to chuck one over us when I emerged from the accommodation. Seeing me, he hesitated and ordered,

'Stand back – you're on fire!'

'I am?' I looked about for the evidence of it, but saw nothing. Turning to him again, I saw that his expression had drained to bewilderment and that he was staring at our chimney from which smoke curled into the evening air. He lowered his bucket, allowing it to swing out of sight behind his legs.

'You've got a chimney,' he informed me, weakly. Then, turning to his friends he called,

'He's got a *chimney*...' in a tone that suggested that I shouldn't have one. He sniffed, 'Anyway – as long as you're all right,' and began turning his boat around, deaf to my gratitude as he motored away, discreetly emptying his bucket.

Our cruise to France began by narrowly missing a Dutch coaster – or him narrowly missing us. A purposeful wind was blowing across our beam, filling our sails on freed sheets as we rolled south over the waves in sight of the Lizard Point. We spotted the coaster when he was just a pip on the horizon, heading toward us from the direction of Land's End – and we monitored him for the 15 minutes or so it took him to arrive close by. During the last half mile, realising that what the International Regulations for the Prevention of Collisions at Sea describe as a *close-quarters situation* was developing, we held onto our course, as the regulations require, while waiting for him to take avoiding action. We grew more alarmed but less surprised when he carried on, straight at us... because of his size, it was less likely that he would see us during the last half mile than in the first ten. At the last moment, when nothing but our action could save us, we threw the tiller over, spun the bow upwind, and passed alongside her port to port before altering course back around her stern. As we passed alongside, an alarmed figure, spotting our 50-foot mast and flogging sails for the first time, rushed out to the flying bridge and looked down on us in shock. When he had recovered, he raised a hand feebly in salutation as we lurched over his bow wave – but we were too annoyed to acknowledge him.

It took us a while to settle down after that shock, and we considered what we could have done differently, but there *was* nothing, short of never leaving harbour. Ahead of us lay the shipping lanes – the English Channel is one of the busiest waterways in the world with over 400 shipping movements per day – that's one every 3½ minutes. At night, with only navigation lights to identify the size, direction and speed of a vessel, crossing in front of tankers is, as Libby Purves puts it, like crossing a motorway on a tricycle.

Yet as we got to the shipping lanes at around midnight, 50 miles further on, we were reminded, to our relief, of how courteously shipping *usually* responds to the presence of small craft. Their actions are timely, predictable, and unanimous – when they make a manoeuvre, they exaggerate it to make it clear that they have done so, and once one has taken avoiding action to pass behind, they all do.

'They've seen us! – thank God for those takeaway dishes,' we agreed, imagining that they had given us a good 'blip' on their radar.

During the night we noticed the lights of two small craft following in our wake as we made for the Chenal du Four – the buoyed passage between the Ile d'Ouessant and the north-western corner of France – and as dull dawn crept over the horizon we made out the masts of two yachts, which slowly caught up with us, and we at last recognised both boats as friends of ours from Falmouth, who were also planning to spend the summer in Brittany. We'd left Falmouth unsure if they were a day ahead of us, or would be a day or two behind, and it seemed strange to bump into them out here, 70 miles out. Calling across to them, we found we were all heading for Camarêt; so our banter could be continued later when we were all a bit more awake.

The brilliant morning sun glanced so hard off the water in the Chenal du Four that we struggled to see the marks, big as they were. The tide had just turned in our favour and sucked us in. One or two boats heading the other way – having left it a bit late – belched smoke from their exhausts as their engines ran flat out, struggling against the tide. Le Four, an oversized beacon, lent the passage an important air as we began to tick off the marks, riding over a grand sea until Pointe Saint-Mathieu at the southern end, at which we turned left just as the afternoon breeze climbed up a notch on the Beaufort scale, filling our sails with more wind than we strictly needed so that we began to foam along at racing speed. This attracted the attention of a sleek-looking yacht flying the tricolour, which came close alongside and paced us toward Brest. French boats are crowded with people – the crew of this one was arranged along the side decks with their legs dangling, adding weight there to help counterbalance the press of the sail, but looking for all the world like birds on a wire awaiting the migration. We Brits must look stingy and unsociable in comparison, as we sail along in our ones and twos.

It was then that we heard the first French voice hailing us across the water: 'Hey! *Caol Ila*!' the helmsman bellowed through cupped hands for a hailing trumpet, '...I lurve zis whisky!' Then he clapped a hand to his heart, operatically, before throwing it into the sky. Encouraged by our laughter, he began another mime – forming the shape of a bottle by clenching his fist and leaving his thumb erect; he took a good swig at his thumb, and then kissed his fingertips.

At home our boat's name draws only blank looks: 'Coal ila – what's that?' – so it seemed strange yet somehow plausible that we should sail to France for instant recognition. An accordion player, without whom no French cruise would be complete, struck up 'Greensleeves' in our honour and the crew of 12 sang along, lah-lahing the words they didn't know.

'Welcome to Franze!' they called, before finally altering course to go their own way, and waving their goodbyes.

Carrying too much sail, we stormed arrogantly into the harbour, scanning it in snatched glances and comparing what we saw with our harbour plan, held down on the cockpit seat with a bare foot for fear of it blowing overboard. We spotted a clear patch among the yachts in the anchorage, rounded up into wind, and carried our way neatly into the vacancy while our sails thrashed noisily. *Caol Ila* came to a stop just astern of the next vessel ahead, and threw out an anchor under that boat's transom to settle back in a perfect position. We hauled down all sail, but because the anchor needs to be set into the seabed – a job usually done by putting the engine in reverse and tugging back on it – we waited for a flaw in the breeze when a puff would cross our decks from one side, and when we got one we unfurled the jib again with a crack, holding it aback to send the bow surging away downwind; it stretched the chain and snubbed the anchor deep into the sand. Then we furled the jib once more, did the same on the other side when we got the chance, and knew we were set well enough for any weather.

Our new neighbour, who wore a stylish pair of sunglasses on his well-tanned face, sat watching us from the cockpit of his yacht. I waved him a greeting – he was too cool to wave back, but pushed out his bottom lip and nodded slowly as if to say, 'That was well done.'

Our friends had arrived well ahead of us and were comfortably installed on moorings nearby; we joined them for a beer on board David's boat, a seemingly trivial detail to record – but David supplied the beer.

An attractive woman dressed for a fashion shoot roared up in a RIB and bounced alongside to collect mooring fees;

her welcoming smile made the price irrelevant. With the day's business concluded, we sat back to relax, take in the atmosphere, smell exciting and unfamiliar fragrances wafting to us from the shore, and talk of all the things we'd like to see and do in the months that lay ahead... for Linda, the top priority was to buy some Camembert which would make our boat smell like a rugby-player's boot locker.

The following morning, after a walk ashore, Linda and I set off to explore the tinkling blue waters of the Rade de Brest, an estuary that begins with an important dock, and then probes 16 km (10 miles) into farming country toward Landévennec Abbey, which has occupied its position for 1,500 eventful years. We parked close by, spending an unusual night at Amorique sheltered behind a ship's graveyard of abandoned naval vessels, which had been stripped, moored in the river, and left to rot away in an orderly fashion. We climbed up an almost vertical fragrantly wooded hill to get to the abbey's medicinal herb garden, only to find that we needn't have performed our obeisance, and that the monks strolled in the other way on gently rising paths.

Slowly making our way back to Camarêt the following day, we paused for lunch, dropping anchor in a quiet backwater, and sat in the cockpit looking dreamily out across the glinting water while the kettle boiled. A sailing boat came into view with the unmistakably romantic lines of an historic inshore workboat from the 1800s; a huge tricolour fluttered from her rakish stern, and as we watched she altered course toward us, and came on.

'I think she's coming to say hello,' I muttered to Linda. 'Yes – I'm sure she is...' And with that we heard a distant call across the water: 'Yustin! Yustin!' No one in the world – not even my own mother – knew where we were at that moment... yet here was an historic French vessel, in the middle of French nowhere, whose French helmsman knew me by name. I staggered to my feet.

As he turned his vessel alongside us, we recognised him. We'd met Serge the previous year on a beach in Cornwall, while we were gathering oysters – not on board this historic boat, but on his own aluminium sloop. On our first meeting, he'd rowed ashore from his boat to see what we were up to – he stuck his head in our bucket and came out wearing a Klondyke expression. Plunging his hand into our bucket he picked one out, lifted his sunglasses to the top of his head, and scrutinised it expertly.

'Zees are very good!' he said, waving it under my nose.

We gave him six and showed him where he might find more besides.

Later that day we also gave him a container of water, having learned that he had run out, and it was that action that brought him out of his way to visit us now. When I handed him the water container I felt I had to explain why, having filled it from a tap fed by a Scottish loch, it was the colour of weak tea... I needn't have worried – as I spoke, he unscrewed the cap and subjected it to the same professional scrutiny as he had the oysters; he sniffed it, dipped his finger in it, licked it and then knocked back a mouthful. 'Zis is perfect!' he said, wiping his mouth and examining me for signs of Breton lineage. 'Sankyou... Sankyou very much!'

He had promised to return the container later that week – but the weather took a turn for the worse and he sailed for home without seeing us again.

His message now was that he wanted to apologise for not returning our container; and... could we join them for lunch?

On board were a dozen subscribers toward the boat's annual upkeep, men and women out to enjoy the fruits of their patronage, and today's ensemble, as luck would have it, shared a common occupation. They were food producers – farmers, shellfish-smokers, pâté-makers, wine-growers and whatnot – and each had come along with their best, set aside for this excursion.

Lunch was arranged in a casually colourful display among coils of rope and tanned cotton sails, buffet-style; and the feasting began. There was French stick 'artisan', dusty with flour; smoked duck's breast, dark and rich; sparkling wine in buckets of ice; blushing nectarines, which smelled so lovely you wanted to dab their juice behind your ears; glazed country pork terrine, dotted with black peppers and cloves; almond and peach torte, attracting wasps from as far away as the Loire... all made by people who took food seriously. If French hospitality carried on like this, how would we ever leave?

After lunch, the women began to strip to their bathing costumes and climbed down a rope ladder into the sea, letting out a breathy 'Merde!' when the coldness of the water hit them. How proud I was to see Linda strip off in preparation to represent England; she lowered herself into the water and screamed until we were all deaf.

Rejoining our friends at Camarêt, we sailed to the white sands of Audierne for a night, and then on to Bénodet. Invariably we trail along behind the others, being heavier and slower, but on this occasion we noticed an impenetrable and menacing-looking white curtain of rain sweeping rapidly toward us from seaward, which entirely blotted out the world behind it as it hung down from heaven to the hell of white-capped water it whipped up below, and we knew we were about to meet the mother of all squalls. Our friends only had time to drop their sails and fire up their engines before it hit... we watched their boats jump with the shock of its arrival. On board *Caol Ila*, with exaggerated calm we just eased the sheets a little – this is the kind of weather she was built for. As it hit, we heard the patter of rain increase to a lively hiss; she leaned her shoulder into the waves and, like a train pulling out of a station, we felt a surge of acceleration as she foamed away. For 20 minutes the wind shrieked and the rain fell so hard that there was nothing of interest to be seen but our speed log setting new records. When it cleared, the sun shone once more, and we smugly enjoyed the rare privilege of finding ourselves some way ahead.

At Bénodet we sailed under the motorway bridge, through 10,000 moored boats, and on upriver to throw out our anchor in the quiet tributary of Anse de Combrit. Linda and the girls disembarked from their several boats to follow forest paths and find out if they lead to a shop selling croissants, while I stayed on board, rubbed washing-up liquid onto my dry hands as a barrier cream against engine oil, and set about finding out why our engine was overheating again.

A short distance away, a small yacht with a beardy growth of weed about her waterline and on her anchor chain gave the appearance of having lain to her anchor for a long time. I recognised her from Falmouth, both because of her unusual name and because I myself had owned a boat of her class years before. Built for racing and weekend cruising, she was cramped, yet here she was, home to three adults who lived on board happily enough. They'd arrived in Bénodet a year earlier, decided to stay, and he, Nigel, had quickly got to grips with everyone and everything there was to know about the place. When he heard about my troubles he rowed straight over.

'Got problems?'

'Yes – our engine's running hot again.'

'Right,' he said, raising a hand to stop me from my meddling and pulling out a cellphone the size of a choc ice. 'We've got a very good engineer here – really clued up... I'll get him along straight away – and we'll probably need to get you slipped ashore, too.' Both of which were the very last things on my mind.

His philanthropy – eagerness – to abandon his own plans for the day in order to come and supervise me was a fine example of the brimming goodwill amongst we yachtsmen, and it was only reluctantly that I turned down offers of help from a man of such broad experience as Nigel's. During our conversations in Falmouth he had let it slip that he was a Harvard graduate who had gone on to become a nuclear physicist, Savoy chef, draughtsman, secret agent and rabbi.

'OK,' he said, looking at me doubtfully. 'But you'll find we've got it all here – boat hoists, engineers, chandlery; the yard-staff are friendly; we got shops, really good food... sun...' He used his phone like a speaker's baton to underline all his key words, and kept it in his hand in case it rang.

I never ask anyone how they fill their day – years of indolence have made me quite sensitive on the matter and produce a bead of sweat on my brow whenever I'm asked to account for myself by someone whose worry-lined face marks them out as a real grafter; but it doesn't stop me *wondering* what they do with their day; and I wondered it now of Nigel, unshaven, creased, and looking as though he'd been lying in bed for four days.

Almost as though he read my mind, he volunteered the information in his next sentence: 'Only problem is that I can't enjoy it, I'm that busy – only last week I had to pilot a yacht coming into harbour.'

I knew the man back in Falmouth who had skippered Nigel's boat over here for him – so I was surprised to hear how well he had progressed with his seamanship and navigation.

'Well,' he said, brimming with charity, 'it was a German bloke who didn't know these waters very well. You might not think you need a pilot – but the waters round here are very perilous. You can't just come straight in, you know!' he warned. 'Even the yacht I was piloting stranded on a sandbank.'

The following day we *ourselves* dried out on a sandbank – careening her so that I could clear the clump of seagrass – the cause of our overheating – from our cooling water intake. We finished our work in an hour and left her high and dry to go ashore exploring for the rest of the day with our friends – the tide wouldn't be back in until late afternoon. As we walked by him, a fisherman on the beach called us over to his boat, reached into the doghouse, and left his hand there, teasingly. 'Only for the men,' he said. 'The women must turn away.' Having divided us into the privileged and the oppressed, he produced, to my relief, a bottle of cider liqueur, a local speciality, and invited us to take a swallow straight from the neck... girls first, he insisted, after all. It was good – even at that time in the morning.

When he learned that it was our boat that lay on the sandbank back along the beach, he threw both hands into the air and turned away in an expression of hopelessness. 'Août quinze,' he said, with the meaning that our boat wouldn't float again for over six weeks. Now, my own calculations were that it would be afloat at five o'clock, and I told him so, but he wouldn't hear of it.

'Août quinze,' he insisted, walking round in little circles of despair. My confidence ebbed when I took into account that he was a local fisherman, had local knowledge, and that he was 'Absolutement certain!'

I didn't enjoy my day at all for worrying, and it wasn't made any better by everyone asking me, 'Do you think he's right?' every time I'd managed to put it to the back of my mind.

Août quinze rang in my ears all day, so an hour and a half before HW, with the boat not quite afloat, I climbed on board, started the engine, and span the propeller ahead at full revs, churning the water behind me while pushing the tiller from side to side to work the keel and plough a little furrow. She slid off the bank and, gathering speed, shot out to deep water; suddenly there was an alarming 'clonk' and the bow went down as we appeared to hit an underwater obstruction... then she spun round to face the way we'd come with her chain stretched out ahead of her. In my nervous condition, I'd forgotten to bring the anchor in.

We explored upriver, winding our way inland between steep, cliffy banks; the air was still and the summer temperatures soared to record levels – at Nantes Airport close by it peaked at 44°C (111°F). Branching off the Odet into a tributary, we motored on from a little sink providing anchorage for one or two craft to a point beyond navigational limits where the outflowing water chatters over stones, and anchored by the bow and the stern to keep the boat afloat in what at low tide was a thin gulley of water. Here, mature oak trees on either bank almost formed a canopy over us. I swam the few yards ashore, sat on a boulder to dry off in the warm air, and then took what I planned would be a short walk among the trees, enjoying the sensation of treading barefoot on a soft carpet of leaves and pine needles; but the countryside was so cool and delicious that I walked on.

Further along the riverbank, among willows standing between water and pastureland, I chanced on a fish trap. It consisted of a man-made pool the size of a city-dweller's garden, which flooded with the incoming tide, but which could be 'locked' off with an elaborate gate raised and lowered by a winding handle, now rusty and overgrown. Water reed and flag iris grew from the wet mud, and blue-banded dragonflies buzzed low over them, hunting on the wing for flies. The interest of that, and other pieces of social history littered about, led me on. Fringing a great lawn, which soon became a well-cultivated flower garden, and then in a clearing, I found myself standing in front of an enormous chateau. The ground floor was punctuated by grand bay windows, with their smaller cousins rising vertically through successive storeys until the eye arrived at the ridge of a steep roof interrupted by spires and by towering chimneys, each terminating in a cluster of ornamental red clay pots of points and curves. I stood admiring it for a while, until the crunching of wheels on gravel brought me to my senses and I turned to see a classic Rolls Royce convertible approaching, with the chrome work of its running boards glinting in the sun and its top down, revealing opulent cream-coloured leather as it glided past me and on toward the chateau. I suddenly realised that I probably shouldn't be there – that this must be private land – and so turned to look for the path back to the boat, and only then noticed that I was dressed in just my underpants.

Motoring back downriver the following day, we turned a corner to find one of the riverbanks was on fire. The roar and crackle from the leaping flames came and went in waves to echo back across the river as it consumed the parched vegetation on the near-vertical bank, and spat embers over us as we passed underneath, gawping up at it. How hopeless it would be to try to tackle a blaze like that, far from any road, and inaccessible from the water.

A continual highlight that summer for all of us was the French markets with their colour, abundance, and the care with which the stalls were dressed. We were dazzled into spending five times what we'd intended without a moment's regret. They seemed to be the very heart of the community in those half-timbered towns, connecting farmers, producers and consumers; a celebration of farming. In England, anyone introducing himself as a farmer is greeted with snorts of derision, and quips of 'Get orf my land'. In France, they are worshipped.

Linda dressed the boat with hanging garlic, sweet pepper, and several thousand *saucisson*. It's strange – she won't tolerate a single white strand of connective tissue on the prime cuts of meat she eats – but an odd reversal takes place when she catches a whiff of some slowly rotting saucisson. She hops about like a carrion crow in front of the stall to ward off competition and orders the stallholder to bring out all he has... and then sends him home to fetch the rest. Back on board, she nails them to the deck beams by their strings until the boat looks like the kitchen/abattoir in *The Texas Chainsaw Massacre*. Over the weeks and months ahead she ruminates on a distressing mixture of eyeballs, snout, tooth, claw and beak, heavily spiced to mask their decay.

At La Vilaine we anchored for the night in a promising-looking spot every other yachtsman seemed to have over-looked. The reason for that became clear at about 3 am. I'd been using an old chart, which I hadn't kept up-to-date – entire continents had been discovered since it was printed – and, unbeknown to me, a dam had been established just upriver from where we lay. I awoke in the wee hours to a sound I knew, but couldn't place. Then I recalled that popping sound you get from mud at low water, and thought how curious it was that we should hear it now, anchored in several metres of water. Then the penny dropped.

I scrambled out of bed without waking Linda – so as not to alarm her – and went on deck to the shrouds where, peer-ing through the darkness, I noticed that the dinghies among which we had anchored seemed a long way down, and were cast about at odd angles as they lay alongside the plump balls of their mooring buoys. We alone stood upright, balancing on our keel, which was partly submerged in the soft mud – no thanks to me throwing unnecessary weight out to one side as I leaned over the edge, from which I now jumped back to creep down below and await our fate. As I lay there I wondered why I had ever taken up boating.

At dawn the tide lifted us on its swelling bosom and after breakfast we motored upriver to discover the frighteningly grand wall of the dam, where we copied all the other boats who were milling about until they were beckoned into its lock. Inside there was a worrying notice, written in both French and English, which read, 'Keep your engine running'; it brought to my mind images of the pandemonium we were about to experience – boats whizzing around in the fill-water like bubbles in a liqui-diser, as we were all lifted 20 or 30 feet to the river above us.

At that time we had a modified exhaust pipe, following an incident whereby seawater had back-siphoned and flooded into our engine cylinders. The disadvantage of our new arrangement was that the exhaust was incredibly noisy; echoing now against the walls of the lock, it had the effect of a stun grenade that kept firing. We saw the crews of other boats diving for cover – but being used to it ourselves, and three-parts deaf because of it, we were looking around for a clue as to the cause of their alarm when our eye was caught by the lockmaster's frantic waving. The miming and gesticulations that followed were hampered by his strong accent, but eventually we understood him to say, 'Pleeza – put off ze engine.'

In the silence that followed, our fellow boaters began to emerge looking dazed but relieved, and even managed a half-smile for us on account of our boat's historic appearance and their supposition that they had been treated to the sound of one of the earliest examples of a marine engine.

At Roche-Bernard, temperatures rose to 42°C (108°F) and settled down for the long haul. The air hung, and the sun scorched the earth and every living thing upon it with Old Testament ferocity – things clean and unclean; the fowls of the air; things that creepeth; and things that go by the belly. Our dark-coloured decks – on which we couldn't walk barefoot without severe burning – attracted and held the sun's heat until the accommodation below became hot enough to bake bread. We were obliged to leave the boat altogether and lower ourselves into the water for hours on end, wallowing like a pair of hippopotamuses in hats until sunset when we crawled out, grateful to still be in possession of our lives... a privilege not granted to everyone, judging by the news bulletins.

Douarnenez hosts a classic boat festival every two years. If French markets are exciting, French festivals are a riot. The town buzzed with the enthusiastic chirruping of coutured visitors discovering an interest in all things maritime, while high up on the harbour wall groups of lusty men dressed in blue boleros and white breeches sang sea shanties to an accordion. Below them, descendants of Vikings smoked herrings in steel drums which had been up-ended on the cobblestones and lidded with sack cloth, through which oak smoke slowly reeked across a harbour backdrop of red-tanned sails hanging from spars hoisted at odd angles – like the hands of a Victorian clock.

There were demonstrations of longboat carving using hand tools (though a chainsaw could be heard making helpful cuts through the trunk, out of hours); maritime artists worked in watercolour, oil and wood; while coils of hemp rope snaked onto the cobbles in front of stalls selling nautical supplies of shining brass; and finally, the illusion of an historic harbour visited in its heyday was perfected by the smell of Jamaican rum on everyone's breath.

Rum and rigging

On the water a race had been organised. Not a race – more of a rally. To enter a 'race' the 400 rakish craft, from skiffs to ships, that lined up for the gun would have needed insurance policies paid for by mortgaging their houses – though for a rally it was bitterly fought. Sadly for the crowds who thronged the waterfront, it wasn't going to be the spectacle that the organisers had hoped – banks of fog drifted in and out, obscuring everything but the crow's nests on the loftiest spars. My French isn't that clever, and I'm not very punctual, both of which counted against me as I prepared for the start – so when at 3 pm sharp I heard the flag I'd been looking out for go off with a bang, I happened to be 200 m (220 yds) behind the start line and sailing away from it. We watched everyone splash over the line and into the fog to look for the first mark, turned around, and followed them. At every buoy a press of boats bumped alongside each other like sampans in a floating market, without a voice being raised in complaint, nor so much as a banana lost overboard. *Caol Ila* seemed to be doing miraculously well in the light airs, and moved through the fleet like a champion racehorse whose rider has either fallen off or missed his chance to get on. By the time we closed with the finishing line, there were only three boats ahead of us, though we wanted to hiss the English winners of the race for employing contentious tactics – because of the fog you couldn't see the marks (you couldn't see much at all, actually), so just before the start of the race they sent a RIB out with a satellite navigator to get 'fixes' on the positions of each buoy. Not that I'm bitter… I suppose someone had to show us where they were, and it meant that everyone was back in time for an aperitif.

The following day a friend of ours from Falmouth set out for the long sail home in his 28-foot gaff-rigged sloop, built in the 1930s. We like to watch him because his boat has no engine and so he is well practised in the salty business of handling under sail. We were in for a treat, because everyone has a sweet tooth for a disaster. A momentary flaw in the wind as he attempted to sail off his mooring caused the jib to fill from the wrong side and sent his boat into, rather than out of, the harbour. Before you could sing '…*and we're bound for west Australia*' his boat had gathered speed and plunged its bowsprit through the rigging of another moored vessel. For those ashore, it made up for the action they had been unable to see on the water the day before. At first it seemed that the boat he'd hit had no one aboard, and that his embarrassment would be limited; but in an unexpected development about which it is best not to elaborate, two men – naked except for their underwear – rushed on deck to fight off the unwelcome attention of his bowsprit. Realising that no harm had been done, and that they were now themselves the focus of everyone's attention, they retired discreetly below...

A river flows through Douarnenez, which is canalised for a short distance and locked to maintain water levels in the harbour known as Port Rhu. We went in and moored up for a few days to explore the local area on foot, and to see if we could procure a cargo of wine at commercial rates for our homeward voyage. Douarnenez has a long maritime history, which flourished with the sardine industry; and today boatbuilding workshops – which public funding barely maintains in a state of suspended animation – are interspersed with boat graveyards as the river winds inland. Great baulks of hardwood – fine boatbuilding timber – lie hidden under the encroaching bramble, waiting for jobs that may never come.

In the town we slipped into a promising-looking *Cave* – the bleak shop window revealed three or four huge vats of wine standing out back in a block-built garage with whitewashed walls; in the foreground, dimly lit emptiness was interspersed by a few racks of dusty wine bottles here and there. Peter Mayle's book *A Year in Provence* fired our imaginations with glimpses of the proprietor we were likely to meet – alert blue eyes watching us from a craggy face, and dark-stubbly lips wetly clamped around the yellow corn paper of a hand-rolled cigarette; instead we were met by a cheerful woman in her thirties. 'Bonjour!' she sang, smelling of bath oil as she wafted past us in a light cotton dress and flip-flops.

During the next hour we tried each vat and browsed the bottles while she nodded her enthusiastic agreement – 'Oui! Oui – exactement!' – with whatever words we used to describe the wine we tasted. We really couldn't put a foot wrong with her. We left with half a dozen bottles to try with food over the next few days, in preparation for our smuggle.

Following another Peter-Mayle inspired whim – to walk to a country village in the middle of nowhere and pop in for lunch at the auberge we knew would be waiting for us – we selected a village from the map with the charming-sounding name of St Germain (two-and-a-half hours away by foot, to ensure we arrived with a good appetite), and set off at ten o'clock one morning in sunshine that continued to beat mercilessly on the cracked earth. The walk was long, not particularly interesting, and – as we had brought no water with us – extremely dehydrating. So we felt a bit of a slump in our spirits, God have mercy on our souls, when we arrived at St Germain and discovered that it was not a village, but a church.

Parishioners carrying in huge floral arrangements for a harvest festival they planned for the coming weekend seemed delighted to have visitors and insisted on showing us what they had achieved so far; they ushered us in – wobbly-legged, dripping with sweat, and with heads banging from the effects of sunstroke, praying to God we would find an opportunity to steal a pineapple. Inside, the displays of chrysanthemums and gladioli were truly magnificent, and I hope we didn't seem disappointed with them. We turned our faces toward Douarnenez, and began the long walk home.

'I'm going to knock at this door,' said Linda, as we passed a farm in an advanced state of dereliction, 'and ask them for a glass of water.' I hung around by the gate so as not to intimidate the owner who must be old, frail and not used to visitors. On the un-mown lawn, slabs of plaster lay where they had fallen from the walls; shutters slumped across windows, hanging on by one hinge; and the front door seemed to be missing entirely. Linda stood a polite distance from the porch, and the moment she called 'Hello?', two dogs – one with rabies, the other with scab – raced around to the front of the house and began snarling at her menacingly. The silhouette of a middle-aged man filled the doorway, remaining concealed in the half-light… he didn't speak. He seemed to be the disastrous result of a long-running experiment his ancestors had hit on in selective breeding, and had wildly angry eyes, no teeth in his open mouth, and a manner beside which the dogs seemed friendly.

'Could I have a glass of water?' Linda asked hesitantly, in English to gain his sympathy... and when that didn't work, translated. The man stared at her, motionless. For a few moments nothing happened, and then I saw Linda back away, fearless of the dogs.

'It's OK!' she smiled, 'don't worry!' She got to the gate and walked quickly past me – I saw goosebumps on her neck. 'Come on, Alfs – let's go,' she whispered.

A few minutes later, when she had put the farmhouse some distance behind her, she let out a sigh of relief. 'Now, he was *weird*.'

Back on board we drank water until our bellies rang like pigskins.

Over the next couple of days we smacked our lips ostentatiously at the wine we'd bought, made our choices, haggled good-naturedly with the *Cave* proprietor, and arranged delivery of 24 cases of red nectar. I helped her load a van, which sunk on its springs and which, when she started it, sounded as though it was powered by a moped engine; we bounced our way round to the harbour, sending sparks flying every time the exhaust pipe grounded on a bump, and then built a wall of boxes at the foot of the pontoon ramp. It took Linda and me until midnight to remove every bottle from its box and find a home for it deep in the bilges, cupboards, and lockers where it couldn't shake, rattle or roll when the time came for us to plunge over the waves for home.

Our friends now kept a discreet distance from us, not wishing to be accessories to a crime – but we'd done a bit of homework. We were sitting on board our boat in the Scilly Isles the previous summer – minding our own business on a quiet afternoon – when a customs 'cutter' of about 70 feet motored into the sound and anchored. A few minutes later, through our hull we heard the distant scream of powerful outboard engines churning water and approaching fast. I climbed up the companionway steps just in time to see a black-clad customs officer leap from his speeding RIB onto our deck with his government issue boots and the rather unnecessary request: 'Customs! Permission to come aboard?' Before he had finished speaking, three more officers had leapt through the air to crash uncertainly on our deck. He watched closely for my reaction.

'Come on down,' I greeted him, with a wry smile.

He asked if we had any drugs, tobacco or alcohol on board, yet I could tell that he had already given up on us.

Linda made tea while a couple of them prodded disinterestedly around the accommodation; then we all sat on deck, chatting in the sun with our tea and biscuits. In answer to our questions they told us about a pursuit they'd recently made in fog around the north coast of Scotland, how the fog had suddenly lifted, exposing them, and the drama that followed of getting back into cover. Their stealth paid off, and they made a haul. That was when we took the opportunity to ask about importation limits. We explained that we drank a bottle of wine a day and had a plan to go to France and bring back a 'couple of hundred bottles' – was that too many? They were non-committal.

'Well, it depends...' 'There isn't a specific number...', '...if it's for your own use.' But by their lack of surprise, we guessed we'd probably be all right.

Eventually the radio that one of them was wearing on his lapel crackled into life with a message from the mother ship. He pressed the button to transmit, and answered with his call sign. 'Go ahead,' he said, cocking his ear. His radio crackled again: 'Do you guys want me to send over the suncream?' There was embarrassed laughter among the officers as they got to their feet, thanked us for the tea, and left.

We motored away from Douarnenez in poor visibility, only to find when we came to the hardest part of our navigation – the rock-strewn Pointe du Toulinguet – that the fog was so thick we could scarcely see the front of our boat. Linda stood on the bow, keeping watch as we inched forward.

'I can hear a fog horn!' she called back. Eventually, out of the fog loomed a smart yacht flying a white ensign – the flag of the Royal Yacht Squadron. As they passed us, the helmsman bellowed, 'Haven't you got a horn?'

'No – but we've got a whistle,' Linda chirped.

'Pharking-well blow it then!' came the incensed reply.

He was quite right, of course – we should have pharking-well blown it. We were paying too much attention to everything else, I suppose. But – contrast that with what happened next. A French boat appeared alongside, out of the gloom... like the Yacht Squadroners, his boat was equipped with radar – and he could tell that ours wasn't by our cautious speed.

'You are going to Camarêt, no?'

'Yes.'

'Zen follow me – I will show you.' He motored away at 6 knots – half his cruising speed, for our benefit – while we followed close in his wake. Forty minutes later we were floating quietly in the harbour at Camarêt. He dismissed my profuse gratitude with a 'C'est normale' sweep of his hand, and then left us to continue his journey to Brest – he'd come out of his way to help us.

In preparation for crossing the Channel back to England, we jumped onto the north-going tide in the Chenal de Four and rode it to L'Aber Benoît, striking in toward that rocky entrance when we were certain of our position – which we weren't for a long time, because one rock looks like another. By now, it was September; the hot summer was over and the river was in mellow mood. That night we were woken by drips of water on our faces and woke to find that our pillows were wet, while outside the rain fell in torrents. We could hear it dripping elsewhere on the boat and got up to investigate – bedding, seat cushions, the floor... everything was soaking wet as rain dripped through the wooden decks, where the boards had shrunk over the hot summer. We might as well have been lying under a sieve. We put saucepans and bowls under the drips, until eventually there were more than 20 containers plip-plopping as they caught water. It was miserable. We had had deck leaks before, but nothing like this. In the morning, we found that the brutal parching we had received had opened up some of the boards so much that you could see daylight through them.

In the sunshine we swung quietly in the deserted river at L'Aber Benoît, and opened the hatches and portholes to begin to dry ourselves out. At low water we watched beachcombers – middle-aged Frenchmen – turning over stones, looking for fruits-de-mer. They didn't seem to be finding much. Whereas in England you are an oddity if you low-water forage, in France everyone does it, and by late summer only the occasional winkle remains. Instead of competing with them for the last snail, we walked through the woodland that fringed the river on one side and fields of wheat and maize on the other, to a mussel farm and restaurant for a late lunch. On the beach by the restaurant's terrace were cairns 10 feet high, made from the discarded shells of many dinners. We planned to climb them after lunch with our own contribution for the summit – but the restaurant was closing as we arrived, a development that only added to the end-of-season feel; it was time to think about heading home.

We motored out of L'Aber Benoît as soon as it became light one morning when there wasn't a breath of wind, and were just picking our way through the littered rocks, shoals and islets – allowing for the strong tide – when the engine suddenly stopped. We'd run out of fuel. I had a spare container – but it was going to take me five minutes to set it up, and we were being swept toward a large rock. We waved and yelled at a fishing boat a couple of hundred yards ahead – but he was oblivious of us. Suddenly a vessel we hadn't noticed arrived at our stern.

'Is it all right?' he asked.

'We've just run out of fuel – could you tow us to that sandbank?' Although the water here was over 40 m (130 ft) deep, we were tantalisingly close to a bank with only 4 m (13 ft) over it just upstream.

He willingly and easily got us to the bank, where we dropped our anchor and set about replenishing our tank. We offered him payment, which he refused with a shrug as if to say, 'For what?'

* * *

When we arrived back in the familiar waters of Cornwall, which felt like home, we allowed autumn to enfold us with its gentle mists and luxuriated up creeks among the wildlife – just

Linda, me, and the wood-burning stove – dreaming back to our colourful summer, and congratulating ourselves on choosing our little life.

The silent mornings started so agreeably that we would take it in turns to lie in bed in the gloaming while the other stoked the fire, put the coffee on to percolate, and made breakfast. I heard Linda splitting wood rhythmically with the kindling axe – clonk... clonk... clonk...

Suddenly the very timbers of the boat shrilled to a chilling scream. 'AHHHHHHHHHH!' – so loud it knocked me senseless with confusion.

I leapt out of bed. 'What's happened!?'

'F—king hell!' Linda cried, in disbelief. 'I've just chopped my finger off!'

As wave after wave of pain thrilled through her body she called my name, imploring me to help... and I didn't know what to do.

'I'll call an ambulance...' On the radio I called the coastguard, trying to remain composed, and gave him our details while Linda wailed in the background.

'Where would you like the ambulance to come to?'

There was a vehicle chain ferry half a mile upriver from where we lay at anchor, known as the King Harry Ferry. It was perfect – we could ground ourselves on the slipway and be within a few yards of a road, and the ambulance.

Tripping and falling over everything, I hauled up the anchor, started the engine, and blasted away upriver. As we approached, the ferry was heading toward the same slip, but stopped when he saw us coming – he would have heard our radio conversation with the coastguard – and allowed us to go ahead. We grounded ourselves on the ramp, where the ambulance was already waiting. I threw the dinghy into the water, fell into it, helped Linda down, pulled away with the oars and then fell off the seat when the dinghy snubbed up short because I had forgotten to untie it.

'Alfie, calm down!' Linda said. Ashore, the medic put an arm round her; I gave him her fingertip which I'd put in a freezer bag, and they drove away.

I'd grounded hard in lieu of anchoring, and it was only with some difficulty on the falling tide that I got the boat back off the slip, motored out into the river, and turned to thank the ferryman, who only raised a sympathetic hand.

That afternoon, relaxed, cheerful and back from hospital, Linda stood on Falmouth quay explaining to Ron and Maureen, two friends of ours – live-aboards themselves, and in their sixties – how the accident had happened and how, in spite of her claims to be the next violin virtuoso, the hospital had refused to reattach the missing part of her finger because it was too small. Behind their backs, I was making urgent paddling movements to get her attention, putting a finger to my lips to get her to shut up. Ron, who nodded sympathetically at everything Linda said, had been walking along a railway line as a youth, on his way home after a night out, when a train he hadn't heard approaching rushed past him. It was only when he went to open his front door that he realised his arm was missing; and he stood now listening to Linda with an empty sleeve tucked in his pocket.

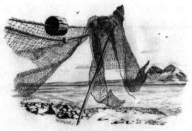

9 A GHOST FARMHOUSE

Autumn brought its gales thundering along the Cornish coast, sending us and all the other wild animals in search of harbour from the storm. There are pockets of beauty along the secret creeks that are so protected from the ravages of the wind that the trees that crowd them carry last year's brown leaves through to March, and only drop them when the green buds of spring emerge.

Linda had found 'bank' work for the winter as a health visitor based at the hospital, filling in for a member of staff on long-term sick leave – very agreeably working just three days a week. My first little job for the winter was found for me by my good friend JFW, in a cathedral – not a building I frequent – and I pushed open a pair of opulent smoked-glass doors expecting a holy rebuke from above for only turning up now that there was the chance of some money in it. But the good Lord spared me, seeing as how I'd taken time out of my busy schedule to help install a new two million pound organ for him.

The paved foreigns leading up to the cathedral had mature bushes along one side, and it was discreetly close to those that the works van was parked so as to cause as little nuisance as possible to visitors who rushed in to hear the Petrine liturgy. Going to fetch some wood from the van, I startled a tramp who staggered out of the bushes doing up

his fly, and who greeted me with the words 'Fine building...
beautiful, in fact!', as though he had just completed a very
thorough survey of it, assumed I was the bishop indulging in
a spot of DIY, and wished to congratulate me on my choice
of residence.

One evening toward the end of the project, JFW was pointing out to me the scrolled marquetry on the organ case which
was now emplaced on a blue-carpeted gallery which overshot
the congregational pews, his finger reflecting in a rippled-
maple console so immaculately polished that it appeared to
be entombed in glass. Behind us, a thousand organ pipes were
secured in a huge fretwork case which looked like a ballistics
cabinet containing long-range missiles, and towered into the
vaulted roof.

'What I've got to do,' he whispered reverentially to me
and the musical genius who was standing with us, and
who was there to direct the windy side of the installation,
'is to attach this rosewood music stand above the keyboard.'
In addition to his career as a Devon sheep farmer, JFW
had been a primary school teacher, and had developed a
style of speaking that suggests you are about to witness
a miracle.

'So!' he barked, to keep our attention, 'I'm going to drill
a hole, just... here.' Since his boatbuilding course he'd under-
gone another metamorphosis and emerged as a fine cabinetmaker; trusted overseer of some of the most prestigious jobs
in the ecclesiastical world... and it was as a piece of charity
that he'd managed to wangle me the job of passing him tools.
It was a virtuous circle for me as I was getting paid *and*
receiving a primary school education.

Having divined by triangulation, executed with microm-
eter accuracy, where the first hole was to go, he asked me
to pass him a tiny 2 mm drill bit – a cobalt, I believe – which
he unwrapped from its waxed paper and installed into
the keyless chuck of his drill with a whiz, followed by an
obedient clunk. He carefully lowered the drill to the case, and
gently squeezed the trigger; in the background I was sure

I could hear the steady beep of an electrocardiograph. Three pairs of eyes – his, mine, and those belonging to the pipe-smoking professor of music – watched as the slowly revolving drill bit bored its way first through the lacquer, and then on into the precious timber, producing miniature corkscrew-shaped swirls of wood as it did so. JFW stopped of a sudden, and his eyes grew to the size of dinner plates... then he rolled them up to a stained-glass window depicting the Passion of the Christ on the Cross set high in the cathedral's gable wall. Remembering that he was in the house of the Lord, he stopped himself halfway through a sentence that began, 'Oh! Fu—'

'Everything all right, JF?'

He didn't answer at first; but began swaying as in a swoon. When he did speak, his voice was just a rasping whisper: 'I have drilled that hole in the wrong place.' Then, finding new strength, he allowed himself to finish his earlier sentence in full.

I attempted to lighten the mood. 'Why don't you stick a match in the hole – no one will notice – Ian, you've got some matches, haven't you?' Ian pulled a box of Swan Vestas from his overalls and handed a match to JFW; to my surprise, he took it.

'Thank you,' he whispered, and pulled out a knife to trim its end, which he carefully started into the hole, its little pink head reflecting oddly in the glassy finish of the case. Using the flat of a chisel, JFW gently tapped the match home. Suddenly there was a flash as the match ignited – illuminating the maple beautifully – and the sulphur flared up, spitting little satellites of flame in all directions to sizzle and boil where they landed.

'NO!' he yelled at the match, puffing gust after gust of spitty breath at it until only ragged smoke remained. He'd started the job quite late in the day; it was by now gone 7 pm, and JFW announced that he was clocking off – and sadly that happened to be my last day, so I never discovered how you go on from there.

JFW

There followed a winter of delirious satisfaction; we spent our time alone at anchor within earshot of the seabirds, and watching the tinkling water through the portholes. I filled my days by drawing the maritime scenes and objects around me in order to build up a portfolio of artwork for the increasing number of shoreside galleries who'd offered to take my work, and to populate the pages of my website. The waters around Falmouth are steeped in maritime history, and at the top of every creek there lie the remains of classic wooden workboats and gentlemen's yachts, floated up on a spring tide decades ago to be 'retired'. And it was the sculptural remains of these wrecks – weathered by wind and tide, together with the rope and seaweed that hung from them at each low tide – that inspired me most, and which I found in such abundance.

On the days on which Linda worked, from where we lay at anchor I could poke my head out of the hatch in the evening to watch for her torchlight flickering through the woods and know that I had five minutes to turn the heat down under everything on the stove, jump in the dinghy, and row the few yards to wait for her in the darkness on the beach – taking an extra plastic bag with me for her to sit on if it had been raining. Some of the nights were so black – even before 6 pm – that she would emerge through the usual gap in the trees, but be unable to see me waiting in the dinghy.

'Alfie?' she would call.

'Hello, duck!' I would say, waving an oar.

'Oh – you're there!'

Around the corner of the winter river one morning came a slow boat. It was a small yacht, dumpy and yellow, well built from plywood in the 1960s or 70s, but stricken in years. It would never have been a flyer, and dragged itself along now at a pace that took account of its age, taking for ever to cover the quarter mile to where we lay at our anchor. It's a curious thing – but if one boat anchors in a thousand miles of open ocean, the next boat to arrive will anchor right alongside, bobbing on the water like a gull looking for a mate. Yet when it reached us, a figure – a man of about 50 – climbed forward through the rigging, dropped his anchor, and went anonymously below; a second face emerged for a cursory glance at the surroundings, and sunk back down below. Smoke began to rise from a chimney, telling us that it was *home* as well as *boat*.

For a week, the couple on board managed to avoid acknowledging us, and when our paths eventually crossed it was as they walked their dog along by the shore. Although they would have avoided us if they could, now that we had met they chatted softly, but stuck to generalities and didn't give anything away. They were academics with bad teeth who loved their dog – all three living on board in such close proximity that they would have shared one another's breath; and having withdrawn themselves from the world lived contented lives of extreme frugality – their clothes lending them an air of shabby gentility.

Over the coming weeks, signs of their industry began appearing in the woods – a little work table made from pieces of flotsam, and tied with binder twine; a firewood shelter roofed with a scrap piece of PVC, under which hung a rusting bowsaw.

They stayed in the same spot for the whole winter, weighing anchor once a week to go on slow voyages to the shops. On my birthday they gave me a copy of Cervantes' *Don Quixote* – it was an old but well made stitch-bound paperback Penguin Classic, published in 1947. Books were the central theme of their lives; their trips ashore always included a visit to the library, and when I went on board their boat – which I was invited to do just once, to chew the cud over an engine problem – piles of handwritten manuscript in the neat hand of a fountain pen were littered over the age-stained cushions and scratched plywood table in the accommodation, in preparation, he mentioned, for a literary competition. The advantage of their life of reclusion was that nobody bothered them, and we knew from our own experience the sanctuary that provides, together with living simply surrounded by the few necessaries of life – it's only when some prying eye obtrudes that disquiet stirs the calm pools of the mind.

I say nobody bothered them – there was a shed further along the shore, lost among the trees and apparently abandoned (but which we knew to be in very occasional use by a retired oyster fisherman), which they began to covet. One morning, when the forecast warned of a severe storm, they took the opportunity to move their vessel from the already protected water in which she lay to the muddy shore in a bite of riverbank at the very door of the shed, where the shelter from the wind was so perfect that swans very regularly used the spot to sleep, anchoring themselves overnight by one toe. Here they stayed for a week or two; then built themselves a gangplank connecting them directly to the shore.

Most river authorities are surprisingly sympathetic to the needs of folk who live on boats – and even those which aren't have very little power over a boat at anchor when all warning shots have been fired – but as soon as she attempts to make her home on the shore, she hasn't a leg to stand on, as it were, and they swing into action to remove her. We saw the harbour master call on them and had no doubt that it was to tell them they would have to move. The remedy for most of us who don't like authority is to avoid it; and soon after that confrontation their boat disappeared from the river – presumably finding a new home elsewhere.

Plockton workboat

Recognising the echoes of their lives in our own, we pondered on what plans we had for the long term – would we live on our boat "til death us do part"?

We knew of another couple still living on board a wooden boat in their seventies. Wooden boats need a lot of maintenance and theirs wasn't getting it – it was literally falling apart around them. Motoring across the channel one day over a gently undulating sea, they heard a crash on deck and came up to find that part of the mast had broken off where woodworm had left the wood frassy.

We decided our course would be that when we stopped enjoying the advantages of life afloat, we'd build a house by some shore. It was a decision that added a new interest to our cruising over the following years, as we kept one eye open for a plot on which we could build a house; still enjoy the seabirds, the wind and the waves – and keep our boat moored nearby. It was a rich man's dream – ludicrous on *our* income, and with *our* assets. When we sold our house we put all our money into the hands of a local financial advisor to invest in bonds, stocks and shares – after two years (during which time investors all over the world were enjoying unprecedented growth) he lost almost 70 per cent of our money.

We got the details of three or four plots in Ireland, starting at €14,000. Ireland was still enjoying its boom just then, and the property market had not yet collapsed, so we weren't too hopeful that we'd find our bargain in Ireland... and in any case these plots were nowhere near the sea – but we decided to sail out to have a look at them the following spring. Once in Ireland, our summer cruising plan was to sail up the coast and on to Scotland, where we would stay for the whole winter to see if we could 'survive' a Scottish winter on board – the winter with which I began our story.

**

We watched the greening of the trees, felt the warming and lengthening of the days, and made preparations for our summer cruise, while waiting for a spell of fine weather to get away.

Sitting in the upstairs bar of the Quayside one lunchtime, with our pints of Doom Bar, we and a handful of friends were enjoying the views across the harbour when a mutual friend of all of ours, Rolf, hove in sight, foaming past the docks at 8 knots. We didn't recognise his boat at first, his hallmark being his bare poles with tan sails brailed up aloft, motoring gently by – yet here he was, for the first time to our knowledge, with all sail set, cracking on into the harbour with a gale behind him and leaving a furrow in his wake. He was in his seventies, and happened to be alone on board his 22-ton yacht that weekend; and we knew that his engine was in bits waiting for a part. He was running out of room, and things weren't looking good.

The harbour is bounded on three sides – the docks; then a marina, with its expensive line-up of craft on the outside pontoon; and finally by the stone wall of the town quay below us. Coming to the end of the docks, Rolf turned late, just in time to avoid hitting the outside line of yachts on the pontoon – which he passed so closely, with the wind on his beam, that boat owners were having to dive for cover as his boom swept low over their decks... and he romped on, leaving them plung-ing over his bow wave.

He spotted a gap between the moored boats into which his boat might fit with a foot to spare and, taking a fancy to it, hailed a passer-by to catch a rope. We saw the passer-by cross-ing and uncrossing the open-palms of his hands in front of his face in absolute refusal. Attempting to moor at that speed would be like parking a car in a space on the high street as you drove past it at 30.

Seeing himself now embayed in a corner, he made one last desperate turn and to his own and everyone else's astonish-ment missed braining himself and ran along the third side of the harbour – the stone quay below us – with only just enough room between him and the wall for a fender. The final miracle was that his boat, which now faced the wind, sails shaking, came to a stop right alongside the disembarkation steps, where it kissed the wall so gently that it wouldn't have broken an egg. Recognising the opportunity to pretend that this was his intention all along, he stepped casually ashore with a rope – the wrong rope, but a rope – to be met immediately by our group, which had rushed down to help. He stood uncertainly for a moment, darting a furtive eye at each of us from under a shaggy eyebrow to see what we knew, deciding whether to play the part of a grateful friend, relieved to see us at the height of his ordeal, or the sea-scourged galleon bird who behaved like this most days. Choosing the latter, he leaned quietly against the railings.

'How are you all? Lovely to see you,' he said, brimming with his usual charm; and followed it with a kind word for each of us. Behind him, the wind backed the sails of his boat and set it off on another voyage without him.

'Rolf! Your boat!' someone yelled. Turning to see what was happening, he cracked on the rope he was holding and shouted, 'Whoaaa!' like a cowboy does to a horse he's lead-ing, which has just reared. Then, realising that the rope he'd brought ashore didn't do anything, he and a couple of the others ran down the steps and threw themselves desperately on board. From nowhere a RIB arrived, grabbed a bow line, and towed him to the anchorage, where he stayed until the engine was repaired.

A few days later, when the weather had entered a settled phase, we prepared to leave our friends behind for a year or two. We would miss the characters, incidents and accidents of the port we loved.

Lay up mooring

We sailed from the Helford River at seven one sunny morning and headed out onto a flat sea. We never skirted the jagged black teeth of Manacles rocks without thinking of Hamish and his boat running on to them. The Manacles bell buoy was having a lazy start to the day and gave a half-hearted dong with its clapper as we rippled by.

Off Black Head we caught two small mackerel, set them aside for later in the day when our stomachs were able to take strong meat, and drifted round Lizard Point, turning west for the Scilly Isles while the sun rose to dazzle our world of yellow and blue. The overfalls off the point lifted and fell eerily like boiling tar, pitching and rolling us in slow motion, and sending our boom crashing from side to side; we hauled it in tight so that it would be quieter – in 2 miles we'd be through, and normal service would be resumed. Near Wolf Rock a fisherman out of Newlyn was hauling his pots with a hydraulic winch; we waited for him to look up so that we could give him a friendly wave, but he didn't – out of Newlyn they never do. Instead he turned his back ostentatiously when we were at our closest.

We'd spent a night in Newlyn Harbour once and it was one of just three occasions when we'd felt unwelcome; a second occurred close by when we were at anchor off Mousehole, a couple of miles south of Newlyn – just inside St Clement's Island. Mousehole is a quintessentially Cornish fishing village, whose beauty has been her downfall – around 70 per cent of her houses are now second homes to city-dwellers and locals can no longer afford to live there. In summer, the streets are choked with expensive cars; in the winter they are utterly deserted – if the locals resent moneyed incomers, then perhaps it's not surprising, and anyone who seems to fit that bill can be a target for their contempt. At leisure on our brightly painted boat anchored off Mousehole – sparkling after our winter refit – we must have appeared to be just two more members of the idle rich. I noticed a fishing boat of around 30 tons, steaming full ahead and pushing a huge white bone of a bow wave in front of her, alter course to come inside Clement Island, putting us right on her bow... we were about to be thrown violently. I called a warning down to Linda who was preparing supper below and, in the half-minute she had, she clattered the plates and glasses safely away, coming on deck just in time to see the hulk of the fishing vessel sweep past us within 6 m (20 ft). My hackles were up but Linda, in a moment of genius, said, 'Don't give them the pleasure,' and waved a generous greeting. The malignant crew was wrong-footed by her action and their sneers melted away as they returned her greeting and shot past. When the foaming wave hit us we reared up as if a depth charge had exploded right below us... the movement was so violent that even though we were expecting it, it nearly threw us clean off the deck.

The following day we arrived at the Scillies just as the sun was slipping below the horizon, and breeding birds that had spent the day fishing to feed their growing brood were settling down for the night. We can't call in at the Scillies without staying for a fortnight... visiting new friends; walking again the circular walks that take us past the exotic shapes and colours of flora and fauna on all our favourite islands; we soak up the sun on white-sand beaches fringed with the green of sea holly and marram grass behind, and the turquoise water in front; and – greatest of joys – visit the Turk's Head.

During our visit, an uncommon summer storm was forecast. The Nautical Almanac says of the Scilly Isles: *It is not a place for inexperienced navigators or poorly equipped yachts. Normal yacht anchors may drag on fine sand, even with plenty of scope.* So it wasn't surprising that at its first promulgation the storm warning caused a mass exodus of yachts from the islands like rats from a sinking ship – the one thing certain in a storm is that damage *will* be caused, and the best anyone can hope for (if they are diligent) is that *their* boat will escape unharmed. Having begun our voyage we had no intention of turning back, and set about planning where we would ride out the storm.

There are relatively few places to shelter in the Scillies when the wind is expected from the south-west to north-west – and in any case a storm will make its presence felt everywhere. The harbour at St Mary's has heavy-duty mooring buoys facing open water from the west, which is unusual for a UK harbour because that's the direction of the prevailing wind – though St Mary's is protected from the worst of a storm by the outlying islands of its archipelago – but wild horses wouldn't induce me to spend two days riding over even the modified combers of storm waves. To our surprise, we found a vacant spot lying against the quay wall, which runs north–south and hooks round slightly at its end to provide line-of-sight protection from open waters to any craft tied inside it.

Next to us was a larger wooden yacht, on board which were four adults and four children; so we waited for the storm to arrive buoyed by the cheerful camaraderie of the adults and the gay abandon of their playing children. The depression arrived slowly, bringing with it a long blow that built large waves and sent them crashing into the harbour wall, where they erupted into the air and fell on us in salty showers. But this was just the start of it. Over the following 24 hours the wind veered into the north-west and rose to storm force.

The first casualties were smaller dinghies on moorings, which broke their lines and were swept ashore by the surf, to be met by island vigilantes who hauled them up to safety.

Looking at the seas that now rolled in, and watching the hundreds of moored craft leaping uncertainly over them, it was sobering to remember that these were the conditions in the *harbour*.

A steel fishing boat was next to break her mooring, and the islanders – who are famed throughout history for facing any conditions at sea to save lives or livelihoods – jumped into action. Two of them motored out in an unsuitable inflatable dinghy – one steering and one bailing – and crashed through the surf, making painfully slow progress toward the stricken boat. Reaching it, one got on board and began searching all the usual spots for the key to start the engine, while the other remained in the dinghy motoring hard against the wind, towing the fishing boat away from the shore – it was a losing battle, of course, but it bought more time. Finding no key, the man on board pulled off the engine covers and began hot-wiring the engine.

'Have you got a spare line?' a wiry man of about 65 shouted down to me. Catching the one I threw him, his yellow wellies ran along the quay, jumped aboard our neighbour and he threw one end of the line out to the stricken vessel, secured it to a cleat and saved it just feet from the rocks.

Aboard *Caol Ila*, we felt a bump, and frowned at each other. A minute later it came again, harder. Each low water where we were tied against the wall left us high and dry... the tide was ebbing fast and *Caol Ila* was pounding on the bottom as she fell in the troughs of the swell that rolled into the harbour. For half an hour the pounding grew, until we shuddered in every timber – glasses and crockery rattled in their lockers; the tinny oven-shelf vibrated; and cupboard doors burst open, spewing out their contents. Out on deck I hailed the skipper of our neighbour.

'Jesus – how are you getting on with this?'

'Oh well...' he said, with a shrug.

'It's jangling my nerves,' I told him, 'and I hope it doesn't go on much longer.'

'What can you do?' he said. 'I'm off to the pub – let it play out.'

At last the tide ebbed and we rested firmly on the bottom.

A floating yacht pontoon in the harbour emphasised the severity of the swell by snaking over the incoming waves like a fairground ride. The mooring line of a catamaran secured to it parted, and she began to break away – she would have been the next on the rocks had her owner not been watching out for her from the shore and hitched a ride out through the surf to save her. Unable to stand on the pontoon, he lay down to work, and when he had made her safe continued to lay there for a long time, being sick.

Then we heard the 'boom' of a maroon calling the lifeboat crew to their station; someone somewhere was in trouble – but who would be out in these conditions? Dressed in orange survival suits, the crew shuddered like toys as they sat along the inflated hulls and their RIB crashed through the surf toward their offshore boat, which waited for them at its mooring; moments later a cloud of blue smoke belched from the dual exhausts of the all-weather boat to be whipped away on the wind, and her bow reared into the air like a porpoise over the combers on her way out of the harbour.

The casualty, we heard, was only a mile away – two yachts were anchored in Porthcressa, a bay just around the headland, well protected from the sea but, like the rest of us, exposed to the strong wind. One of them – a Dutch boat – had dragged her anchor and would soon be on the rocks. The danger had been reported not by the Dutch boat, but by the other yacht in the bay – a French boat, concerned that the Dutchman had been 'behaving strangely'. The lifeboat arrived to find the Dutchman precariously close to the rocks – seemingly unperturbed, alone on deck in just a T-shirt, and attempting to hoist some sail; his wife and daughter remained below. The boat looked unprepared for sea – and these weren't sailing conditions. The skipper refused to be helped by the lifeboat when it arrived, so they stood by to observe, before deciding to intervene. They took the vessel in tow to another bay on a different island where there was a heavy mooring, and were just leaving him secured to that when they noticed that he was preparing to launch his inflatable dinghy. Returning, the yacht skipper told them he was planning to row ashore. The shore lay only 100 m (110 yds) away, but there was no prospect of him reaching it in an inflatable dinghy in the prevailing conditions – he would have been flipped, or swept offshore – so the lifeboat confiscated his dinghy, promising to return it the following day when the storm had abated.

We bounced up and down on the next two tides, but the only damage was to our nerves; and 36 hours after that, summer returned.

A week later, on a day that began with a grey dawn, we hoisted sail with a single reef in the mainsail and headed out into the heaving Atlantic swell, which sucked at scattered rocks as we passed by bound for Ireland. A few miles out to sea the swell became more regular, and we settled down to a fast passage, taking the south-west wind over our port quarter. The tiller was heavy sometimes when we ran down the face of a large swell, but that too eased as we headed out into the Celtic Sea, whose bottom is a monotonous plateau stretching for 160 km (100 miles). Leaving the Scillies is always hard – bright weather seems to favour them, lingering on their shores; as we sailed away, the horizon became gloomy.

We arrived at Kilmore Quay in Southern Ireland a day later, having only distantly seen a trawler and a cargo vessel on passage across the empty wastes. We were ready for a bit of society as we crabbed toward the port entrance, stemming a strong coastal tide on our beam and following transits set up on the shore – and we got more society than we were expecting. Linda howls whenever we crab across the tide because she finds it disorientating to have the bow pointing in one direction, and yet be moving in another; her shrieks attracted a small crowd to the pier head to see what the matter was.

The harbour was full of boats with no people on them – they'd all left to explore the town – yet when you walk into the town, there's nothing there... no signs lead you to attractions, no roads lead to a throbbing heart. It's like a maze – but it has only two streets.

We rifled through our files for printed sheets detailing the building plots we'd discovered on the internet during the winter, hired a car, and set off to see what sort of a plot you could get for €14,000. We weren't expecting great things, but because it was remote – which wouldn't appeal to everyone (though it was fine with us) – we thought we just might find a bargain. It'll give us a 'baseline', I told Linda, from which we could assess other plots.

Three hours out we drove along a very minor road, up into the hills, passing fewer and fewer vehicles until we got above the treeline, drove into a thick fog, and began to wonder if we should have left word where we were going. Crawling along in second gear with my head out of the driver-side window so I could see the road better made the journey seem endless, and still we climbed. As I drove I thought of the two French drivers who had met quite literally head on by both doing what I was doing now, coming at each other from opposite directions... but oncoming traffic never came.

The plot lay to the right of the road, next to a double bend – we could see that from the map – so when we got to a promising-looking bend and saw a pile of stones (even though there was no estate agent's sign, which must have blown down, or got caught in the wheels of a passing jet) we knew we had arrived. As I turned the ignition off I imagined the fantastic views that would be ours on fog-free days, and already liked it.

'Are you coming?' I said to Linda, who seemed less enthusiastic.

'You go.' I climbed out of the car and breathed in the clean air with exaggerated pleasure, and then stepped into a bog so deep that I when I looked back at Linda, who was at last beginning to enjoy herself, my chin was level with the driver's seat. Having managed to get one leg out, I pulled out the other to find an eel in my lap.

'Anyway,' I said, when Linda had stopped snorting long enough for me get a word in, 'now we know what you get for 14 grand.'

The other bargains we crossed off our list either because they were in someone's back garden, because they were a few yards from a road on which everyone seemed to be attempting a land speed record, or because they were on a bend blackened with skid marks, which began on one carriageway and ended on the other among a litter of broken glass and bits of bumper. We'd got a couple of days with the car, so we went exploring to see if we could find an unadvertised plot just by being in the right place at the right time... you never know your luck.

Just across the River Sheen, County Kerry, a homely looking board nailed to a post banged into the ground at an odd angle advertised *The Falls B+B*, so we followed it and pulled up at a modern bungalow farmhouse on the outskirts of Kenmare, scattering some free range ducks, and gravel; and opened the car doors to the roar of tumbling water. We arrived just as the farmer's wife was coming out, wearing a matching coat and hat and carrying a wicker basket.

'It's a lovely day!' she greeted us. It certainly was, and we all stood around admiring it for a few moments.

'Do you have a room available?'

'Well now, sure we do,' she said, undoing the buttons of the coat she'd just done up. 'It would be just the two of you, would it?' She opened the front door and led the way into the house. 'Let me just make you a lovely pot of tea, and would you take a few sandwiches... or scones?' Only with the greatest difficulty did we persuade her not to let us interrupt her original plans.

The falls

'Well, if you're sure…' she said, doubtfully. 'I was just away to the shops – so if there is anything in particular you'd like for your breakfast?'

'Ooh – black pudding!' Linda said, emphatically. I looked at her to see if she was being funny – but no.

'You like the black pudd'n? Well, you're in luck. Sneem, not too far from here, is famous for the makin' of the black pudd'n, so it is.'

We enquired about the waterfall, and left to go and explore it; and then drove back into town for dinner in a pub that had been styled on an American ranch and used that as an excuse for a menu offering eight variations of steak, chips and peas.

The soft marshmallow bed consumed us and we arose the following morning, warm as dough, smacking our lips and trying to remember what planet we were on. We sat alone at breakfast as Nora – our hostess – carried in two plates each piled high with bacon, duck's eggs, tomatoes, mushroom, and two enormous slices of Sneem black pudding, with the triumphant smile of a woman who knows that her breakfasts satisfy the passions they arouse.

'There we go!' She folded her hands gracefully in front of her. 'Now then – is there anything else I can get you?'

'Not a thing in the world!'

When she had gone, Linda and I beamed at each other, I secretly scanning her for signs of misgivings about the very bloody-looking black pudding which clung wetly to our plates, and which I had up until that moment assumed were eaten cooked. I felt sure Linda wouldn't eat it and watched her from the corner of my eye as I put a morsel into my mouth. My stomach heaved; it tasted like you were mucking out a pigsty with your tongue. Linda put a piece in her mouth, chewed it, and then stopped... as did my heart.

'Mmm!' she said, looking at me with an appreciative smile, 'not bad, are they?'

I slipped my two slices onto her plate, but she wouldn't accept them – two was enough, she said – forcing me to wrap mine in my napkin, sprint along the corridor to our room, throw them in the luggage, and sprint back to the table before my absence was discovered.

After breakfast we sat chatting with Nora and Johnny, her husband, getting along like a house on fire for a couple of hours – and when I was sure they wouldn't resent us, I told them of our secret purpose, that we were interested in buying a ruin. Did they know of anywhere? Yes, more than one – and described in detail one in particular, a mile or two away; gave us the address of the owners in case we liked it, and told us how much they were looking forward to having us as neighbours.

You could see the ruin from the road, sitting on elevated ground at the top of a long, hedged field, white-peppered with grazing sheep and bordered on one side by a stream. The house looked over a valley four or six miles wide to the Killarney National Park and on to the distant blue-tinged summit of Carrauntoohil beyond. It was hard to imagine how anyone could choose *not* to live here, but all that remained inside the stone-walled house, with its sycamore saplings growing from the roof, was an iron bed frame, some aluminium saucepans in an old cupboard, and a pile of leaves heaped by the eddying wind that came in from the gap under the door. A swallow, who laid first claim to the house, flew in at the window to add to her nest stuck to the side of a floor joist above our heads.

Following directions to the owner's spanking-new farmhouse – a sprawling bungalow at the end of a tarmac drive, defended by what looked like a pair of Second World War machine gun emplacements topped by statues of eagles – I walked past a picture window and saw both husband and wife, discussing something important judging by their irritated glances when they spotted me. It was too late to turn back. The farmer's wife came to the door, listened to me explain myself nervously, and then relayed my message rather unnecessarily to the man who sat a few feet away from her.

'Well now,' he said, joining us, 'no, we hadn't thought of selling – but since you ask, perhaps we could give some thought in that direction.' The conversation grew warmer as we talked back and forth; Linda arrived, and soon we were invited in to discuss the practicalities: 'What would you do for water, I wonder?'

The farmer's wife had introduced herself as Catherine, and her husband as Johnny, that evidently being a popular name just there. Keen to sweep away all obstacles, I told her of the arrangements Fausty had made at her church by boring for water… but regretted it when I thought I saw in her face sacrilegious shock that England had become a Gomorrah where you could buy yourself a church as a house.

'The borehole is in the graveyard,' I explained.

'Stopitttt! Stopittt!' she said, not sure if I was teasing.

'Don't worry – it goes down about 300 feet,' which brought me to another thought: 'but now you mention it – it does always smell a bit funny…'

'Stopittt!' she said – certain by now that I was joking. It does, though.

Catherine turned to her husband: 'I wonder, now, should they go to see Moira's ole place – seein' as they're here like?'

Moira and her husband, she explained, had lived in a remote farmhouse on the other side of the mountain – not far as the crow flies – but 20 miles to drive. She lived there until her husband died, quite suddenly; and on the very *day* he died, she moved out and never went back.

'And when I say "moved out",' Catherine underlined, 'I mean she just *walked out*, like… not taking a ting with her.

You'll find everything just as she left it – 15 years ago... you'll be in for a shock, mind,' she warned.

'Sounds exciting,' I said.

'It's just a ruin now,' she cautioned; and then, remembering what had brought us there, added, 'but you obviously won't mind that.'

They gave us instructions on how to find the place, and a key to the front door. As we were leaving, Catherine called out mysteriously, 'You'll be all right going in – I wouldn't go there myself, mind – but just you get your courage up and you'll be fine.'

Round the other side of the mountain we turned off the 'main' road – a single-track road with potholes – onto a boreen badly in need of grazing. At the junction there was a close-cut field with a stack of silage wrapped in black plastic, on which the farmer had experimentally tried to solve the perennial problem of crow damage by scrawling in white paint – one letter to each bale – 'FEK OFF CROWS!' Our lane wound on for eight more miles before petering out in the mountains – near the distant end we found the rusting iron gate we had been told to look out for and parked up, as advised, to complete the journey on foot.

In the still air a buzzard shrieked distantly as it rode a thermal up the mountain; a rabbit the other side of the gate ran for cover; sheep stopped browsing; and everything seemed startled to see a human – even the gate squeaked with surprise as we opened it. My pulse raced with excitement as we walked down the mossy concrete drive, which had been contoured to drain surface water – of which they obviously got a lot – into a stream. In the meadows, the long grass blown by eddying winds had collapsed into stooks; hedges were choked with bramble; and a small copse of scrubby trees hid an inky interior in its shadows. It was when we crossed the ford that we caught our first glimpse of the sagging ridge of the small farmhouse, hidden among a stand of spruce trees planted to offer protection from winter gales. The single-storey house had been extended into the roof space and a pair of crumbling dormer windows stuck out of it amateurishly; each had a dirty-grey net curtain, water-stained and drooping with age.

Unpainted render clung to the walls of the house and a scattering of barns and sheds, whose gaping doors hung from baler twine in frames so low you had to duck to get in them. Signs of former use lay neatly stacked inside each: a wooden pail for milking; feed troughs; old leather harnesses; 'peats' – still tinder dry, indicating a fuel store; bales of straw, dusty dry; and a copper for clothes-washing... together with hundreds of other interesting but unidentified knick-knacks accumulated over generations of smallholding.

Linda didn't want to go into the house – so I slid the key into the sturdy padlock that secured a broken front door, at which the latch came away in my hand. I pushed my head in.

'Hello?' I was startled, first to hear my own voice in the house, then by a noise whispering in my ear; it was the mechanical chattering of an old electricity meter mounted, very practically, next to the front door in what was the sitting room – and which had been waiting 15 long years for someone to turn on a light (but who would pay the bill?). Its noise exaggerated the stillness of the house. The first room – the first of only two rooms on the ground floor – had a sofa, stained and torn, together with two wooden chairs, huddled into a group in front of a large open fireplace of rough-hewn stone, their legs buried in several inches of soot, which had collapsed from the chimney to spew over the floor. The fire had also served for cooking – a cauldron hung from a blacksmith-made wrought-iron arm, which was swung incongruously over the sofa... inside, a few bones, and the same black dust as had settled on every surface in the room, even obscuring the gaudy images on crockery propped up for display in a Welsh dresser by the door. A pair of mouldering leather shoes had been set to one side of the fire to dry, and an outdoor coat hung from the back of one of the chairs.

The room above this one had partially collapsed into it – its floor was supported by the top shelf of a second Welsh dresser. The back door, which was 12 feet away from the front door and faced it, was badly gnawed at the bottom and no longer reached the ground.

The spiral stairs came away from the wall when I tried to climb them, and swayed under my weight – so I stopped on the fourth stair by a window, on the sill of which lay the cardboard sleeve from a tube of Colgate toothpaste advertising *threepence off* – in old money. From there I could see into the gloomy bedroom where the doors of a hand-built wardrobe had burst open, spilling piles of clothing onto the floor. An adult 'cot' bed had been built from three sheets of white-painted plywood bolted together... it was unmade, and a brown woollen cardigan sagged limply from where it had been hung at the bedhead. Placed conveniently on the floor next to the bed was a cylindrical tin with a perforated lid, labelled 'Louse Powder'.

These images made a striking impression on my mind and gave me a glimpse into the deeply personal life of a poor Irish family who had lived on a remote mountain farm – whether in struggle or blissful contentment it was hard to guess... but I envied them its location, at the very least.

Returning the key to Johnny and Catherine, we told them we would be interested in knowing what price they had in mind for the farm, at which they promised to get it valued – but even as they spoke I sensed something had changed; they had remembered something, perhaps, and weren't selling. We arranged to phone them in a month.

Back at Kilmore Quay, where we had left our boat, I returned from having showered to find Linda – who is one of the most peacefully contented people I know – standing on the pontoon involved in a yelling match with one of the harbour officials. The argument seemed to be that he wanted cash, and Linda wanted to pay by card; but at the end of it, I don't think either of them knew what it was *really* about.

We sailed up the coast and put into Arklow to see if James would remember us, and whether he had any cloakroom tickets left. The place hadn't changed at all, though it seemed quieter.

'Ach – de fishin is dead. Ders no one doin' it any more,' James told us, casting his eye around the oily walls of the harbour where rusting fishing boats lay quietly in their berths, hanging from limp mooring lines. The air smelt of rotting fish, doubtless coming from the shells of whelks that stuck out from where they were jammed in hamster wheels – contraptions used to sieve the right-size whelks out from the muddy detritus dredged up from the bottom.

'Anyway – you're in luck,' he continued, never failing to strike a note of hope; 'ders live music goin' on in town.'

From Arklow we sailed out on a cheerless morning toward Howth, rolling over an agitated sea that rose and fell in grey hummocks, reflecting the sky. If every day were like this, the glamour would go out of yachting. In order to beat the tide, which flowed against us, we motor-sailed.

Sitting down below to re-solder a joint on the GPS aerial, I was aware that Linda – who had been calling me on deck – was beginning to get grumpy; finally she announced, in a voice that suggested it was beyond her control, that we were about to run over a pot buoy... and moments later I heard the engine revs slow down and begin to labour as the polypropylene line from the buoy wrapped itself around our propeller. I pulled the decompressor and allowed the dying gasps of the engine to expire, then went on deck to find Linda unrepentant and pointing in the direction of the damage I'd caused – there was a taut blue line streaming away from our propeller, plunging down to the depths where there might be as many as 400 pots on the sea bed. I got a carving knife from the galley with the intention of cutting the line, but hesitated when I wondered if cutting it meant that some struggling fisherman would lose 400 pots.

I called the coastguard to ask for advice.

'Nah – cut it,' he said. 'How yoos going to do it?'

'With a kitchen knife – I might be able to reach it from on board; otherwise I'll go over the side.'

'How many people do you have on board?'

'Two.'

'Whoa – now just you hold on there!... stand by for five minutes.' I liked the way this was beginning to sound, and told Linda so – the water didn't look too inviting as it sucked past us; it looked cold, and the line was under considerable strain from the tide, which wanted to carry us, and the pots we were now attached to, away. We heard our name again on the radio.

'OK, just hold on where you are – the lifeboat has launched and will be with you in 10 minutes. Are you wearing lifejackets?'

'Yes – both wearing lifejackets.' I thanked him, and then we set about putting our lifejackets on and making everything else aboard the boat look seamanlike for their arrival. Within a few minutes we saw the unmistakeable orange-over-white of a lifeboat on a 'shout' with a bone in its mouth, still about 3 miles away. Ten minutes later their boat roared up and then dropped off the plane as the engine revs were wound down to idle, surfing the last 20 yards to us on its own bow wave, and stopping alongside with well-practised precision.

'Is everyone OK?' a voice hailed.

'Yes – all fine.'

'And – where is de rope?'

'Streaming away here,' I indicated by lowering and raising my arm from our stern in the direction of the line.

'OK – we're going to go ahead of yoos, and see if we can pick it up from der.'

'Righto!' I said.

'Where are they going?' Linda asked when she emerged from below – having attended to a crashing noise we'd heard on their arrival – and saw them motoring away.

'Ahead – he says he's going to try to pick the line up from there.' We shrugged at each other and settled down to watch how they did it. A grapnel was being tossed through the air and into the water to be retrieved repeatedly from different directions according to the enthusiastic chorus of suggestion from eight of the crew who lined the safety rail.

'Try dis side! Try dat!' Then, calling up to the coxswain, 'Go round again.'

Twenty minutes later they called to us, 'Where was it you saw the line?'

'It's here – trailing away from the stern.' I pointed it out again.

They motored to the stern, saw the line, cast the grapnel, picked it up, and with the help of many hands in tug of war formation, got it close to the surface by the grapnel line.

'Tie that off! – Tie it off on that cleat back there.' Their man shouted the orders then lay on his belly on deck and tried to reach the line with his hand, but couldn't.

'Everyone... hold my ankles!' He got his hand within inches.

'Lower me down!' He grabbed it.

'Pass me de knife!' One of the crew ran back inside the boat to fetch a knife, while the group holding his ankles froze like athletes on the starting block.

'Here!' said the runner, passing a knife.

'Got it!' For half a minute he sawed energetically at the rope without cutting a fibre; he stopped, looked at the knife, and then sawed a bit more.

'Get me a sharp one!' he yelled, passing up the blunt knife, and sounding irritable. The runner took the knife and ran back to the accommodation. The rest froze again. Another knife was passed to the dangling man, red-faced from inversion, and as soon as he touched it against the rope it parted with a wet crack. Our boat, released from her tether, became animated once more and heaved away on the tide, released, but with her propeller still badly fouled.

The lifeboat crew pulled their man back on board; he got to his feet, turned to us, and with a comical wave of his hand called, 'OK – see yoos,' and walked away to a chorus of laughter; then he ran back. 'Only joking! We're going to trow you a line. Now dis first one is just de heavin' line, you'll need to pull it all on board and you'll find de end is tied to a ticker rope, de hawser – dat's the towing line – attach dat one to a strong point on your boat – d'ya onderstand?'

'Yes – got that.'

A monkey's fist – a decoratively tied ball of rope – arced through the air, whizzed past my head and struck the deck behind me... it sounded like it had a bronze nut in it. It was a great shot – the ball was attached to a lightweight fluorescent line, which covered me like party string sprayed from a can, and which I pulled in-board hand over hand, shortly coming to the end of it – there was nothing attached. I looked up to see the lifeboat crew leaning idly against the rail in the way that people do when they're watching someone work. I held up the empty end of the string questioningly; they admired it for a moment before jumping visibly. 'Where's de hawser?' someone shouted at me accusingly.

'Here!' came the answer from someone on their boat, and he willingly held it above his head for inspection.

'Well, why didn't you...' He cut his question short, and recomposed himself.

'Right – get anudder heavin' line.' Before long another well-aimed shot came arcing through the air, following exactly the trajectory of the first, and leaving me once again in a tangle of pink line. I hauled away at this second rope hand over hand as before, but by inspiration stopped early and, looking up, saw the crew member with the hawser settle himself down to make a really good job of a sheet bend, while we all looked on patiently.

I dropped the 'eye' of the hawser over our Samson post, secured it, and then called across that we were all set, adding to it the sign they'd shown me – crossing my forearms into an 'X' – by way of confirmation. A shout went up that we were ready; the helmsman spun his wheel for home and threw down the control lever to produce an alarming jet of foam and black smoke as the engine roared away... We reached 12 knots and I fought with the tiller to keep from sheering.

'I've just heard them on the radio,' Linda said, half-climbing out of the hatch and leaning toward me with a confidential whisper, 'they were telling "base" that it would be a while before they were back because we didn't have a suitable towing point, so they were having to go slowly.'

'Jesus... this is slow?'

Passing through Dalkey Sound, our speed set up a scour in the shallow water and the boat became the very next thing to uncontrollable – bending our bowsprit perilously each time the straining tow rope got under it. We passed close by a group of motor cruisers who were casting lines into good fishing water, judging by how many boats had congregated on the spot; on board one of them a Chinese man caught my eye and covered his mouth with a cupped hand, bouncing his shoulders as if to let us know that we were the ridiculous object of some joke.

The lifeboat placed us quietly into a berth in the mirror-calm waters of the marina at Dun Laoghaire, where we had a chance to thank the crew for getting us out of danger.

I dived over the side with a carving knife, cleared the propeller from its welded ball of polypropylene – and even in that controlled environment still managed to cut the back of my hand.

The following morning we heard our name called on the radio as we were motoring out – it was the marina office, asking if we'd left.

'We're leaving now.'

'My name is Hal Bleakley and I've just heard that you were brought in to us by the lifeboat – we never like to make money out of someone's misfortune, so if you can hang on for five minutes I'll come out to you in a launch... I'd like to refund part of your mooring fee.' We stopped, spent a few minutes hoisting sails, and sure enough the general manager, looking quite regal in a piloted launch, shook me by the hand, gave us half our money back, and handed us a compliment slip wishing us a safe passage and apologising for 'not acting more quickly'.

Next stop was Strangford Lough, and sailing back through the entrance felt like coming home – we tied up to the same mooring buoy, guessing that its owner was somewhere in the Arctic muffled in the warmth of his beard, and sat down in the afternoon sun to reacquaint ourselves with the scenery. Black guillemots flew past us, their wings whirring, on their way to nesting boxes hung from the stone-built harbour wall; in their beaks, silver fry still flapped their tails. Having delivered the food to their nest, they would emerge to preen, then whir down once more with their red webbed feet stretched out before them, braced for a crash landing on water. The harbour wall surrounded the well-manicured lawn of an old house, set back a discreet distance from waterborne activity. In fact it must have been a very old house – occupying the position that you would choose if you got here first.

Inspired by the success of the guillemots, I cast a rubber lure into the clear water and allowed my line to be swept out into the whirlpools at the edge of the swift current. Casting and retrieving mechanically, I couldn't believe my eyes when a large sea trout came to the surface with my lure, but I tugged and found that he wasn't on my hook, merely curious. I cast again, and again he followed it up from the deep – then a third time. He was interested, but not so interested that he could be induced to strike – or at least, not by me. Eventually I tried every pattern of lure in my box and he took a polite interest in them all… but when he'd seen all I had to show him, he finned idly away.

The following day I went into the town to see if the beauty salon was still open for business – it was. I opened the door; inside, the hairdresser turned when she heard the door, and had no sooner clapped eyes on me than she called, 'And how are you keeping?'

'You amaze me… you surely don't recognise me?'

'Of course I do – and if it's a haircut you're wanting, I can do you in ten minutes.'

As her scissors clacked we got quite carried away, comparing notes since we last met; exhausting that topic, we moved on to the doings of near, then distant relatives; and finally onto that old saw, the meaning of life. By the time we bade each other cheery farewells I was as bald as a coot, and looked thuggish. Louts crossed the street to avoid me.

Walking out of town to breathe once again the balmy air of Audley's Wood at Castleward, I had the good fortune of finding a £10 note blown into the brambles at the side of the road, and at first counted my blessings; but on reflection imagined the mournful face of someone even poorer than I, if such a one exists, who had perhaps lost the note; and so walked back a quarter of a mile along the road to the newsagent, handed it in, and asked if they would keep it behind the counter in case anyone came for it. Happening to be in there again a couple of days later, the newsagent called to me from across the shop, 'Was it you who brought the £10 note in the other day?'

'Yes.'

'Well, a man came in for it, he lives at Cedar Wood [name changed to protect the innocent] – do you know it?' From the description that followed, I knew the house – it had electric security gates, which opened onto a drive of white gravel sprinkled with lapis lazuli leading to a garage the size of a tithe barn, and on to a vulgarly ostentatious house concealed among the trees – all in all, the glittering reward for a lifetime spent milking hard-working people of their money as an ant will an aphid.

'He tells me it was 20 pounds he lost, and I was to ask you – are you sure it was just the one note you found?' The newsagent wore a suspicious frown; and from all corners of the shop, customers threw glances in my direction to know what a thief looked like.

My reward will be in heaven.

To be absolutely candid – I did come close to stealing later that day when I walked further along the road and saw what I took to be artichokes growing in someone's garden. I'd never seen them growing before, and had to wait until I was back on board and could look it up to be sure they were indeed artichokes – I planned to return under cover of darkness and take one, but decided not to risk slurring my name further, having already had a taste of the kind of justice that was on offer in this town.

Our friend Joe – who gave us a lottery ticket on our last visit – told us he was moving inland to the countryside, and that we wouldn't be seeing him any more. We could hear in his voice that he didn't want to move; and Charles the naval man obliged Linda with another bath, but checked first that she had had one between times.

Having exchanged parting gifts with Joe, we jumped on the tide one fine morning and sailed with a propitious wind for the Copeland Islands, passing a fleet of a dozen huge trawlers all ploughing the same furrow close inshore. They seemed to be taking part in a competition to deplete a sandbank against the clock. When they had come to the end of one run at dredging speed, they would turn hard and steam full ahead to get back and begin another; we never saw such frenetic activity at sea.

Late that afternoon we dropped anchor in the quiet waters of the Copeland Islands once again, though we weren't feeling so lonely as the last time we were here – not only were we in brighter mood, but we weren't alone. Four skinheads in a speedboat came roaring up to us, circled us once – which pisses yachties off more than power-boaters realise – and then stopped alongside. Because I always think the worst of folk, I immediately assumed that they had come to hurl some abuse at us, and was more than a bit intimidated by their behaviour – but no, they had spotted my haircut, recognised me as one of their own, and came to greet me with a cheery, 'Focken! Focken! Focken!'

'Yes!' I agreed, and then followed it up with, 'That looks like a fast boat you have there?'

'Ach – it's fast enough, I s'pose… this is the first time we were ever in it,' said one.

'We've no idea what we're doin'!' said another.

'Likewise,' said I. But they didn't believe me – though they might have, had they watched me a day later. In Red Bay my plan was to sail right up to the beach at Glenariff and drop anchor next to the pier. When the anchor had rattled down into eight metres of water by a rusting rail mounted high on a ruined concrete slip, and we had settled back on it, Linda said, 'So where are we?'

I pulled open the chart and prodded my finger at Glenariff pier.

'Right,' she said, unbelievingly. Then she was quiet for a long time, studying it.

Eventually she said, 'I don't think we are there, you know… I think we're *here*.'

'Yes, well, you've got no *spatial* sense.'

'Yes, but look,' she said, and went on to explain her thinking; increasingly as she spoke I realised that she was right, and that we were a mile away from where I supposed we were. It was a rocky shore, but luckily 'clean' where we were, as could be seen by the white sandy bottom. Not needing to move, we stayed put but it was salutary for me to look back and see where I had gone wrong, particularly as the next leg of our trip would deliver us to the wild west coast of Scotland, where one shore looks much like another, and the navigation needs careful attention.

10 FILM STARS AND GYPSIES

The hotel bar looked just as we remembered it – but there was a confident, cheerful, even slightly blasé manner, which hadn't been there before – the islanders of Gigha had bought out their laird and now owned all they surveyed. I fell into conversation with an islander who commutes for two days a week to Hertfordshire – a journey of about 500 miles each way. He was softly spoken and tolerant of all my questions, as he looked down at me through spectacles with thick lenses that made his eyes look small and him look wise. I didn't ask him what he did, but I knew it would be something clever. I envied him his happy combination of interesting employment and stress-free living – five days every week spent on a quiet Scottish island with a population of 150, I mused. As he was extolling the virtues of the island with its many conveniences, he mentioned the visiting GP's surgery. I pricked my ears up at that, I'd been wanting to see a GP myself, and gathered that if I went along to the village hall – an unlikely looking building about the size of a lock-up garage – at 9 am the next day, I would be seen.

'Just go in and sit down in the waiting room – you'll see the doctor will come and get you himself,' he told me.

At 9 am I was pipped to the post by just one other patient; she went in, I waited, and soon we were six. Quiet greetings were exchanged, and then silence fell again. A man in his eighties came in and sat next to me, greeted me with a warm smile, and fell asleep. When he awoke a few minutes later, he jumped to see me sitting at the foot of his bed, as he supposed, and looked me up and down reprovingly. He was just about to ask me what on earth I thought I was doing there when he noticed the others, and pieced it all together.

'Is there anyone in there?' he asked me, tossing his head impatiently in the direction of the surgery.

'Yes,' I smiled.

'God – if you're not ill when you arrive, you'll die waiting,' he said, and fell asleep again.

Waking a few minutes later, he went through the same routine – the startled jump; reproval; recollection; and then: 'Is there anyone in there?'

I nodded.

'If you're not ill when you get here, you'll die waiting.'

After a third performance he woke more fully, and gazed contentedly out of the window at the serenely twinkling azure water and hills beyond, lit by almost impossibly bright sunshine.

'What a lovely day to die,' he said softly. Embarrassing as *I* found it, no one else in the waiting room stirred at his remark.

A few seats away I followed a conversation between two women, enjoying their soft island accent as they compared notes on how they went about the hoovering. Eventually I asked the old man next to me – whose accent was English – 'How long have you been on the island?'

He interrupted the hoover conversation.

'How long have I been on the island, darling?' His slightly cynical 'darling' suggested they'd been together for many years, not all of them harmonious.

His wife broke away from her conversation just long enough to call, 'Forty years.'

'Forty years! Ha!' The old man slapped his hand on his thigh. 'No, come on,' he said, 'how long?'

'Forty years!' she snapped back.

The old man was startled.

'Forty years?' he asked, weakly; then more assertively: 'No, come on, I was living in New Zealand for 12 years – when did I go out there?'

'1952,' she said, without looking up.

The old man did the mathematics and then sat playing with his hands, lost in his own thoughts. 'Forty years,' he kept repeating, as though trying to come to terms with it.

On our way to Tayvallich, which was to be our next stop, *Caol Ila* raced along with a bone between her teeth; the island of Jura lay on one side, the mainland on the other, as we spanked along through a stretch of water historically known as the Sea of Disappointment owing to its contrary tides and the fluky winds, which eddy in the shadow of the high ground. On the day we passed through the tide was behaving itself, but on our left the dark hills of Jura were soon blotted out by a white wall of rain as a squall swept down from its summit and approached us across the water. I had only time to put on my wet-weather gear when the first generously sized drops of rain began drumming on deck and firing into the surface of the sea, blurring it in spray.

As off the coast of France, we simply eased the sheets rather than taking in sail, but it took something to hold our nerve. Violent squalls of wind seem almost to have a personality – not entirely malevolent, but sobering. When this one hit, *Caol Ila* reeled like a punched drunk. Rain fell with biblical abundance, overwhelming the scuppers and double cockpit drains and carrying away coils of rope to trail in the water astern. I eased the sheets until the sails flogged, then started them back in until they just drew; and set like that we crashed along at 10 knots over a foaming sea blown flat by the wind. Five minutes later we burst through to the other side of the squall – the rain stopped, *Caol Ila* righted herself, and sunlight danced off the water. Within a minute the dark wood of our decks began to steam from the sun's heat. The weather in Scotland isn't 'bad' – but it *is* changeable.

We sailed into the smooth waters of Loch Sween, saw the thousand-year-old castle with a caravan park set incongruously alongside it, and heard the voices of excited children playing at their imaginary sea adventures, drifting to us across the water. Suddenly the authoritative voice of an eight-year-old – realising that we had come to take the castle from them (or what remained of it since its destruction by the Irish in

1640) – shouted: 'Look, there's a pirate ship!' The air was rent with blood-curdling screams from girls who had seen the truth of it with their own eyes and now ran for cover; the boys made a momentary heroic final stand before giving up their position as hopeless, and followed them.

The village of Tayvallich sits on the shores of what is virtually a salt lake, cut off from the main body of Loch Sween except by two small openings a few yards wide. Hurricane-force winds roaring over the top of the steep hills that surround it have no more effect than to ripple the surface of the water with cat's-paws. Locals warned us that they were exposed to easterly winds, yet the grassy banks that roll down to the water's edge and face east were thriving, so we reasoned that it was all relative.

The village is surrounded by green pinnacles of hills thickly wooded with mature beech and oak, and carpets of bluebells and white wild garlic grow from the rich soil in due season – conditions that must equally have suited the luxuriant moustache of a rugged and powerful man of about 50 who composed himself against his pick-up truck as we walked up the slip to stretch our legs and breathe in the warm vegetation.

'She's a fine-looking boat ya have there,' he said, without looking at us as we passed. I'd seen his face before, but couldn't remember where. Then the penny dropped – his was the sober, handsomely chiselled face of the Scottish Dragoon Guard who looks out from every box of shortbread, cigars or whisky when their manufacturers want to stress the peerless nature of their brand. 'Build her yarsell?' Although his Highland accent was thick, it was easy to follow because of its organised delivery, like volleys of musket fire. He'd been a boatbuilder – owned a timber yard, too; and was knowledgeable about both the style of our boat and about wooden boats in general.

Over the next few days we often saw him cruising along in his white pick-up truck, being one of those villagers whose veiled work kept him continually circumnavigating the bay in third gear. I imagined him to be fiercely patriotic, willing to defend his country to the last drop – particularly when the invader was an Englishman – so I hesitated to ask him the question most on my mind, but plucked up courage one evening when he was just leaving the pub, and I was just going in.

'We're interested in buying a building plot hereabouts, Duncan – would you happen to know of any?'

An iron hand gripped my shoulder and manoeuvred me into the shadowy corner of the entrance porch where he crowded me in, breathing alcohol over me, and blotting out what remained of the twilight. I watched a stubbly chin as rough as a badger's arse move toward my ear; and after leaving a significant silence, it said: '*I've* got some land for you...' Then he withdrew his face to watch my reaction.

The next time we met Duncan it was on an anonymous apron of tarmac used for three-point turns by vehicles that have discovered that the single-track road they've been following doesn't go anywhere. We walked up to his pick-up truck with hopeful smiles, glancing at the empty fields around us.

'This isn't it,' he said, reading our thoughts. He tapped the side of his nose: 'Walls have ears.' He led the way up the road, dressed in a Tattersal check shirt, stained with blood at the collar from a bad wound received while shaving, and the plus-four tweeds of a gillie. After a couple of hundred yards he stopped and turned to face us, gazing into the middle distance over our heads to disguise us as three people standing around waiting for something more interesting to happen.

'If you look over my left shoulder,' he said, without moving his lips, 'you'll be looking at the plot. You'll have to get planning permission – no problem there – and I'm selling it to you for £40,000. That-is-an-absolute-*bargain*, round here.' He articulated the last part in staccato to help us realise the privilege of the position in which we found ourselves.

The location was pleasant. A 'wee burn' tumbled through the middle of it, busily chattering like children on their way to the beach. It didn't have much of a view, being in a cleft; and it was overlooked by a couple of houses – the occupants of which wouldn't fail to object to a new development outside their front gate.

'Do you mind if I jump over the fence and take a closer look?' I asked.

'Be my guest.'

I vaulted over the fence and sunk to my knees in soft mud. I was about to take another step when I noticed that this was the driest part of the plot... nearer the burn, surface water stood about in muddy pools. Linda and I exchanged an 'Irish Plot' look, and a cartoon came into my mind whereby a huntsman on horseback, up to his saddle in a bog, complains to a farmer who is looking on: 'I thought you said there was a bottom to this bog?' 'Aye, an' so there is – but you ain't found 'un yet.'

Duncan didn't comment on the mud just then – but on the walk back to his truck he decided it was only fair to bring it to our attention.

'You'd need to do something a bit different wi' the foonz...' he said, using local site language for 'foundations', and went on to describe a piece of ground-breaking technology developed by a friend of his to give firmament to a shed – and for which he might grant us a licence. Hundreds of scaffold poles are set 'end on' in a slab of concrete and lowered, spiky side down, into the mud. An alternative idea, I thought, was that we could have our boat lifted onto the site, and tie it to a fence.

We left Tayvallich to explore the coast for more winter anchorages and, entering one, surprised a dozen basking seals as we slipped into it between spurs of rock set just far enough apart to allow our passage, and which formed themselves into rocky canals. The seals threw themselves into the water in disbelief, bobbing to the surface a moment later to blink their astonishment and turn to one another as if to say, 'Well, I never did!'

The channel lead to a plashy pool only as deep and as wide as an ornamental duck pond in a municipal park, enclosed by fingers of Forestry Commission land on which the tall trees sheltered its mirrored surface from the ravaging wind – and promised us a never-ending supply of winter fuel into the bargain. Recluded in the protective womb of our newly discovered anchorage, we found ourselves floating above a tangled carpet of black spiny starfish. Drifting about the rocky islets in the dinghy one day, I noticed a shape in the silty sand that I thought I recognised as I wafted over it, and stopped to pick it up, using the blades of both oars as tongs. At the surface I found I'd got an oyster the size of a side plate, and that other members of its extended family were sprinkled on the silty bottom all around. Nearby, a colony of giant mussels clung to rocks, and I gathered some for supper. Back on board I opened the oyster and noticed among the huge frills of meat that a part of it was quite dark in a speckledy sort of way, which I hadn't noticed in any others, and so tried a morsel very cautiously... It was utterly delicious; for the first time in my life I didn't have to pretend to be enjoying an oyster straight from the shell. It seems that oysters thrive in brackish water where they get a rich diet, and their livers grow like those of French geese. The water hereabouts, too, would certainly be more pure than most of the sites from which we gathered shellfish.

We discovered a footpath in the forest within half a mile of where our boat lay, and found that if we followed it for 2 miles – past the ruins of a village abandoned a hundred years ago – we came to a road. Half a mile beyond that our phone beeped to let us know it had found a signal. Another hour's walk brought us to a village store. Four buses per day passed back and forth to the town with its supermarket – but local information cautioned against depending on it.

'Och – they don't always run... you're just as well hitchin' – someone will always stop,' we were told. And they *did*, sometimes to offer us a lift, sometimes to explain why they couldn't.

From where we lay at anchor, I noticed a petrified oak tree, long since expired, atop a little cliff which overhung the water; its bark and pulpwood had rotted away, leaving only the harder heartwood. It was as spare as an antler. A tree like that, parchment dry, would keep us alive for a month in the winter, and so I set about sawing it down. I didn't use the chainsaw for fear of disturbing the wildlife or the rangers.

Linda posted herself on the footpath as lookout and I began the long process of felling it with a carpentry saw, shoving it from time to time to see if it was ready to topple into the water, from where I could get at it by boat. At last I was able to push it very nearly off balance and had it swaying back and forth like a drunk, teetering on the edge of the cliff, but never quite falling. As I picked up my saw to apply myself to one last bout of sawing, something caught my eye, and I peeped over the edge of the cliff to where 20 feet below I was staggered to see, in this remote spot, a solitary canoeist floating directly under the tree, lying back on his boat, sunbathing. How long he had been there I don't know – he appeared to be asleep... there can be no other explanation for the fact that he hadn't seen my tree swaying above him. I tied the tree securely back with a rope to continue work another day, and the canoeist's life was prolonged.

Back at Tayvallich, I was just telling Shona – who spent summers aboard her boat with her husband Iain, now that they had retired – about the abandoned village nearby: '...A collection of six or eight stone "black" houses and a mill – all roofless – but otherwise intact, and a drover's road rising up the hill beyond.'

The Forestry Commission had bought the land and planted it in the 1930s – but even though the forest now crowds up around it, it's possible to imagine life in the village set in an inexpressibly sweet little dell, surrounded by lush grazing and salt marsh.

'The village is believed to have been continuously inhabited for at least a thousand years, and was abandoned less than a hundred years ago,' I said, thinking I was telling her something she didn't know. 'There's a well, too, marked with a cross slab, and the water is still sweet – I myself drank from it and survived, as you see.' She listened patiently. 'Do you know whereabouts I mean?'

'Aye, I do,' she said, bouncing the grey curls of her hair; 'and was my ane grannie not one of them that was the last to live there?'

Shona and Iain planned to spend a day helping a friend to take his boat through the Crinan Canal, and Linda asked if she could join them. The Crinan Canal, a few miles from where we were speaking, is a 9-mile waterway dug 200 years ago to provide access from the Atlantic waters in the Sound of Jura to the Clyde, and on to Glasgow – saving a 130-mile detour. On the canal, Linda, Shona and Iain were held back at the locks by the boat ahead. Linda says that they stood out as an unusual crew from first glance... in spite of the streaming rain, the four people on board – a woman in her forties and three teenage girls – were dressed for the high street in their heels; coatless; and shivering from the rain. The two boats shared crews to make lighter work of the lock gates and, as the conversation between them grew, it transpired that there had been more of them on board – some boys – but they had left because they'd been unhappy with food shortages and lack of dry clothing, while the girls stuck together to support their aunt.

At Ardrishaig, the distant end of the canal, Shona bought the girls fish and chips; took them to a laundry to dry their clothes; and gave them money for food later in their journey – but the journey didn't go on for much longer. We read in a newspaper that the Clyde coastguard had a call from a yacht asking on which side they should pass the buoys in the Clyde – which is a bit like asking a policeman which way you should drive round a roundabout, and is bound to raise an eyebrow. The Clyde is busy with shipping for Glasgow and dogged by fast tides and shoals, so the coastguard asked a lifeboat to look for them. They found the yacht aground, and the crew attempting to wade ashore, which – owing to gullies, soft mud and rip tides – they could not have reached.

We spent the rest of that summer cruising among the jagged peaks and spectacular wildernesses of the west coast, where history litters the shore – every protected hollow conceals tumbled stones set up for a forgotten purpose by wee crofters or early Christians, who left only these signs. We loved all we saw. In preparation for spending a winter on board here in Scotland – the winter with which I began my story – we had nosed our way into countless rocky pools to inspect them for the security they offered against howling winds; and what we had found assured us we would be safe. We'd made a mental note of standing deadwood that would be ready seasoned for the fire, and which would be essential to keep and cheer us. And as autumn arrived, we carried out maintenance jobs on the boat, which would be difficult when the weather was wetter and colder and the days short.

Back in the days of working sail, boats would be beached as part of their daily routine; today, you almost never see it. Far less often do you see boats beached under sail. Four people walking their dogs along the sandy shore as we hove in sight stopped to admire our sail, but their faces turned to incredulity when they saw us alter course for land. By the time our bow bumped onto the sand, they were speechless – they had actually witnessed a 'boat crash'. I needed a battery for my camera and approached them for ideas of how to solve the problem – but at the sight of me they hurried away, not wishing to intrude in our disaster.

We dry our boat out between tides every couple of months, against a quay when there is one, careened on the beach when there's not. It allows us to scrub away any early weedy growth, and I wanted to investigate a vibration from the propeller shaft. When the tide had left us high and dry, I could see that the cutlass bearing – a sleeve through which the propeller and its shaft emerges, and which is prone to wear – needed replacing; more worryingly, we noticed a swelling between the laminations of our rudder, which indicated that water had become trapped in there, and would need attention. Linda wondered if I could repair it before high water, but unfortunately it was too big a job.

'We'll need to dry it out thoroughly for a week or two before filling it with resin,' I said.

She pulled down the corners of her mouth, knowing that meant having our boat lifted out at a marina, and might cost £1000.

Things happened quickly – the marina we phoned wanted to pluck us out of the water before they got busy with winter liftings; and so a few days later we found ourselves propped up on the tarmac of a dusty yard, with our rudder drying out in a shed. Two or three weeks after that, I could see that the repair, when it was complete, was worth the expense of bringing her ashore. And there were a couple of unexpected benefits from our stay at the marina, too.

Someone came out of the office with a message for us to 'Ring Hans about some film work'. Intrigued, I called the number. 'Hans? – this is Justin.'

'Oh ay! I was wondering – would ya boat be available for some film work?' I was particularly flattered by the note in his voice which implied it might not, and without sounding too desperate, I hope, assured him that it would. The voice on the other end of the telephone belonged to a fisherman who had seen our boat sailing around in the area, and whom a film company had asked to muster 'historic' boats to his pier in Carsaig to make a film set for a 1920s fishing village. He asked how much we *usually* charged, at which I suggested a couple of hundred pounds... and he heard the price without astonishment.

We giggled at the possibility of some film work without really expecting it to come off, but were wide-eyed when the fisherman called back just as we'd completed our repairs to say: 'Are you still at the marina? – only, there's the Art Director coming up to see you jess noo. Take care what you say about the money,' he cautioned; '...I've told 'em you'll do it for a thousand a day.'

'A thousand *pounds*?'

'Yes.'

'A *day*?'

'A day.' You could have knocked me down with a fender.

'How did you pull that one off?' He explained that in putting together the rest of the flotilla, he'd only been able to find old-looking rowing boats and daysailing craft; and that he'd charged *them* out at a couple of hundred pounds a day – which left him no choice but to name a higher price for the 'big boat'. The Art Director arrived, fell in love with our boat, and told us that they would be filming in November.

The second piece of luck we had at the marina was meeting the interesting gypsy caravan owner and ex-drug abuser, Graham. His boat was chocked next to us in the yard as he was chainsawing out the accommodation from his Folkboat; and it was he who offered me the prospect of employment with the words: *There's a bloke wants some work done on his fishing boat, and he's heard I'm good with wood... I'm going to see him tomorrow morning; d'you want to come along?*

We got the job, you'll recall; and on the first morning we were to start work, I was up early, Linda handed me a packed lunch, Graham's truck pulled up – and suddenly it seemed a long time until evening.

'I can't work Thursday,' Graham croaked as he swept the rubbish off the passenger seat with his hand and onto the floor to allow me to sit down. 'I've arranged a blessing for *Moonbeam*.' *Moonbeam* was his boat. I clunked the door, but it didn't shut.

'Slam it. Really hard,' Graham told me. I did, and it shut this time, but the handle came off in my hand. I looked at him apologetically.

'It always does that.' He started the engine and we began the first of 30 terrifying journeys to and from work.

'Who's doing the blessing – a vicar?' I was struggling to refit the handle.

'Mike's gonna do it... and I've written a poem. – Just chuck that on the floor.'

'Who's Mike?' Graham snatched the handle from me and chucked it on the floor.

'He lives at Ford – used to be a Hell's Angel.'

'Reverend' Mike

For the next three weeks, Graham and I worked side by side in harmony. It took us a couple of days to discover each other's strengths and to organise ourselves so as to make the most of them. At first, Graham did the measuring: '54¾... 54¾... 54¾,' he repeated as an aide mémoire as he skipped up the ladder. I heard the quick, light fall of his receding footsteps until they stopped in front of a pile of plywood sheets; heard him drag one onto the saw horse; and then his footsteps tripped back until he poked his head through the fo'c'sle hatch above my head. I looked up to see his face framed in a toothless portrait: 'What did I say it was?'

Adding up was a problem area, too: '17½ plus 5 is 23½ .'

By inspiration, he gave up measuring and threw himself on his sculptor's art. Needing to snug a plywood sheet into the sweet curve of the boat's side, he cocked his head at his subject this way and then that, like a Dutch Master; and then drew it freehand onto the plywood sheet with a flourish, using a black marker pen. He pushed his jigsaw along the line, and offered it up... it wasn't even close; he turned the sheet over – that was worse. Soon we had piles of cut, re-cut, and finally discarded pieces of plywood heaped in one corner of the boat, and if I'd let him carry on much longer we would have capsized and sunk.

His inability to remember things set me thinking.

'I read the other day that people who smoke marijuana can suffer short-term memory loss – what do you reckon, Graham?'

'Yeah, I've heard that too.' He thought for a while then shrugged. 'It's never affected me, though.'

Spending so much time with him, I came to know him quite well. He was a very spiritual man and, perhaps, *allowed* me to get to know him on the basis that a closer acquaintance would be instructive for me. No day was without its illuminating revelation. One morning, when the conversation had taken a philosophical turn, I remarked that a life-altering experience can sometimes be just what we need to 'bump' us into our senses.

'Yeah...' he said, sawing a sheet of plywood with the rhythm of a pendulum, 'prison teaches you that.'

'Have you been to prison?'

'Yeah,' he said, without looking up. I waited for him to elaborate... and was rewarded with: 'Twice.'

'What for?'

The sawing continued.

'Oh, silly things... you know,' he said, with a final air.

'What sort of silly things?'

At this Graham stopped and, looking past me into the emptiness of that corner of the boat that wasn't filled with scrap plywood, began to explain, in the manner of a barrister for the defence, the simple circumstances that had led to his client's needless three-year sentence. His mouth was distorted into an ironic smile, and his eyebrows were raised almost to his hairline.

'You know what it's like when you're taking drugs,' he began, as though citing a universal experience, 'you see a wall and you think to yourself: "I wonder if I can climb that wall?" and you find – "Yes, I *can* climb that wall!" Then you see a window, and you think: 'I wonder if I can get through that window?' and you find – "Yes, I *can* get through that window!" Then you see a safe and you think: "I wonder if I can open that safe?" And you find – "Yes, I *can* open that safe!" '

He turned to me with an angelic smile: 'Silly things... you know.'

I shivered at the thought of imprisonment – the very furthest thing from the life we were leading – and told him that of all the things that could happen to me, losing my freedom, being locked up in a cell while the bright sun shone on the green hills outside, was the thing I thought I could bear least.

'Me too!' he said passionately, 'that's why I escaped!'

By the time I arrived back on board in the evenings, frost would already be forming on deck and I'd be greeted by the smell of home cooking; the cosy red glow of the wood-burning stove; Linda's smile, and the flitting shadow of a bottle of wine dancing from the flame of our lamp.

'How was your day?' Linda would ask, and then wait for the smile that played around my lips.

Some nights we moored at the marina, from where I would often disturb a heron fishing by the glow of a pontoon light.

During the winter I never saw any fishy movement in the water, but the heron knew better: he would stand motionless, watching for ten minutes at a time; then suddenly his head would swing the javelin of his beak toward a target and gather his neck into an 'S' shape, before unleashing his strike. If he was successful he would throw back his head to swallow his catch with a couple of peristaltic jerks of his neck; if he missed, he would shake his head disdainfully and spit out the water.

Cormorants, too, were successful. They need to be because they expend so much energy on their fishing, constantly diving and chasing their prey, finally bobbing to the surface with an eel – which even cormorants find slippery customers as they try to turn them head-first into their throats. Frequently dropping them, they dive again and recapture them – and they *never* give up. Even when they have swallowed an eel the battle isn't over – the struggling eel will emerge unexpectedly and reverse back out of their beaks, which the cormorant answers with some more exaggerated swallowing. At last, the struggling ceases, and after an excited and splashy ritual bath, the cormorant will fly noisily away, banging the silent water with his wings as he struggles to get airborne, and land on a low water rock to digest his meal and hang his wings out to dry.

Cormorant

That weekend we had a visit from Graham's girlfriend – or ex-girlfriend. She was doing all she could to bring about a rapprochement with him, and her plan this week was to buy herself a boat – our boat.

Ten years Graham's senior, our first glimpse of her was when we heard a voice outside on the pontoon apparently talking to itself, and looked through the porthole to see a woman of about 60 standing next to our boat, her wild grey hair tugged by the wind across a blood-red Tudor bonnet. Linda emerged through the hatchway to ask whether she was looking for us, then invited her on board, at which she hopped down the companionway steps like a sparrow. The blue satin of her ankle-length dress peeped through a crocheted cardigan only a few inches shorter – the knee-level pockets of which bulged with tissues. She wore a poncho of naive colours, and strings of shells rattled as they patted against her flat chest. 'Right! How much do you want for your boat?' She stood blinking at us like a benevolent aunt about to get out her purse, twitching her face expectantly from me to Linda and back again.

'Why do you want to buy our boat?'

She let out a long and painful cry: 'Oh! – I'm sick and tired of living in a house,' she sobbed, and threw herself down dejectedly on one of the seats, where we noticed for the first time her tear-stained cheeks. She pulled a tissue from her pocket, wiped her eyes, and began to pour out her troubles.

We have learnt that when we have a guest on board, and they are sitting under our lowest deck beam, it pays to point out the obstruction and the danger it poses to their head. 'Oh don't worry about me – I was *born* on a boat. My father used to own the...' – here she gave us an account of all the famous old sailing boats she'd lived on, which we hadn't heard of – but probably should have. 'I know more about boats and the sea than most people are *ever* likely to – crikey, I didn't know what a house was until I was forty!'

'Would you like a cup of tea?' Linda asked.

'Thank you!' she said, leaping to her feet at Linda's kindness and head-butting the deck beam. The boat shuddered to the sort of crack you hear when someone is splitting wood with a maul, and Annette sunk back to her seat dazed, her blue-framed glasses dangling from one ear. We chimed our sympathetic 'oohs' and asked her if she was all right – when she had recomposed herself, she calmly raised a hand. 'It's all right – when you've spent half your life at sea you do that once and you don't do it again... A landlubber would do it a second time,' she said, wagging a cautionary finger at us, 'but a seaman doesn't.'

While Linda filled the kettle and lit the burner, Annette looked about, smiling her approval at each of the appurtenances and declaring how perfectly it all suited her. In answer to her questions, we described what our boat was like to sail – all of which met her requirements exactly; what she was like to live on – at which she observed how the coincidence of her tastes and ours left her longing to replace us as owners; how easy she was to handle – here she embarked on an essay of the priorities a boatbuilder should keep in mind when considering deck layout, and congratulated us on having avoided all the pitfalls; and when we came to describe how happy we were living on her, Annette had something approaching a religious experience: 'And I know I shall be, too!' she said, launching herself to her feet and cracking her head so hard that I found myself surreptitiously examining the beam for damage. When she slumped back in her seat, she was silent and her eyes were pointing in different directions.

'Ooh! Poor you,' Linda said.

'Gosh – are you OK?' I asked. She propped herself up uneasily on one elbow like a patient in a hospital determined to make the most of her visitors.

'Don't worry... don't worry,' she said weakly, looking at both of us simultaneously, 'I've learnt it now.' Linda and I turned the conversation between ourselves for a while to allow her time to recover. After a few minutes, Annette began to show interest in life again, even throwing in an occasional contribution to the conversation. We asked her about the village, what it was like to live there, and about the work she did, and listened as she began to tell us about her interesting life.

'Here's your tea,' Linda said. Annette leaped from her seat to take it, there was a third, sickening crack. It was a long time before anyone spoke.

Annette

Arriving back at the boat one memorable evening after work and listening to the Maritime Safety Broadcast from the Clyde Coastguard as usual – with the wind already blowing a gale – we learned that it was expected to increase: 'Storm Force 10 or Violent Storm 11 – perhaps Hurricane Force 12 for a time...'

That was the first time we had ever heard Hurricane Force 12 mentioned for an *inshore* waters forecast – we'd obviously been having an easy life in Cornish winters. No sooner had we doubled our mooring lines than the storm arrived with a bang, sending *Caol Ila* bouncing out on her lines as though they were elastic. We went below and sat by the wood-burning stove, watching its brightness pulse with the wind and listening to the note of the whistling rigging rising until the mast juddered, and shook the boat like a train crossing the points.

A gap above our washboards, about the width of a couple of letterboxes, kept us intimately connected with the weather, summer and winter, bright and rain; it was never closed – and through it a healthy stream of fresh air always flowed, but that night the wind drove rain into the accommodation as if from a hose. I stuffed a bath towel into the gap, but in less than a minute it was soaked; it sagged, and blew in with a wet slap onto the table in front of us. We went to bed where we would be dry.

Intense storms soon pass and after a few hours of lying awake, listening to the creaking ropes, we realised the sound was becoming less urgent, the wind was dying away, and at last we fell asleep.

That morning, as we drove to work, I wondered if Graham had had a disturbed night in his gypsy caravan; he looked wretched and drove in contemplative silence, until at last he said, 'I think I've got to make a confession to John...'

Our commute had fallen into a pattern – slow in the mornings, when it was getting light, and recklessly fast in the evenings, when it was growing dark. I had asked him about that. 'Well, I'm tired in the evenings, and need to get home quickly,' he explained, with unfailing logic.

This morning's drive was particularly sober and as we pootled along I tried to imagine what he had to confess.

'Why?' I asked. There was a long silence. Then he cleared his throat, and croaked out what was on his mind.

'Do you remember John telling us that his prawn catches were down?' John kept meticulous records: caught weight, ground fished, date, bait, and market prices; and he'd mentioned to us the previous day that his catches over the last couple of weeks were the worst he'd known for 11 years. 'I jus canna explain it,' he'd kept saying, by way of explanation.

'Uh-huh,' I said.

'Well,' said Graham, morosely, 'I think *I* know why. I was sitting at home last night thinking about it, and I suddenly remembered that a few days ago I had a sort of dream... and in it I taught the prawns how to get back out of the pots.'

***

The accommodation on John's boat was taking shape nicely – it looked fresh and homely, even without beanbags. Graham had been teaching me some of the things he'd learned at Osborne House – Queen Victoria's palace on the Isle of Wight – where he was apprenticed to the cabinetmaker; and told me how his first assignment had been to make a pretty chair – 'It wasn't perfect – but quite good,' he said; and how his boss had smashed it up before his eyes, then told him: 'Now do it properly.'

'Did you ever think of taking up furniture-making?' I asked.

'Sort of. People won't pay for good furniture – so I imported some once.'

I'd often looked at the low prices of chunky furniture from China and India, and wondered how any UK furniture-maker could compete, even though the joinery on imported furniture is often awful – nailed, or strapped with pieces of tin.

'You imported furniture to sell in the UK?' I asked.

'Yes.'

I was impressed – every time I thought I was getting to know Graham, he'd say something unexpected. He explained how the bank had lent him £10,000 to go and buy two container-loads of furniture from Sri Lanka and import them to the UK. He spent three months visiting factories, placing orders, and awaiting fulfilment. Finally, when everything was ready for shipping, he watched them loaded into containers and, in his words, 'made sure it would all be a financial success by chucking in a couple of bales of marijuana.'

Arriving back in the UK, he arranged to sell the marijuana to someone he described as 'a bit serious', who phoned him every day to ask if the shipment had arrived.

It all started to get a bit bad-tempered when the ship was a few days late, and Graham had to stall him.

'You're making me look bad,' the drug baron told him.

He went to the docks every day – yet on the day the ship actually arrived he was feeling under the weather and stayed in bed. In his stead, a friend of his went, and on claiming the shipment was arrested by customs officers, and later sentenced to eight years in prison. In spite of his failure to produce the goods, the drug baron was sufficiently impressed – perhaps by Graham's ability to avoid arrest – to offer him 'a plane and couple of flying lessons' for the next attempt. He'd thought about it long and hard, but made the decision that he didn't want the big life, and had turned the offer down.

That weekend we finished our work and John the fisherman came to inspect. His gaze roamed over the accommodation and he landed an approving thump on everything he saw. 'Aye,' he kept saying. And then summed up: 'Aye, you've done a good job, boys.'

Taking this opportunity to compare him, as he stood there, with the size of the holes we'd cut in the faces of the bunk beds, at his request, I couldn't help wondering how he was going to get in… but when I raised the matter and we offered to make them bigger, he wouldn't hear of it.

'Ya ken yarsell – if it was any bigger, you'd fall oot.' I myself struggled to get through them and he was about three of me… but then, if he managed to squeeze himself in and became trapped, I suppose Graham could teach him how to get back out.

***

The entrance to the pool in which we now moored *Caol Ila* was formed by a gap between two uninhabited islands, one of which was half a mile long and ridge-backed, craggy, and thick with vegetation. It was easier to walk along the ridge of the island than in any other part – its west face being boggy, and supporting dense thickets of flag iris and impenetrable scrubs of silver birch, while its east face was littered with huge boulders the size of Minis, and was so deep in fern, marram grass and bramble that it was impossible to see where to set your feet. My mind was preoccupied with that problem as I clambered onto the roof of one of the boulders, so I wasn't prepared for the shock that greeted me on the other side – two

Spanish ibexes, dreamily chewing the cud, jet-black and with breathtakingly large horns, suddenly jumped to their feet and faced me off. I braced myself to be butted off the summit.

The only other time in my life I remember standing so close to a goat was as a result of one of Steven Thomas's capers – the film-maker who had such happy memories of the dirty weekend he spent alone in St Mawes. He'd called unexpectedly at my house one day as a birthday surprise, but there was a surprise for him too when I told him he was eight months early. I happened to look out of the window and saw him climbing the steps to our house holding a newspaper folded open at a page of interest, and wearing the look of someone who had reached a decision. He went to bang on the front door, but I opened it simultaneously and he fell in.

'Come on!' he said by way of greeting, as he climbed to his feet. 'I'm going to buy you a goat!'

'A goat?'

'Yep – a goat!' He swiped the newspaper with the back of his hand. 'This ad is from a goat farm saying they've got loads of the bloody things, and they're right on your doorstep – about... two inches away on the map.' He beamed with generosity while waiting for me to realise that a goat was what my life had been missing all these years.

For the next two hours we threaded our way cross-country to the farm. It's exhilarating being driven by Steve – it's like facing a firing squad where you are sighted but the artillery is blindfold. The journey was embarrassing, too; whenever we met oncoming tractors, lorries, cars, cyclists or pedestrians in the narrow lanes, Steven was unyielding and shooed them back into a gateway because he hadn't yet found reverse gear on his new Volvo T5, and was convinced it didn't have one.

We pulled up at the farm to be met by a herd of musky goats, which crowded us, clamping their teeth on all parts of our clothing from the waist down and forcing us to protect ourselves by driving our hands into our trouser pockets and facing one another.

'Hello?' we called pleadingly, at which a man appeared.

'Are you from the ministry?' he asked.

'No,' said Steve, 'we've come to buy a goat.'

The farmer laughed with relief to hear that they'd sent someone with a sense of humour.

'Plenty of choice...' Steve noticed, approvingly. 'It's not for me, of course, it's for my friend here – his Flymo's broken and I thought it would do his grass.'

The farmer roared.

When the confusion was cleared up, and the farmer realised that we weren't in fact from the ministry, but a couple of hoorays, he let us know, rather pointedly, that he wasn't just *a* goat farmer – he was none other personage than the foremost goat authority in Britain.

'Ahh!' said Steve, who has an enquiring mind, 'in that case you may be able to answer my question: Billy/Nanny – what's the difference?'

After lecturing us on gender, and the not-so-obvious husbandry requirements of each, I chose a billy. The goat expert seemed to harbour misgivings about our suitability as parents – but stuck with us on the grounds that he *was* absolutely overrun with goats. He selected a tall, forward-going billy from the flock as the most suitable for our purposes, and named his price.

'When will you come for him?'

'We'll take him right now,' said Steve, beaming with pleasure.

'How will you get him home?'

'In the car.'

'Have you got a trailer?'

'No – he can sit on the back seat.'

'Hang on a second...' said the farmer.

He didn't let us have a goat that day – and he told us he never would – but time is a great healer.

I didn't feel I'd spent enough time with goats on that occasion to get used to their company; and facing two wild ones now on a deserted island – both of whom had a couple of giant corkscrews on their head – made my heart bang like a bass drum. As it turned out, they felt equally uncomfortable with me, and leapt away from rock to rock as though they were hopping along the thoughtfully laid out stepping stones of an ornamental roof garden.

It struck me as odd that a deserted island should be home to a pair of goats – particularly Spanish goats – and I later discovered that Iberian goats have been found living wild in a number of locations around the Scottish and Irish coasts. The theory is that they swam ashore from wrecked boats of the Spanish Armada in 1588 – aboard which they were carried as food – and that the goats seen today are the descendants of those originals.

The forecast warned of a spell of bad weather, and at the same time Hans rang to tell us that we would be needed for filming the following day. I knew that Linda wouldn't be keen, and even as I told her we saw the first harbingers of a gale whizzing overhead. We only had to get ourselves 12 miles along the coast, and since the wind would be blowing off the land there would be a relatively calm sea. Privately I was more concerned by the prospect of spending three sleepless nights lying to our anchor in an open bay that would get rough if the wind changed direction; we might lose our boat – or worse.

The next morning, as we began lifting our chain, and the wind was blowing a severe gale with violent squalls tumbling down from the hills, a man dressed in green overalls and a waterproof jacket passed through the loch in a workboat, with his head bent double against the wind. Noticing us lift the chain, he turned back. 'You ganning oot?'

'Yes.'

'Have you no heard the forecast?' We told him we had, but we'd got some work to do.

He looked at us for a moment – as though taking a long last look – and then motored away, shaking his head. I found his lament discouraging, and wondered once again if we should stay put, out of harm's way; but I'd thought the thing through and felt sure we were equal to the challenge.

Motoring past the protective islets and out to sea, we began to feel the full weight of the wind. We rounded the boat up to windward, hoisted a triple-reefed mainsail and a reefed inner staysail – the least amount of plain sail we could set – and when all was pulled taut and ready to try, and we'd got our ropes coiled down, we turned the bow across the wind. The first gust to arrive span across our deck humming like a top and threw us on our beam ends like a toy boat – Jesus, but it was lively – still, *Caol Ila* lifted herself up each time she was punched down and we began to surge over the short waves. When occasionally a bigger wave arrived, looking for trouble, it found our stem at a cunning angle lying close to the water, got no purchase on it, and we smashed through it like a shop window.

In the strongest blasts, it was a struggle to keep her on course – but once I'd heaved the tiller to windward, and thrown a hitch round it with the rope that was always ready in my hand, we enjoyed that thrill of all sailors – the exhilarating power of the wind. We stormed along! Foam sang in our wake! We read the warnings for each new squall in their footprints approaching us on the water – or by the spray torn from the white-capped waves that raced across the surface of the sea like wet smoke. At that speed, and with all that excitement, it seemed but a few short minutes until we were off the bay where the filming was to take place; and from the mouth of the bay came a blast to greet us – stronger than the rest, which knocked us down until our sails lay on the water. Before we could recover, our stem tripped the top off the next wave which rolled across the boat into the hammock of our sails, so that we staggered under the weight of the water. With a shudder *Caol Ila* burst powerfully through to the other side of this watery chaos like a fly-half still holding the ball as he wrong-foots his last opponent and runs unchallenged for the line. It was an heroic arrival for Hans to look out on – his house having commanding views of the bay – and we were more than proud of our vessel as we turned in toward the rocks that would give us shelter.

The filming had become a community event; all who lived in the bay were in some way involved, and looked for our arrival.

'Here they come!' we imagined them saying; 'and *how* they come!'

In a little channel between two huge rocks – which so protected us from the raging wind blowing overhead that you could have lit a candle on deck – our anchor chain rattled lazily into the mirrored surface of the water to sit on a patch of white sand amid the kelp forest. In that spot, in which we were to stay for three days, we were relieved to find that it offered better shelter than the pool we'd left behind.

Nothing stirred ashore, though we looked for signs, and so with time to kill that afternoon I went for a walk, found an old drovers' road, and followed it. For hundreds of years this road was used to drive cattle and sheep, landed from the islands of Islay and Jura, to market – sometimes 100 miles from here. A stone wall lined one side of the road, and a natural cliff ran along the other; between them, trees sprouted among the grass on the disused lane, and opportunistic low-hanging branches reached to the ground. I was struck by how well fitted the wall was and what labour must have been required to build it – only to fall into this redundancy. Just a drystone wall, stretching for mile after lonely mile – but the intention was that it should stand for centuries, and so it has. It's a blessing that the skilled craftsmen who built it can't climb from their graves to inspect the quality of our 21st-century buildings.

Nothing stirred that second morning either. Linda and I pottered at our chores, peeping through the porthole from time to time to look for signs of activity on the beach. After lunch Hans arrived by boat, greeted us with a cheery 'How ya doing?' and told us that the film company would like to see our boat moored at the pier at around 4 pm; they wanted to get an idea of framing the shot for filming tomorrow. We motored to the pier, skirting rocks hidden by the high tide, and moored alongside the stone pier, but no one came. As the light began to fade, Hans came by.

'OK! All done! The director's just driven by and when he saw you at the pier he says, "Perfect!" He's really pleased with it and wants you tied alongside the pier all day tomorrow – will you be OK drying out?'

'No problem with drying out – we do it all the time – but we'll need to come on to the pier at high water, which means 4 tomorrow morning – it'll be pitch black and I'm not too sure about navigating round those rocks in the dark… can you come on board at 4 and be our pilot?'

'Nay bother at all… see you at 4.'

'Four? – Jesus,' I said to Linda when he'd gone, 'I can't remember the last time I was up at that time.'

It was now – just as we were pulling away from the pier to return to our anchorage – that we discovered Carsaig Pier to be the perfect place for a strange meeting. A good-looking, dark-haired man in his late thirties, immaculately dressed in a dark suit and trilby, strode down the pier toward us, his steel Blakey's clacking against the concrete. He looked as though he had come to meet a steamboat, but was 80 years too late. As we swung our bow out to sea the smiling stranger reached the end of the pier and called after us, 'I've heard the whole story!'

I looked about me to see whom he was talking to – but there was no one else. 'Who on earth is this man... why is he dressed like that... and what the hell is he talking about?' I wondered – but managed only a feeble, 'How are you doing?'

He expanded a little: '...about the fire... and the boatbuilding, and everything... And I just wanted to say – if ever you write a book about it all, I want the first copy. I'll see you tomorrow!'

'Oh!' said Linda, 'you're in this film, are you?'

'Yes... look forward to chatting then!' he said with a wave.

That night I couldn't sleep; I got up at 2, dressed, and sat next to the glowing stove, quietly drinking tea and listening to the soft purrings of Linda's snore. Shortly before 4, I climbed on deck into the inky blackness of a dry November morning and began dressing the boat with fenders made from knotted coconut fibre, and setting up mooring lines made from hemp rope – the genuine article, supplied by the film company. I stood for a moment in the utter stillness of the morning – only the sea licking at unseen rocks made any sound. It felt like an important day, and I knew I would remember it for the rest of my life. A light came on at Carsaig Pier a few hundred yards away – they were the navigation lights of a fishing vessel, and I answered them with my own. Dougie – Hans's fishing partner – motored out to us and dropped Hans off on our deck, and then carried on out of the bay for a day's prawn fishing. Hans talked us past the rocky hazards of the bay and up to the pier where we tied alongside, had a cup of tea, chatted, and at 5 we were alone again.

A couple of hours later ten film extras, ten crew, and the contents of a removal lorry crammed with props – wooden creels, hessian sacks, sailcloth, racks for air-drying fillets of fish and wooden crates filled with salt herring – were dropped off at the pier head to begin transforming it into a busy fishing scene from a hundred years ago. Among the props were antique clothes – a costume for each of us, which we climbed into; and then began to dress our boat to enhance her antique appearance: slackening the rigging, drooping the sails, hiding modern rope behind those of older appearance. As we worked we became aware of the confident clacking of Blakey's striding along the pier toward us, turned, and there was the stranger from the night before, dressed once again in his trilby, and crisply-pressed suit, beaming at us like an old friend. 'I can't believe what you've done here – is that right that you built this boat yourselves?' he said, holding his palms open on outstretched arms as if beholding a wonder.

'We did... starting with a lot of trees and no experience!'

'In a word – how?'

As we filled in the details he asked us a hundred questions, about the boatbuild, our life on board, and about our house fire, teasing out the fibres of our story through his wide-eyed attention, like a child hearing of the adventures of King Arthur. Eventually I wondered if the film crew were eager to get on and that our indolence was somehow holding them back:

'Ah – they'll shout when they're ready,' he said with a dismissive wave of his hand.

'Have you done a lot of "extra" work?' We were struck by his cool air.

'Yes – that's my job – I work as a professional extra.' It sounded like a great way to earn a living – he told us he was on-set, somewhere, most days, and began to tell stories of his own life – the exotic and unusual locations, and the variety of his work: he was a horseman, he told us, and that skill was often in demand – in *Braveheart* as a shining example, in which film he'd been Mel Gibson's stand-in; being of similar stature, and bearing a passing resemblance to him. As he had predicted a shout went up from the director, and everyone fell silent. 'Don't forget my book,' he whispered, and clacked away, striding confidently along the pier.

The film was a sequel to *Walking with Dinosaurs* and was to be another natural-world dramatisation – this time about the deep-sea life of a sperm whale, to be screened by the BBC with the title *Ocean Odyssey*. The sequence being filmed here was of a tsunami – which *actually happened* on 24 January 1927, destroying the Norwegian community we were playing.

When the director shouted 'Run!' – our cue to spot the tsunami rolling in and leg it – I treated him to my thousand-pound-a-day run... along the pier, and uphill for a hundred yards; vaulting over props, overtaking my fellow extras – always passing them on the camera side – until I sat gasping for breath on a boat which had been whelmed over a pile of fishing nets when the rout was over and we had run off-set. I hadn't run like it since the school sports day, and my heart nearly gave out when I heard the director call, 'Take Two!'

On the second take I fell – I don't know why it always happens to me. I felt myself falling forward as I ran but couldn't save myself. I tucked my head down, landed on one shoulder, and a moment later found that I had rolled head over heels and was back on my feet... and so carried on running. We did six takes in all – I felt the last four were superfluous... how could they improve on my roll?

We had a pub lunch followed by more filming in the afternoon, then as night fell we took *Caol Ila* back out to anchor, and rowed ashore once more as the last of the sun's blood-red rays set fire to the sky above Jura's dramatic paps to attend a barbeque Hans's wife had arranged. On the menu was £400-worth – two cases – of langoustine, which had earlier been filmed leaping somersaults in an open basket. And to wash them down, a few bottles of whisky. Rising red embers from the fire illuminated the happy faces of all our company as we huddled round for warmth, whisky tumbler in hand, waiting for our langoustines to cook. We didn't have long to wait, and it was heartening to hear even the fishermen smack their lips wetly as they wafted yet another crimson shell in front of the assembly and declare, 'That's the Prince o' the sea – that is!'

In the darkness I saw myself and Linda amid this happy throng and stepped back to take stock. We had arrived in Scotland as just two more visitors by boat; yet everywhere we went we had been made welcome, received hospitality, and found new friends. We looked forward to the winter ahead without the least trepidation – we had the feeling that Scotland would look after us.

Rowing back to our boat late that evening over the glassy waters of a black, black night, we had a carrier bag full of fresh langoustine, our share of the oversupply, with which we planned to make the best prawn curry in the world; and we had a second carrier bag full of cash – pay for three days' work.

I stopped rowing and the trilling water at the bow soon fell silent as we slowed, leaving only the dripping of water from the blades of the oars. We looked at the stars in their millions, above our heads; our blood still pulsed with the excitement of the day. The warm sanctuary of our boat floated between protective rows of rock a little way off, silhouetted in the starlight – we could smell the oak smoke of our wood-burning stove even from here. Linda's eyes met mine. 'I don't think life gets much better than this.'

Justin

ACKNOWLEDGEMENTS

Every towering literary achievement, such as you now hold in your hands, owes its success not so much to the person named on its cover as author, but to those among his or her friends who have by brute force kept him if not *on* track, then as close to it as their strength would allow. Accordingly the names which ought to appear on the front cover of this book are:

Janice Benning; Georgina Fitzgerald; Steven Thomas. Steven contributed the film which appears on my website www.justintyers.co.uk in spite of the scurrilous slur occasioned against him in the pages of this book. Thanks Piers Murray-Hill for expert advice.

The contribution Linda, my wife, has made is too great even to be hinted at by mere words – simply put, without her not only would this book never have been written, but the events it describes would never have taken place. She is one of the bravest people I know.

Thank you Donnie McNeill for the back cover photograph.

Thanks to John Hesp, boat designer, for allowing us to reproduce the lines of Caol Ila. See more of his work at www.hesp.co.uk

Thank you Peter Chesworth, photographer, for allowing me to use the images 'Work begins on the accommodation', 'She sails like a dream' and 'Romping home into Falmouth Harbour'. And thank you to Lindy Harding for the photograph 'Typically narrow Devon lanes'.

Thanks to everyone at Bloomsbury who has worked on *Phoenix*... I marvel at all the feverish activity in the editorial, design, and marketing departments even though I can only put names to a handful of the people responsible for it:

Jessica Cole; Jonathan Eyers; Hannah Leech; Elizabeth Multon; Janet Murphy; James Watson; Naomi Webb.

And thank you to everyone who appears in this book – wherever you are now, thanks for making us welcome, we will always remember the fun and the good times.